SERVICING MORTGAGE PORTFOLIOS

STRATEGIES &
APPLICATIONS
FOR BUYING,
SELLING AND
**MANAGING
MORTGAGE
LOAN
PORTFOLIOS**

TIM COHANE
LARRY RAFFERTY, EDITORS

PROBUS PUBLISHING COMPANY
Chicago, Illinois

Library of Congress Cataloging in Publication Data Available

ISBN 1-55738-109-7

Printed in the United States of America
KP
1 2 3 4 5 6 7 8 9 0

TO A GREAT TEAM—

**The Employees of
Cohane Rafferty Securities, Inc.**

Contents

Preface   vii

Acknowledgements   ix

1   Strategic Planning   1

2   Packaging   13

3   Marketing   39

4   Economic Analysis   47

5   Bidding and Closing   101

6   Due Diligence and Portfolio Transfer   139

7   Transfer of Servicing   153

8   Hedging   163

9   Practical Application: The Plain Vanilla Deal   191

10 Flow Deals **213**

Appendix I Normal Paper Trail in Servicing Sale **221**

**Appendix II Due Diligence and Transfer
Procedures** **271**

**Appendix III Procedural Guidelines for Transfers
of Servicing** **357**

Appendix IV Delinquency Calculation **397**

**Appendix V State Servicing Information
and Laws** **401**

Index **433**

Preface

The portion of the secondary mortgage market called the "servicing market" has experienced dramatic change since 1984. The servicing market involves buying and selling mortgage servicing portfolios. Servicing portfolios of $50 million and more have been traded with increasing frequency.

The interest rate spike of April 1987 created several factors that affected this market concurrently. Mortgage bankers who lost money because of this rate spike had to liquidate some of their servicing portfolios to stay afloat. Large servicers who could weather the storm decided to come into the servicing market aggressively. Meanwhile, increased liquidity had been created by specialty brokerage operations, and increased value and prepayment horizons improved with the higher interest rates.

The overall effect was an explosion in the trading of mortgage servicing portfolios. The trading of mortgage servicing is now an integral part of the banking industry and will continue to be for the foreseeable future.

How are mortgage servicing transactions achieved? What do you need to know to get into this market? What is the best way to go about this type of deal? These are the kinds of questions this book answers. Studying it and understanding the principles and structure involved in the servicing market will help prepare you to become a player.

Tim Cohane
Larry Rafferty

Acknowledgements

We want to thank the following employees of Cohane Rafferty Securities, Inc.

Erma Evans who did a great job assembling all parts of the Book.

To contributing writers: Elizabeth Workman, Daniel Thomas, William Lahart, John Racy, Mark McAfee, and George Lee.

To Derek Park and Peter Cohane who were contributing editors.

To Irene Tansey, Jacque Day, Ted Davis, Steve Downey, Hilary Renz, Matthew Monahan, Nick Caratzas, Don Parris, Roger Vogt, Bob Toppe, and Michael Scanlon for added support.

And to all those mortgage servicers who have made the evolution of this market occur.

Strategic Planning

During the late 1980s, buying and selling mortgage servicing burgeoned into an important and sometimes vital part of the banking business. In the banking industry, the obvious need for liquidity is a constant challenge, haunting the sleep of mortgage bank presidents and CFOs. In this area, mortgage servicing provides the uncommon: a steady, predictable, reliable income stream.

In servicing mortgage portfolios, it is the contractual obligation of the mortgage bank to perform administrative duties such as payment collection, payment of property taxes, and payment of interest. This obligation carries with it, in exchange for services rendered, a specific fee collected monthly that provides income to the mortgage bank.

Aside from the cash flow generated, mortgage servicing holds even greater value for a mortgage banker. Mortgage servicing is both a tangible asset and a transferable one, one that can be sold for cash to bolster flagging income or viewed as the payoff, the golden egg that has been growing and developing during some portion of the mortgage bank's history. The owner(s) can cash in for millions of dollars and continue to conduct business as usual.

As an ongoing endeavor, on the other hand, a business can improve productivity and, therefore, profitability in several ways through the purchase of a mortgage servicing portfolio. Buying mortgage servicing establishes the steady, predictable, reliable cash flow everyone needs. Moreover, by adjusting the mix of loan types being administered, mortgage bankers can streamline and tailor their operations to produce maximum economies of scale. This translates directly to black ink on the bottom line.

This is not news to the mortgage banking community. These lessons, if they weren't known before, were clarified for all during the mortgage banking boom between 1983 and 1988. Not only was there a chicken in every pot, but that pot was increasingly situated on John and Mary Doe's new electric range, in John and Mary Doe's new kitchen, in John and Mary Doe's new home. And all these homes had lovely mortgages attached to them.

Mortgage originations were flooding in everywhere. Mortgage portfolios were swelling at the seams. Mortgage servicing fees were providing comfortable amounts of operating income. Almost everyone in the business was sporting a satisfied smile.

The smart ones quickly realized that their swelling mortgage portfolios were money in the bank. They saw and seized the opportunity to play these assets into additional profits. Selling and buying mortgage servicing became not only big business, but smart business as well. It became an important operational instrument to the mortgage banking industry.

However, even during the boom years there were those who misused this instrument, who unwittingly hurt their business in the longer term. Now, when mortgage markets are falling into their predictable, cyclical downswing, the ability of a mortgage banker to structure, maintain, and efficiently buy and sell mortgage servicing can mean the difference between self-sufficiency and survival, assimilation and mandated sale, collapse and complete extinction. Those who are failing are generally doing so for one of two reasons: they don't fully understand how the instrument can and should be used, or they don't fully understand how their own business operates.

Why Sell Mortgage Servicing Portfolios?

Mortgage bankers sell mortgage servicing portfolios for two reasons:

- to generate cash; and
- to streamline their portfolio.

A mortgage servicing portfolio has a definable cash value to the institution that owns it. In fact, it is estimated that over eighty percent of the net worth of a mortgage bank is attributable to its servicing portfolios. A servicing portfolio valued at $200 million may sell for two points in the market. The $4 million generated by that sale is the reason for the sale. It means cash flow, an improved profit picture, or a comfortable retirement for the private entrepreneur.

Properly structured and administered, mortgage servicing can offer a higher yield than other investment instruments. The effect of mortgage servicing is like buying an annuity stream, but it must be actively and professionally managed. Mortgage servicing is both an investment and a part of your business. To make mortgage servicing work well as a specific part of your business, you must incorporate it efficiently into your business plan. For example, you may assess your mortgage portfolio and find that its variable tax payment schedules place an added and perhaps unnecessary burden on your administrative setup. To relieve this burden, you may need to restructure the timing of other required payments.

Another reason for restructuring may be found in the types of loans your institution services. FHA and VA insured loans require substantial and specific reporting procedures. If your computer system isn't set up to generate the required style of report, it may be wiser for you to sell all your Ginnie Mae and service only Fannie Mae or Freddie Mac loans. Streamlining your portfolio to fit your operation makes it more efficient.

Why Buy Mortgage Servicing Portfolios?

Mortgage bankers purchase mortgage servicing portfolios for a variety of reasons:

- *To augment cash flow.* Mortgage portfolio servicing provides a preset, stable cash flow. Especially when loan originations are down, servicing can offset lost income flow with a more reliable, steady income flow.

- *To broaden the customer base.* Thrifts are required to keep a certain percentage of their assets in real-estate-related investments. Once a thrift obtains a mortgage, it has a good probability of getting the mortgagee's entire basket of financial obligations. Buying mortgage servicing provides an opportunity to broaden the institution's customer base.

- *To gain float from escrow.* A mortgage bank not only acquires cash from the set monthly servicing charge but can also profit from the float while holding escrow payments.

- *To achieve administrative efficiency.* Determine what it costs you to service each loan, each investor type. If you find it's costing $90 to service Ginnie Maes and only $65 to service Freddie Macs, you should consider selling your Ginnie Maes and buy Freddie Macs, because you do it more efficiently. Also consider your utilization of personnel, finding your average costs, and your marginal costs (average costs being the average cost per transaction, taking all cost factors into account; marginal costs being what additional cost you would incur to add on a loan). If you have underutilized personnel, the operations cost incurred by adding loans may be near zero. In this scenario, adding loans also reduces your average cost—a double advantage.

- *To supplement productivity.* If you operate most efficiently at $500 million and normal levels of prepayment will reduce that by $100 million, then you will want to supplement your portfolio by $100 million. If your business plan calls for the origination of only $40 million of new loans, then you'll want to go out and get another $60 million.

Strategic Business Planning

The reasons for purchasing mortgage servicing are many. To determine which reasons apply to you and to decide between buying or selling, you must establish goals and objectives for your business based on a detailed cost and operations analysis of your current business and future expectations. The building or restructuring of a servicing portfolio is a process, not an overnight decision followed by an immediate action.

To stay in control of operations, nearly everyone uses some form of business planning. These plans run the gamut from educated guesses to well-structured, fully integrated, carefully monitored strategic plans. The rest of this chapter will help you structure a business plan. It also offers a complete outline of an alternative method of strategic planning.

Strategic planning is nothing more or less than an exercise in applied logic. It is a matter of identifying who and what you are as a company, where you are as a company, where you want to be as a company, and the changes or steps necessary to get there.

Consider the ten elements of strategic planning:

1. Statement of purpose—management philosophy
2. Statement of company goals—long-term directions
3. Company appraisal—strengths and weakness
4. Strategic assumptions—economic operating environment
5. Business objectives—short-term goals and directions
6. Business strategies—tactics to achieve objectives
7. Business action plans—formalization of assigned responsibilities
8. Pro forma projections—testing phase
9. Contingency plans——what if....; fallback positions
10. Monitoring phase—the proof of the pudding

Statement of Purpose

Management philosophy can only be dictated by the chief executive officer, with input from the executive committee and senior management. A statement of the company's management philosophy should deal with the two critical resources of any organization: people and money. While it is a general statement, it should provide all employees with an understanding of the character of the company.

Properly approached and worded, the statement of purpose presents business parameters (—a mortgage bank offering retail banking services in Northern Westchester County—), human values (—we shall differentiate by providing personalized, quality service at all locations—), and profit mandate (—we shall endeavor to provide the best possible economic rewards to stockholders and employees, with a minimum R.O.I. of 16 percent—).

This "reason for doing business" serves as the ultimate test of all that follows. Does this goal objective assumption activity meet with the mortgage bank's statement of purpose? Any that do not demand rethinking.

Statement of Company Goals

Here you address long-term goals as they relate to your stated purpose for doing business. Goal-setting always begins with the answers to a series of questions involving people and money.

On the people side you might ask the following:

1. What are our compensation and benefit goals?
2. What are our training and management incentive goals?
3. What are our personnel training approaches?
4. What is our attitude toward promoting within?
5. What professional organizations are important to us and who should belong to them?

On the money side, your questions may vary somewhat from these, because they must relate specifically to where and how you do business:

1. What geographic areas do we want to service?
2. Are there related business lines we should be selling, such as life or mortgage insurance?
3. What position do we as a company take on risk?
4. Do we want to reduce operational costs without affecting personnel morale or service?

Care should be taken in structuring and answering these questions because they are a reflection of your own particular corporate culture. Ask a thousand questions if you feel the need, but don't overburden yourself at this point in the process by generating a long, precise list of goals.

Remember, this is only the second step in strategic planning. The specific steps necessary to meet these goals will be developed logically later.

A set of company goals might read as follows:

1. Expand influence into Southern Westchester by opening strategically located branch offices.
2. Increase servicing portfolio by 20 percent per year.
3. Improve image through increased local advertising and promotion.
4. Achieve lower levels of servicing costs.
5. Maintain competitive compensation and benefits package for all employees.
6. Increase in-house training programs to facilitate promoting within whenever possible.

Company Appraisal

The company appraisal is undertaken at this stage of the process because "you can get there from here, but only if your know where here is." To reach long-range goals, management must understand the company's current business posture.

The self-appraisal process demands a thorough cost analysis of the operation. It should analyze the functioning of each department separately and then relate it to the whole. For this reason, it is wise to involve representatives of all departments on the appraisal committee.

The company appraisal will help management identify and capitalize objectively on strengths while reducing weakness and risk. The key word here is "objectively." Now is the time for cold, hard analysis of your personnel and operations. That doesn't mean ruthless. It means removed.

The appraisal covers all aspects of the business. Analyze each profit-and-loss component for every department. Then determine whether a particular function has greater profit capabilities, either through increasing gross revenues or reducing expenses. For example, to determine the number of loans an employee currently services and could service most efficiently, you must examine productivity. At this point, managers will find many operational procedures that must be changed or implemented to increase productivity and efficiency.

Properly conducted, this company soul-searching will probably reveal some surprising and possibly exciting facts. For example, a cost analysis of the servicing function might show that one person can administer $50 million of mortgages under the current portfolio mix. The mortgage bank has a total portfolio of $500 million, with thirteen people assigned to the task. The possibilities for improved efficiency are suddenly obvious: take three people off the task and assign them elsewhere, or increase the portfolio to $650 million. Good ideas, perhaps. But wait. An error people commonly make at this phase is to assume that this isolated piece of information is conclusive and that an action can be taken before the entire planning process is complete.

Those actions suggested by the servicing function cost analysis may prove to be the way to go. But what if your appraisal also demonstrates that the capacities of these particular thirteen employees administering the servicing portfolio are somewhat different? Perhaps they are already working to capacity. If that's the case, the action suggested might be substantially different. Accelerated training to improve their efficiency and capacity might be the best option. Examine all factors before drawing conclusions and before taking action.

Another facet of this appraisal as it relates to the mortgage servicing function is a detailed valuation of your current mortgage portfolio. It should be analyzed by investor types, location, loan maturities, length, turnover rate, foreclosure rate, etc. What are the state laws on foreclosure? What's the redemption period?

When all is said and done, the appraisal committee should create a list of strengths, weaknesses, and potential opportunities. Taken together, the items on this list constitute the state of your company's health and establish the limits of change that can reasonably be implemented.

Strategic Assumptions

Now that you have an intimate understanding of the current strengths and weaknesses of your own business, it's time to examine the context for future change and growth. What will the economic environment be like one year out, three years out, five years out?

Strategic assumptions as part of strategic planning are educated guesses about the future, guesses about things over which you have no real control but which you believe will have a predictable impact on your business. While they are guesses, they can be vitally important and should be addressed as such.

Critical economic factors such as housing starts, inflation rates, and interest rates will have a dramatic impact on your bank's loan origination volume. These factors, taken alone, should have a predictable influence on your business. If you believe housing starts will rise over the next three years and then decline during years four and five, it makes sense that originations will follow that trend proportionately. Naturally, interest and inflation rates should have the opposite effect.

Economic factors are generally viewed on a national basis. You, however, must relate these indicators to your own operating area. Look at the economy of Houston, Texas, during the mid-1980s and compare it with Stamford, Connecticut, for the same period.

Of equal importance to key economic indicators are projections of what will occur in the mortgage banking industry during the next five years. Trends, competitive environment, and costs of doing business must be considered. What laws or regulations might government impose on the industry in the near future and how would they affect you? Will the recent trend of assimilation of smaller banks by larger continue, and if so, how might it involve you?

Assumptions concerning your mortgage bank's position in the industry must also be made. What will be the trend in your business regarding single-family production, commercial and construction loans, and loan servicing and administration?

Mortgage servicing is the only source of income that can be relied on over the course of the business cycle. It is, therefore, a worthy assumption that servicing can play an important role in your present and future business.

Many experts in the field of strategic planning suggest that assumptions be created for three scenarios; best case, worst case, and most probable. Effective strategic planning is an acquired art. It takes familiarization and practice. As a result, the challenge of creating one set of solid assumptions may be sufficient for most. If, however, you're up to the task, there is no doubt that three scenarios are better because they provide a more precise blueprint for action.

Business Objectives

The caravan is formed. You know where you want to go in the long term. You understand the basics of what and with whom you have to work, and you have painted a picture of what color you expect to find the grass on the other side of the hill. Now you set about establishing the landmarks, the interim objectives that will take you there.

Objectives can best be defined by "If; then" equations. The objective will result logically from certain facts already assembled, couched in assumptions concerning the business environment.

For example:

IF

- Senior servicing representatives undertake an intensified training of subordinates during the next year, increasing capacity to administer loans by $100 million without additional cost.

- Data processing expands its capacity during the next year to handle quarterly payouts using current systems, as their cost analysis indicates.

- An additional $100 million of New Jersey loans are bought.

  THEN
- The servicing portfolio can be expanded by $100 in one year, without incurring marginal costs.

Because one of the business's long-term goals is to improve productivity and profitability of the mortgage servicing function, this objective is appropriate and should be adopted. It not only supports an established goal, but it also dictates a specific direction, a targeted set of actions.

The number of objectives set is totally at the discretion of those doing the planning. As a rule of thumb, set enough objectives to meet the stated company goals but not more than are manageable given constraints of time and personnel.

Business Strategies

Objectives are the landmarks for your future growth, and the specific strategies are the stepping stones. They are the selected tactics employed to meet objectives.

Using the objective stated previously as our model, what strategies will be necessary to expand the mortgage portfolio "by $100 million in one year, without incurring marginal costs?" To some extent, though not entirely, the answers are found in our set of "IFs."

In-house training was mentioned. Therefore, a specific training program must be developed, a training timetable established, and some method for measuring improvement implemented.

An additional $100 million of New Jersey loans are to be purchased. What type of loans do you want and what will be your method of acquisition? Do you want to buy on a flow basis or bulk basis? What discount rate are you willing to pay? What mix of loans do you want to buy based upon types of loans you service most efficiently?

The answers to these questions provide the strategy. For example, you might determine that you want only Fannie Maes and Freddie Macs, that you want to buy on a bulk basis, and that you can pay 195 basis points for the package. You also might decide to use a securities firm that specializes in mortgage service brokering. Finally, you might decide to purchase during the ninth month to assure internal readiness. Now you have developed a strategy.

Business Action Plans

Action plans are the formalized timetable for execution of the strategy. Some people call them a timeline, clearly assigning specific tasks to be completed by a specific date, under the direction of a specific person or department. As incidental and unnecessary as they might seem, action plans are important yardsticks to completing strategies, because they provide order and assign responsibility, elements that are central to a successfully executed plan. They are also, at long last, the chance to put your efforts to work for you.

Pro Forma Projections

Every phase of strategic planning discussed so far has dealt with analysis, goal-setting, assumption, and facilitation of goals. Will they really do what you expect them to do? When you hash it out, will the anticipated profits generated through a larger volume of mortgage servicing really add twenty percent to the bottom line? Does it all make financial sense?

Pro forma projections will tell you. They are a simple set of financial projections based on your anticipated changes in operations.

Do not make your pro forma projections too complex. Using past performance criteria for your company will help you judge the relative impact of the changes you intend to implement.

Contingency Plans

Contingency plans are required because of the vital what-ifs that exist in the economic assumptions and projections you have made. During the development of your business assumptions, you might have created three scenarios. If you did, then your contingency plans should be created around the "worst case" scenario. If you did not, then this is the time to address the question.

Consider factors that are not currently a part of your plan but that could conceivably occur. What is the probability of such factors falling into place? If they do, what strategies could you employ to offset negative consequences or take advantage of the situation?

Contingency plans are often viewed as defensive reactions to negative events, but they can as easily be aggressive steps taken to maximize unexpected opportunities. Look at it from both sides.

Monitoring Phase

Monitoring your business with an eye toward the strategic plan is important and can be very gratifying. When you see the fruits of your efforts reflected in actual performance, you'll become an advocate of the strategic planning process.

Strategic Mortgage Servicing

Strategic planning over a longer time cycle allows flexibility and orderly development of staff and support facilities. Whether planning is applied on a company-wide basis or on a departmental basis, the same rules and approaches apply. Consider some of the planning factors endemic to the mortgage servicing function.

An appraisal of the firm's servicing portfolio provides managers with the information showing what operational improvements have to be made and the areas and functions in which the company services loans most efficiently and economically. Because optimal efficiency in the servicing operation will maximize income stream, the company will maximize profit by both increasing fee income and minimizing expenditures while providing quality service to customers and investors.

Managers will implement operational improvements during the operational phase before embarking on strategic goals—buying or selling servicing. The operational and appraisal phase will allow managers to make a better reasoned decision on the type and amount of servicing they should sell to increase operational efficiencies and which servicing it should acquire to increase economies of scale and profitability. If the operational and appraisal processes are ignored, managers may decide to sell servicing that is very profitable and purchase servicing that it administers inefficiently.

2

Packaging

Once the decision to sell servicing has been examined and included as part of the company's strategic plan, packaging the portfolio is the next crucial step. In fact, it can be argued that packaging the portfolio is the most important step.

In any type of sale—cars, packaged goods, or financial services—product presentation has significant and sometimes dramatic impact on the prospective buyer. This is particularly significant in the sale of servicing, because the buyer is not dealing with a tangible product whose quality can be clearly perceived by the senses.

When it comes to the sale of mortgage servicing, a buyer's perception of quality is often contingent on how well an offering is formatted and presented.

- Is the portfolio pleasing to the eye?
- Does it read smoothly, clearly?
- Is it properly organized and structured?
- Is the data concise?
- Does the offering give the buyer a clear picture of exactly what is being offered?

If even one of these elements is missing, then the buyer's perception of quality falters and the market value of the servicing falters along with that perception.

The successful sale of servicing, like that of virtually any other product, depends on effective marketing. A popular misconception is that marketing a servicing portfolio is a simple matter of sending out data, then sitting back and waiting for the bids to roll in. Little attention is given to the form and appearance of the data. It is too often left to the prospective buyer to sort through, clarify, and interpret.

Marketing means preparation and planning, before and during the selling process. Highly dynamic, the servicing market is a constantly changing network of people and institutions who at any time can be on either or both sides of a transaction as buyer and seller. Because the product is nothing more than a collection of data, the key to working in this market is the ability to accurately store, retrieve, and assemble data. The servicing market hinges on the players having a sophisticated, manageable data processing and telemarketing system.

This chapter briefly explores the evolution of the mortgage servicing portfolio to its present form. It also discusses the essential data needed, its sequence and form, and examples of some typical offerings. Finally, it examines the marketing stages and strategies that can help a seller maximize price.

Evolution of the Servicing Portfolio

The evolution of the form, structure, and content of the servicing offering has coincided with the growth of the mortgage market. Early servicing offerings, like the one shown in Exhibit 2.1, consisted only of scant information regarding the underlying loan characteristics. There was rarely, if ever, a clear picture of what you were buying.

During those days, underwriting was often haphazard at best. No two loans were underwritten according to the same guidelines. As a result, a single servicing offering included many different loan types, maturities, and ranges of interest rates. The lack of standardization caused the market to be extremely inefficient and servicing values to be unclear.

The advent of mortgage-backed securities and the emergence of the secondary market in the late 1970s has given servicing sales a new look (Exhibit 2.2). Sellers provided more information about the loans that comprised the servicing offering, because government agencies had begun to see and capitalize on the benefits of standardizing the sale by specific loan types, maturities, and interest rates.

Despite those efforts, the sale of servicing remained inefficient during those formative years of the secondary market. One of the biggest factors creating this inefficiency was the unavailability of mortgage prepayment statistics to prospective buyers.

Exhibit 2.1   Early Servicing Offering

Unpaid Principal Balance	$100,000,000
Number of Loans	1,000
Interest Rate	10.00%
Gross Servicing Fee	0.50%
Remaining Maturity	28 years
Total Monthly Payment,	
Number of Delinquent Loans	**4**
Location	New York 700
	New Jersey 200
	Connecticut 100

Exhibit 2.2   Late 1970s Emergence of Secondary New Look

Date of Information	July 7
Product Type	FHLMC 30-Year
	Fixed Rate
Unpaid Principal Balance	$100,000,000
Number of Loans	1,000
Average Loan Size	$100,000
Weighted Average Interest Rate	10.00%
Weighted Average Net Servicing Fee	0.44%
Weighted Average Original Term (months)	350
Weighted Average Remaining Term (months)	336
Principal and Interest Payment	
Tax and Insurance Payment	
Number of Delinquent Loans	7
Location	New York 700
	New Jersey 200
	Connecticut 100

Vital questions that would help a buyer determine the true value of an offering could not be answered.

- How quickly do the conventional loans prepay compared to FHA or VA loans?

Exhibit 2.3 Sample Servicing Portfolio Computer Reports

Servicing Portfolio — Summary Information

Description	Wtd. Avg. Note Rate	Loan Count	Unpaid Prin. Balance	Avg. Loan Size	Avg. Escr. Bal./Loan	Avg. Int. Paid on Escrow	Servicing Fee (Net)	WAOM	WARM	Deq. Rate	FCL* Rate
FNMA LASER I											
FNMA 30 YR FIXED	10.670	15	1,828,120	121,875	0.34	1.29	0.3569	360.0	351.4	1.45	0.06
FNMA 15 YR FIXED	10.515	3	144,624	48,208	0.77	1.00	0.4784	180.0	151.1	1.45	0.06
FNMA 30 YR ARM	8.905	33	4,235,801	128,358	0.32	1.00	0.3802	360.0	352.1	1.45	0.06
FNMA 30 YR BI-WEEKLY	10.548	18	1,942,013	107,890	0.18	1.45	0.3750	244.5	238.1	1.45	0.06
TOTAL FNMA LASER I	9.721	69	8,150,557	118,124	0.30	1.14	0.3755	329.3	321.2	1.45	0.06
FNMA LASER I SUBSERVICING											
FNMA 30 YR FIXED	10.607	4	258,245	64,561	0.66	1.00	0.3194	356.6	344.3	0.00	0.00
FNMA 15 YR FIXED	10.413	4	344,159	86,040	0.55	1.48	0.3247	180.0	170.4	0.00	0.00
FNMA 30 YR ARM	8.888	13	1,294,981	99,614	0.38	1.52	0.3750	360.0	350.6	0.00	0.00
FNMA 30 YR BI-WEEKLY	10.523	3	340,613	113,538	0.09	3.16	0.4203	244.5	42.8	0.00	0.00
Total FNMA LASER I SUB.	9.570	24	2,237,997	93,250	0.39	1.47	0.3677	314.3	275.3	0.00	0.00
TOTAL FNMA LASER I	9.688	93	10,388,554	111,705	0.32	1.23	0.3738	326.1	311.3	1.08	0.04
FHLMC ARC											
FHLMC 30 YR FIXED	10.565	387	45,411,885	117,343	0.40	1.25	0.7732	358.3	352.5	0.62	0.06
FHLMC 15 YR FIXED	10.100	90	8,661,640	96,240	0.49	1.08	0.9178	180.0	175.0	0.62	0.06
FHLMC 30 YR ARM	10.265	7	704,082	100,583	0.49	1.72	0.8839	360.0	340.6	0.62	0.06
TOTAL FHLMC ARC	10.488	484	54,777,607	113,177	0.41	1.23	0.7975	330.1	324.3	0.62	0.06
FHLMC ARC SUBSERVICING											
FHLMC 30 YR FIXED	10.518	215	19,515,405	90,769	0.47	2.02	0.6887	353.3	347.5	0.62	0.06
FHLMC 15 YR FIXED	10.028	68	4,441,138	65,311	0.70	1.12	0.9132	175.7	168.9	0.62	0.06
FHLMC 30 YR ARM	10.491	3	250,619	83,540	0.42	1.00	0.6840	360.0	343.1	0.62	0.06
Total FHLMC ARC I SUB.	10.428	286	24,207,162	84,640	0.51	1.79	0.7298	320.8	314.7	0.62	0.06
TOTAL FHLMC ARC	10.469	770	78,984,769	102,578	0.44	1.43	0.7768	327.3	321.3	0.62	0.06
TOTAL PORTFOLIO	10.379	863	89,373,323	103,561	0.43	1.41	0.7299	327.1	320.2	0.67	0.06

* Foreclosures estimated at 0% for year 1.

- How fast does an 11 percent loan prepay compared to an 8 percent loan?

The theories behind how prepayments work were all there, but statistical evidence to prove them was not available.

Since then, computers have revolutionized virtually all aspects of the financial industry. They are the central technology for all successful servicing operations today. Exhibit 2.3 shows sample reports that can be created by the computer in providing desired servicing data. Where in the past lenders had to sort manually and hand calculate an enormous amount of information on the loans they wished to sell, the computer enables lenders to calculate the key information automatically.

Computers also have had a significant effect on collecting, storing, and calculating historical prepayment statistics on mortgage-backed securities. This critical data is now available for many different investor types, coupon rates, loan types, and maturities, where in the not-so-distant past it was difficult or impossible to collect. The result was enhanced efficiency for the entire mortgage-backed securities market, especially the mortgage servicing market.

Another major change the computer brought to the servicing market was in the evaluation of servicing portfolios. Before computers, buyers manually calculated the net after-tax value of the servicing income stream. Today, servicing evaluation computer models perform the majority of these calculations automatically, and these evaluation models have become standardized with only slight variances.

Coupling the growth in the secondary market with the speed, accuracy, capacity, and efficiency offered by computer technology, standardized data is no longer a luxury but a basic tool for packaging and selling mortgage servicing today.

Packaging the Servicing Portfolio

The form, structure, and overall appearance of a servicing portfolio is everything.

Cover Page, Bid Page, Table of Contents

The cover page is a presentation tool showing the type of servicing offering being presented—exclusive (with one broker) or non-exclusive (with more than one broker)—indicating the marketing distribution to the prospective buyer, the deal number, and the date and time on which the auction is scheduled to be held (see Exhibit 2.4).

The bid page summarizes the highlights of the portfolio:

- Dollar amount
- Product type (i.e. FNMA, FHLMC, GNMA)
- Type and geographic location of the selling institution (i.e. savings institution or mortgage bank)
- Broker's disclaimer
- Bid date (reiterated for the buyer's benefit)
- List of features that make the package attractive to buy (such as low delinquencies or high service fees).

Exhibit 2.4   Portfolio Servicing Offering, Sample Title Page

---

EXCLUSIVE SERVICING OFFERING

NO. 497

BID DATE: November 9, 1989/3:00 P.M. New York Time

550 Mamaroneck Avenue
Harrison, New York 10528
(914) 381-6300
(914) 381-6307 (FAX)

The contents page lists the items included in the portfolio offering marketing package (see Exhibit 2.5).

The bid page summarizes the highlights of the portfolio. The cover page, bid page, table of contents format structures the portfolio for the convenience and readability of the buyer.

Essential Details Page

The first section of the offering presents the vital facts about the offering. It permits prospective buyers to identify almost instantly whether this type of servicing fits their strategic plan for acquisition and encompasses the data necessary for their evaluation model.

Consider a typical set of data found on the essential details page (Exhibit 2.6).

Date of Information

This means that "this information was compiled as of (date)." Prospective buyers require information that is current.

Investment Type

This information immediately identifies what types of loans are included in the offering. Some buyers are only interested in conventional loans, either FNMA or FHLMC; others prefer GNMA, government-backed mortgages. Also presented here is whether the product being offered is fixed rate or adjustable rate.

Principal Balance

The aggregate unpaid principal balance of the underlying loans is presented to signal the buyer immediately whether the offering size is appropriate.

Number of Loans

This is the total number of loans included in the sale.

Exhibit 2.5   Servicing Portfolio Offering, Contents Page

Cohane Rafferty Securities, Inc. is acting as an exclusive agent in the sale of $99,903,595.03 of FHLMC and FNMA MBS servicing rights by a northeast financial institution.

The information in this report has been obtained from sources that Cohane Rafferty Securities, Inc. believes to be reliable. However, we do not guarantee its accuracy, as such information may be incomplete or condensed.

Bids must be received by Cohane Rafferty by 3 p.m. New York Time, November 9, 1989.

Some of the features of the portfolio being offered include:
1. 100% fixed-rate non-recourse
2. Low average note rate of 9.82%
3. Low delinquencies of 1.38%
4. Geographically concentrated in Connecticut ($72 million)
5. Average loan size of $76,967.33
6. 95% self-originated, 94% single-family

To facilitate your analysis of the offering, this portfolio contains the following information:

	Page
Summary Information	1
Total Portfolio	
Essential Details	2
FHLMC ARC	
Essential Details Total	3
Essential Details 30-Year Fixed	3
Essential Details 15-Year Fixed	3
Note Rate Distribution 30-Year Fixed	4

Exhibit 2.5   Servicing Portfolio Offering, Contents Page (continued)

Geographical Distribution 30-Year Fixed   4
Note Rate Distribution 15-Year Fixed   5
Geographical Distribution 15-Year Fixed   5
                                                    5
FNMA MBS
  Essential Details Total   6
  Essential Details 30-Year Fixed   6
  Essential Details 15-Year Fixed   6
  Note Rate Distribution 30-Year Fixed   7
  Geographical Distribution 30-Year Fixed   7
  Note Rate Distribution 15-Year Fixed   8
  Geographical Distribution 15-Year Fixed   8
Additional Information   9

Average Loan Size

Another important trigger, this figure is the unpaid principal balance divided by the number of loans. Most buyers prefer high-balance loans and have specific loan size requirements for their portfolio.

Note Rate Range

Note rate can be defined as the actual rate the mortgagee pays. The note rate range represents the range of note rates being offered for sale in the package. The term *note rate* can be used interchangeably with *mortgage rate* and *interest rate*. It should not be confused with *coupon rate*, *security rate*, or *pass-through rate*, which all stand for the rate passed through to the investor after the servicing and guarantor fees are extracted from the note rate.

Exhibit 2.6   Essential Details

Information as of Date
1. Investor (i.e. FNMA, FHLMC, etc.)   _____
2. Program (i.e. Laser I, ARC, GNMA II. etc.)   _____
3. Product Type (i.e. Fixed, ARM, etc.)   _____
4. Note Type (i.e. Conventional, FHA, etc.)   _____
5. Recourse (if non-recourse, indicate; if recourse,   _____
    indicate dollar amount and number of loans)
6. Weighted Average Original Term (months)   _____
7. Weighted Average Remaining Term (months)   _____
8. Weighted Average Term to Balloon (if applicable)   _____
9. Unpaid Principal Balance   _____
10. Number of Loans   _____
11. Average Loan Size   _____
12. Weighted Average Note Rate   _____
13. Weighted Average Net Service Fee   _____
14. Montly P&I Constant   _____
15. Monthly T&I Constant   _____

Delinquencies
(as of date ____/____/____)

	Number of Loans	Percentage of Loans
30 days	_____	_____
60 days	_____	_____
90 days and over	_____	_____
Total foreclosures/bankruptcies	_____	_____

Weighted Average Note Range

While the note rate range gives the high and low mortgage or interest rates contained in the offering, the weighted average note range provides the prospective buyer with the predominant note range level for most of the loans. Specific breakdowns with a corresponding unpaid principal balance and number of loans for each rate are given in a later section of the offering.

Weighted Average Net Servicing Fee

The net servicing fee is the difference between the mortgage interest rate and the security rate less any guarantor fees. The weighted average servicing fee is the predominant servicing fee level for most of the loans. The weighted average servicing fee on GNMA I loans is set at a standard 44 basis points. GNMA II loans are not standardized and can vary from a slight increase over 44 basis points to a huge increase, sometimes totaling 60 basis points net fee. FNMA/FHLMC loan have no standard fee and can run from 25 basis points up to 100 basis points, sometimes more. Private investor servicing fees have no set standard but are usually either 37.5 or 50 basis points. Finally, adjustable rate mortgages often have 50 basis points servicing fees.

Weighted Average Original Term (WAOT)

The weighted average of the original term over which the loans are amortized. Weighted averages are calculated on the unpaid principal balance. The WAOT equals the sum of the product of the unpaid principal balance and the original term of each loan, divided by the total unpaid principal balance of all loans.

Weighted Average Remaining Terms (WART)

The weighted average of the remaining terms over which the loans are being amortized. The WAOT and the WART permit prospective buyers to determine the overall age of the portfolio. Loan terms of 15, 20, 25, and 30 years may be grouped together. However, as a general packaging rule, if the number of 15-year loans exceeds 10 percent of the total, they are often best segregated into one group with its own essential details page. Otherwise, they disproportionately skew the weighted average term figures. Thirty-year loan groups commonly include 20-year and 25-year loans.

Twelve-Month Average Escrow Balance

Average monthly escrow balance—the average amount of prepaid taxes and insurance maintained by the bank until they come due—should be calculated against average principal balance. This figure is usually the most difficult to calculate. Companies don't know in advance which servicing they are going to want to sell, and most don't maintain a history of escrow balances for every account over the past year. However, this figure is important to prospective buyers, because it gives a general idea what income, on average, can be expected from the escrow account balances.

Monthly Tax and Insurance Constant (T&I Constant)

Every month the borrower's mortgage payment includes principal, interest, taxes, and insurance. The T&I constant is that portion of the overall payment that relates just to taxes and insurance. This figure is the sum of all tax and insurance payments collected monthly from the group of loans being offered for sale. You can use the T&I constant to estimate a twelve-month average escrow balance if none is available (multiply the T&I constant by a factor determined by the number of times a year the seller pays taxes in each state). The more geographically dispersed the underlying loans in the offering are, the less accurate this average escrow calculation becomes.

Exhibit 2.7 shows the number of times a year tax payments are required to be paid for each state and the corresponding multiplier that can be used for each state. Of course, buyers may prefer to use different multipliers in their own analysis.

Monthly Principal and Interest Constant

The other portion of the monthly mortgage payment is the principal and interest. The principal and interest constant is the total P&I payments scheduled to be made by the borrowers.

Geographic Concentration

This gives the prospective buyer a quick take on the major state or states in which the loans are located.

Delinquencies and Foreclosures

Delinquent loans can be a source of income as well as an indicator of possible future foreclosure losses. This is a vital statistic that is interpreted different ways by different buyers. Use only month-end figures here,

Exhibit 2.7 Tax Payment Frequency by State (with multiplier)

State	Code	Annual (T&I multiply)	Semi-Annual	Quarterly
Alabama	AL	6.5		
Alaska	AK	6.5		
Arizona	AZ		4.0	
Arkansas	AR	6.5		
California	CA		4.5	
Colorado	CO	6.5		
Connecticut	CT		4.0	
Delaware	DE	6.5		
District of Columbia	DC		4.0	
Florida	FL	6.5		
Georgia	GA		4.0	
Hawaii	HI		4.0	
Idaho	ID	6.5		
Illinois	IL		4.0	
Indiana	IN	6.5		
Iowa	IA		4.0	
Kansas	KS	6.5		
Kentucky	KY	6.5		
Louisiana	LA	6.5		
Maine	ME		4.0	
Maryland	MD	6.5		
Massachusetts	MA		4.0	
Michigan	MI	6.5		
Minnesota	MN		4.0	
Mississippi	MS	6.5		
Missouri	MO	6.5		
Montana	MT		4.0	
Nebraska	NE		4.0	
Nevada	NV	6.5		
New Hampshire	NH		4.0	
New Jersey	NJ			2.0
New Mexico	NM	6.5		
New York	NY			2.0
North Carolina	NC	6.5		
North Dakota	ND	6.5		
Ohio	OH		4.0	
Oklahoma	OK	6.5		
Oregon	OR	6.5		
Pennsylvania	PA	6.5		
Rhode Island	RI		4.0	

Exhibit 2.7   Tax Payment Frequency by State (continued)

State	Code	Annual (T&I multiply)	Semi-Annual	Quarterly
South Carolina	SC	6.5		
South Dakota	SD	6.5		
Tennessee	TN	6.5		
Texas	TX	6.5		
Utah	UT	6.5		
Vermont	VT	6.5		
Virginia	VA		4.0	
Washington	WA		4.0	
West Virginia	WV	6.5		
Wisconsin	WI	6.5		
Wyoming	WY	6.5		

because they are the specific cut-off dates that most mortgage companies use for tracking delinquency ratios.

Exhibit 2.8 shows three methods for determining when a loan is delinquent. Many buyers have real strength in their collection function and can control delinquencies effectively. Such buyers can derive substantial ancillary income from late charges and delinquent loans. On the other hand, high delinquency rates may scare other prospective buyers away; to such people, it translates to possible future foreclosure losses. After prospective buyers have reviewed all the information contained on the essential details page, they should have a clear understanding of what is being offered for sale and whether they want to examine the contents further.

Geography Breakdown Page

We have already discussed the importance of identifying and controlling distribution of loans by state, especially as it relates to effectively administering one's servicing portfolio. This factor is considered of great importance in determining overall efficiency.

After the essential details page, the geographic breakdown of the underlying loan is most important to prospective buyers. Exhibit 2.9 shows a typical geographic breakdown page. The number of loans, unpaid principal balance, and percent of total loans for each state is

Exhibit 2.8 Delinquency Calculation

Mortgage Banking Method

Today Is	Loan Is Due For	Last Paid Installment	Delinquency Rate
4-1-88	3-1-88	2-1-88	30 days
4-1-88	2-1-88	1-1-88	60 days
4-1-88	1-1-88	12-1-87	90 days

FHLBB (Thrift) Method

4-1-88	2-1-88	1-1-88	30 days
4-1-88	1-1-88	12-1-87	60 days
4-1-88	12-1-87	11-1-87	90 days

Odd Due Date FNMA Method

4-1-88	3-10-88	2-10-88	Current
4-1-88	2-11-88	1-10-88	30 days
4-1-88	1-10-88	12-10-87	60 days
4-1-88	12-10-87	11-10-87	90 days

usually enough for buyers to determine whether it fits their strategic plan to purchase servicing.

Note Rate Distribution

Most buyers want to see the actual note rate distribution, as shown in Exhibit 2.10. This page includes the following:

- Note rate (not coupon rate)
- Number of loans at the rate
- Unpaid principal balance for those loans (UPB)
- Percentage of total for the unpaid principal balance

Many buyers also want to see the weighted average net servicing fee for each note rate, especially if the portfolio consists of a sizable number of conventional loans. Buyers care about this because often the high servicing fees are associated with the higher note rates, and these are the loans most likely to repay through refinancing, which has a dramatic impact on overall servicing income and therefore on overall yield. As

Exhibit 2.9   Geographic Distribution

State	Number of Loans	Principal Balance	T&I Constant
Alabama			
Alaska			
Arizona			
Arkansas			
California			
Colorado			
Connecticut			
Delaware			
District of Columbia			
Florida			
Georgia			
Hawaii			
Idaho			
Illinois			
Indiana			
Iowa			
Kansas			
Kentucky			
Louisiana			
Maine			
Maryland			
Massachusetts			
Michigan			
Minnesota			
Mississippi			
Missouri			
Montana			
Nebraska			
Nevada			
New Hampshire			
New Jersey			
New Mexico			
New York			
North Carolina			
North Dakota			
Ohio			
Oklahoma			
Oregon			
Pennsylvania			
Rhode Island			

Exhibit 2.9 Geographic Distribution

South Carolina			
South Dakota			
Tennessee			
Texas			
Utah			
Vermont			
Virginia			
Washington			
West Virginia			
Wisconsin			
Wyoming			
Unknown/Other			

stated earlier, on GNMA I loans, the net servicing fee is always forty-four basis points, so this information is not necessary. But most other loan types carry various servicing fees and these weighted averages should be listed with their corresponding note rates.

Loan Breakdown Section

In the loan breakdown section, an offering begins to take definable shape; here a buyer finds depth and detail (Exhibit 2.11). To begin, loan terms are presented—broken out by number of loans, unpaid principal balance (UPB), and percent of total loans. Next, every type of loan included in the offering is listed—fixed rate, adjustable rate, GPM loans, buydown loans, FHA section 245 and 265 loans. The same statistics are given for each (number, UPB, percent of total loans). Finally, FHA, VA, and conventional loans are given the same treatment.

Probably 70 percent of all mortgage portfolio packages in the market today include this information. For the sophisticated buyer, include additional details about the composition of the offering package (sse Exhibit 2.12).

Supplemental Information

The final page or two of the offering should be labeled Supplemental Information and should include any information of potential importance

Exhibit 2.10 Note Rate Distribution

Note Rate Range	Number of Loans	Principal Balance	Original Term
____.00->____.49	_____	_____	_____
____.50->____.99	_____	_____	_____
____.00->____.49	_____	_____	_____
____.50->____.99	_____	_____	_____
____.00->____.49	_____	_____	_____
____.50->____.99	_____	_____	_____
____.00->____.49	_____	_____	_____
____.50->____.99	_____	_____	_____
____.00->____.49	_____	_____	_____
____.50->____.99	_____	_____	_____
____.00->____.49	_____	_____	_____
____.50->____.99	_____	_____	_____
____.00->____.49	_____	_____	_____
____.50->____.99	_____	_____	_____
____.00->____.49	_____	_____	_____
____.50->____.99	_____	_____	_____
____.00->____.49	_____	_____	_____
____.50->____.99	_____	_____	_____
____.00->____.49	_____	_____	_____
____.50->____.99	_____	_____	_____
____.00->____.49	_____	_____	_____
____.50->____.99	_____	_____	_____
____.00->____.49	_____	_____	_____
____.50->____.99	_____	_____	_____
____.00->____.49	_____	_____	_____
____.50->____.99	_____	_____	_____

Exhibit 2.10 Note Rate Distribution (continued)

Note Rate Range	Remaining Term	Weighted Average Note Rate	Weighted Average Servicing Fee
____.00->____.49			
____.50->____.99			
____.00->____.49			
____.50->____.99			
____.00->____.49			
____.50->____.99			
____.00->____.49			
____.50->____.99			
____.00->____.49			
____.50->____.99			
____.00->____.49			
____.50->____.99			
____.00->____.49			
____.50->____.99			
____.00->____.49			
____.50->____.99			
____.00->____.49			
____.50->____.99			
____.00->____.49			
____.50->____.99			
____.00->____.49			
____.50->____.99			
____.00->____.49			
____.50->____.99			
____.00->____.49			
____.50->____.99			

Exhibit 2.11 Loan Characteristics

Fixed Rate

	Number of Loans	Percentage of Total Loans
30-year fixed	_____	_____
15-year fixed	_____	_____
Other (please specify)	_____	_____
Total	_____	_____
Buydowns	_____	_____
GPM/GEM	_____	_____
HUD subsidiary loans	_____	_____
FHA	_____	_____
VA	_____	_____
Conventional	_____	_____
Total	_____	_____

Adjustable Rate

	Number of Loans	Percentage of Total Loans
30-year variable	_____	_____
15-year variable	_____	_____
Other (please specify)	_____	_____
Total	_____	_____
Buydowns	_____	_____
Other (please specify)	_____	_____

Exhibit 2.12 Composition of the Offering Package

Property Types

Type	Percentage of Total Loans
Single Family	90
Condos	5
Town House	3
2-4 Family	2

Loan Source

Type	Percentage of Total Loans
Retail	95
Correspondent	2
Brokered	2
Bulk Purchase	1

Loan to Value

Type	Percentage of Total Loans
0–80	60
81–85	20
86–90	15
91 percent and above	5
Average LTV	65

PMI Information

Number of loans with each private mortgage insurance company: MGIC, GE, and Verex.

Exhibit 2.12 Composition of the Offering Package (continued)

Specific Investor Information

GNMA

Who is the custodian?
Percentage with final certification.
How long before 100 percent of loans have final certification?

FNMA

MBS or Laser reporting?
How does the servicer remit (scheduled/actual or actual/actual)?

FHLMC

Are they PCs or whole loan sales?
Are they sold via the accelerated remittance cycle (ARC) or the normal
  remittance cycle (NON-ARC)?
Are the PCs 100 percent participation or some other percentage?
What percentage are recourse loans?

---

to the package that does not fall into any previous category. This information might include the following:

Computer System

The type of computer system used by a seller can be very useful information, especially if the prospective buyer is on the same system. Compatibility of computer systems can make a transfer much smoother and more cost efficient. In fact, the ability to transfer data via magnetic tape is becoming an absolute necessity on transfers of more than 300 loans.

Tax Service

Most banks use a tax service (Ticor and Transamerica are the two firms most used by the industry); some do their taxes in-house. If the buyer does his or her own taxes or uses a different tax service than the seller, the result can be costly for either one side or the other.

Cross Selling

Many institutions use the servicing function as a tool to sell other financial services, especially life insurance. Therefore, this information may be desirable to the prospective buyer. It usually will be presented in the following format:

- Have the loans been solicited for insurance (yes or no)?
- What percentage of the accounts have been penetrated?

Ancillary Income

Ancillary income encompasses all miscellaneous income derived from income other than service fees, late charges, escrow float, and P&I float. Examples include late fees and commissions from optional insurance solicitations.

Escrows

The interest income earned from escrow accounts can be substantial. You may have heard the saying, "A mortgage bank is a float machine." Buyers may want to know in what states the seller pays interest on escrow account balances. Exhibit 2.13 shows the states in which interest on escrows are required by law.

Other escrow questions answered here are these:

Exhibit 2.13 Interest on Escrow by State

State	Interest on Escrow Rate
California	2.00%
Connecticut	5.25%
Iowa	5.25%
Maine	3.00%
Massachusetts	5.25%
Minnesota	5.00%
New Hampshire	5.00%
New York	5.00%
Oregon	4.50%
Rhode Island	4.00%
Utah	5.25%
Wisconsin	5.25%

- What are the current escrow advances?
- How many times per year and when are taxes paid in each state?
- When was the most recent escrow analysis performed?

Special Packaging Considerations

In a perfect world, every institution that wanted to sell servicing would have the perfect balance of loan types, terms, rates, and locations to comprise a package that would bring a number of top dollar bids. Of course, this is not a perfect world.

More frequently an institution wants to streamline its own portfolio by getting rid of those loans that are inefficient for it to service. That does not necessarily mean that those loans will always be inefficient or costly to service for others. In fact, there is nearly always some institution with a servicing niche that can profitably and efficiently handle the loan mix being offered. Finding the buyer with the appropriate niche is the challenge.

Aside from giving the package to a reputable servicing broker to move, you can do other things in packaging a group of loans with apparent underlying defects or negative elements. Consider some of these problem types and cosmetic packaging techniques:

High Delinquency

A loan mix with a high delinquency rate can evoke many negatives from a prospective buyer. The worst fear is that the loans were poorly underwritten and that foreclosure losses eventually will mount. If this fear is borne out, the loans probably always will have high delinquencies, no matter how strong the buyer's collection department. For the buyer who is able to capture significant late charges from delinquencies, however, these loans could represent hidden income value, especially if the purchase/sale agreement is written so that the buyer does not pay for loans that are more than 60 days delinquent.

Delinquency rates are relative values. What is considered high by one institution is considered healthy by another. One way of softening this data is to present state, regional, or national delinquency averages along with the portfolio delinquency average, if they compare in a favorable manner. For example, if the delinquency rate for the Texas loans in an offering is 5.7 percent, and the average is 7.25 percent, it is to the seller's advantage to include this information.

The Mortgage Bankers Association of America (MBA) publishes a quarterly delinquency survey that can be quite helpful toward this end (Exhibit 2.14). One other factor that must be considered is whether there is a story behind the high delinquency, such as recent high turnover in the seller's servicing department. Telling the story can only help the seller. In short, the seller should include anything that improves the appearance of or qualified otherwise high delinquency rate.

VA Loans

In the wake of the VA no-bids situation that arose several years ago, many buyers have set acquisition parameters that limit the amount of VAs they will purchase. However, many sellers have never experienced a VA no-bid situation, because their state economy has remained strong. For packages with heavy VA loan percentages, it is usually best to provide all possible information about these loans. Geographic breakdown, delinquency rate by state, and the average VA loss experienced by the lender in the past two or three years should help to clarify and soften this often difficult factor. Also, if the seller will indemnify the buyer for losses due to a VA no-bid situation for a specific term, then this should be clearly spelled out.

Exhibit 2.14 National Delinquency Survey of One- to Four-Unit Residential Mortgage Loans—Sample Page

Expanded

MORTGAGE BANKERS ASSOCIATION OF AMERICA

NATIONAL DELINQUENCY SURVEY OF 1- TO 4-UNIT RESIDENTIAL MORTGAGE LOANS
MARCH 31, 1990

CENSUS REGION	PERCENT OF LOANS WITH INSTALLMENTS PAST DUE														90 DAYS OR MORE (S.A.)		PERCENT OF LOANS IN FORECLOSURE STARTED DURING QUARTER		
	TOTAL PAST DUE			30 DAYS			60 DAYS			90 DAYS OR MORE									
	CURR. QTR.	YR. AGO	QTR. AGO	CURR. QTR.	YR. AGO	QTR. AGO	CURR. QTR.	YR. AGO	QTR. AGO	CURR. QTR.	YR. AGO	QTR. AGO	CURR. QTR.	QTR. AGO		CURR. QTR.	YR. AGO	QTR. AGO
CONVENTIONAL LOANS																		
Northeast	3.07	0.05	(0.45)	2.14	(0.08)	(0.51)	0.49	0.05	(0.01)	0.44	0.08	0.07	0.43	0.10		0.19	0.07	0.07
North Central	2.32	0.13	(0.66)	1.70	0.13	(0.57)	0.36	0.02	(0.09)	0.26	(0.02)	(0.02)	0.25	0.00		0.18	0.00	0.01
South	2.97	(0.51)	(1.09)	2.08	0.01	(0.63)	0.44	(0.02)	(0.11)	0.45	(0.50)	(0.36)	0.43	(0.33)		0.30	0.07	0.02
West	1.90	(0.21)	(0.48)	1.36	(0.03)	(0.44)	0.28	(0.06)	(0.05)	0.26	(0.13)	0.00	0.25	0.01		0.16	0.03	0.04
U.S. Total	2.68	(0.15)	(0.74)	1.89	0.00	(0.56)	0.41	(0.01)	(0.07)	0.38	(0.14)	(0.11)	—	—		0.22	0.03	0.02
U.S. Total (S.A.)	*2.76*	*—*	*(0.39)*	*1.98*	*—*	*(0.26)*	*0.41*	*—*	*(0.03)*	*0.37*	*—*	*(0.08)*	*0.37*	*(0.08)*		*0.21*	*—*	*(0.00)*
VA LOANS																		
Northeast	5.69	(0.39)	(1.82)	4.34	(0.30)	(1.56)	1.10	0.01	(0.19)	1.25	(0.10)	(0.07)	1.17	(0.08)		0.33	0.04	0.05
North Central	6.30	0.01	(2.03)	4.15	0.11	(1.63)	1.05	(0.02)	(0.26)	1.09	(0.09)	(0.14)	1.06	(0.11)		0.45	0.05	0.01
South	5.98	(0.44)	(1.34)	3.89	(0.28)	(1.12)	1.02	(0.03)	(0.13)	1.07	(0.13)	(0.10)	1.02	(0.04)		0.45	0.01	0.02
West	4.88	(0.36)	(1.05)	3.22	(0.12)	(0.89)	1.51	(0.10)	(0.13)	0.85	(0.14)	(0.01)	0.82	(0.01)		0.40	0.00	0.03
U.S. Total	5.81	(0.30)	(1.43)	3.80	(0.14)	(1.18)	0.98	(0.05)	(0.16)	1.03	(0.11)	(0.09)	—	—		0.42	0.02	0.01
U.S. Total (S.A.)	*5.98*	*—*	*(0.58)*	*4.00*	*—*	*(0.49)*	*0.99*	*—*	*(0.04)*	*0.99*	*—*	*(0.03)*	*0.99*	*(0.03)*		*0.38*	*—*	*(0.04)*
ALL FHA LOANS																		
Northeast	7.12	(1.10)	(2.28)	4.65	(0.54)	(1.82)	1.19	(0.16)	(0.30)	1.28	(0.39)	(0.14)	1.16	(0.21)		0.47	0.06	0.02
North Central	6.24	(0.23)	(2.06)	4.18	(0.05)	(1.67)	1.02	(0.09)	(0.27)	1.04	(0.10)	(0.13)	1.00	(0.08)		0.47	0.04	(0.02)
South	6.37	(0.11)	(1.54)	4.15	0.01	(1.25)	1.04	(0.04)	(0.18)	1.18	(0.07)	(0.10)	1.12	(0.08)		0.51	0.04	0.04
West	5.08	(0.22)	(1.15)	3.40	(0.06)	(1.01)	0.81	(0.10)	(0.16)	0.87	(0.06)	0.00	0.81	(0.02)		0.43	(0.01)	(0.07)
U.S. Total	6.07	(0.19)	(1.59)	4.01	(0.03)	(1.30)	1.00	(0.07)	(0.20)	1.06	(0.08)	(0.08)	—	—		0.46	0.03	0.00
U.S. Total (S.A.)	*6.26*	*—*	*(0.69)*	*4.24*	*—*	*(0.53)*	*1.01*	*—*	*(0.09)*	*1.01*	*—*	*(0.06)*	*1.01*	*(0.06)*		*0.44*	*—*	*0.03*

SURVEY INFORMATION AND NOTES

1. The historical data in this issue have been seasonally adjusted using the X-11Q Variant of the Census Method II Seasonal Adjustment program. Some previously published data have been revised. The table on the first page presents the seasonally adjusted figures for last year.

2. This survey includes about 14.5 million mortgage loans on 1- to 4-unit residential properties totaling an estimated $800 billion of debt. These loans are serviced by more than 400 reporters, including mortgage bankers, commercial banks, savings banks, savings and loan associations, and life insurance companies.

3. A loan is considered 30 days delinquent if the March 1 installment has not been paid as of March 31. A loan is 60 days delinquent if the February 1 installment is unpaid as of March 31, etc.

4. "Foreclosure started during quarter" includes loans placed in the process of foreclosure during the first quarter, deeds in lieu of foreclosure, and loans assigned to FHA, VA, other insurers or investors. "Foreclosure inventory end of quarter" includes all loans in process of foreclosure on March 31. Both foreclosure categories are excluded from "total installments past due."

5. National totals include Puerto Rico loans and loans of firms not providing state-by-state data.

6. S.A.—seasonally adjusted data

7. NC—not calculated

8. Changes from quarter ago and year ago are done using unrounded estimates.

CENSUS REGIONS

Annual subscription is $30.00

Marketing

The sale of mortgage servicing has become an increasingly sophisticated process along with the emergence of the rest of the secondary market. Ten years ago this type of sale was conducted something like the way you sell your family's second car; today it is a matter of focused, comprehensive product packaging, professional and strategic product marketing, and skillful negotiation and closing of the deal.

Even the objectives of the sale have been affected by the drumbeat of advancing technology. Ten years ago sellers were satisfied with the best offer received from among the several institutions they or their designees had contacted with the offering—the best offer from among limited prospects. Today the business of selling a package of mortgage servicing demands maximized exposure of the offering to elicit the maximum number of bids, thereby attaining the maximum price for the package. In the mortgage banking industry, that difference between the "best offer" of ten years ago and the "maximum offer" of today can be the difference between success and failure.

As the portfolio size, frequency of sale, and sophistication of mortgage servicing marketing has grown during recent years, the brokerage of mortgage servicing sales also has grown in size and importance. In fact, firms that specialize in packaging and marketing mortgage servicing have become an indispensable part of the industry. This is a function of scale. With a system of more than 10,000 banking institutions that handle mortgage loans as an integral part of their operations, the process of communications, qualification, categorization, and negotiation that attends the sale of a servicing package would be virtually impossible for even the largest from among these 10,000. It is a specialized service.

Without it, the "maximized" objectives listed above can't hope to be achieved. The seller would be relying on luck instead of the more predictable results that mass marketing will produce.

The sellers of servicing portfolios contact mortgage servicing brokers to package, distribute, monitor, negotiate, and accept bids on their behalf. Three factors make mortgage servicing brokers add value: their experience, their database, and their marketing skills.

As specialists, mortgage servicing brokers must stay abreast of the current market climate and trends, significant business and legislative issues, and other events that have impact on the secondary market. Also, as a function of their profession, they are experts in the best methods of packaging, presenting, negotiating, and closing sales to satisfy the seller's maximized objectives.

Experience fuels the engine of the mortgage servicing brokers; their database is the engine itself. Without that database, a mortgage servicing broker is out of business. What goes into that database—the organization and updating of files—constitutes the largest difference in the relative abilities and success among mortgage servicing brokers.

The mortgage servicing broker lives and dies by the telephone. It is the driveshaft, the axles, and the wheels that keep the machine moving forward. On the one hand, the broker conducts the bidding process over the telephone. The broker calls potential bidders to ensure that they received the offering, assess interest, answer questions, accept bids, negotiate caveats, and finalize the sale.

When not pursuing a specific sale, the broker is continually updating that all-important database. For every account on the broker's database—and that could be over 10,000 accounts—specific data must be obtained. For example, what type of institution is it—a mortgage bank or a thrift? What type of mortgage product does it handle, and what product mix? What geographical concentrations or preferences does this product reflect? What computer system does the institution use?

More subjective concerns can have everything to do with identifying an institution as a good prospect for a given offering: How does its mortgage portfolio figure into its strategic plan for the next six months or year? What type of product is it interested in buying and in what geographical areas? And then there is the golden question, "Do you have any product you want to consider for sale?"

Mortgage servicing brokers are always on the lookout for other types of information that can translate to sales opportunities. During the past few years, a large number of banking institutions have been forced to consider acquisition by other banks or banking conglomerates. Brokers have often been the go-between in these acquisitions or mergers. As a result, the broker's database maintains information about the corporate status of many banking organizations.

Mortgage servicing brokers must update their databases every few months to ensure topicality. The sale of a mortgage servicing package is highly competitive and detail-oriented, and it occurs within a relatively short time frame. When pursuing a sale, brokers have to rely on the accuracy and timeliness of their databases. As in most businesses, stale or incorrect information is tantamount to a total system breakdown.

Finally, brokers are valuable to the prospective seller (and buyer) because of their market expertise. Trained in telecommunications, mortgage servicing brokers know how to conduct business via this medium. This is no small capability. Hundreds of business courses are offered every year on telephone sales techniques. Within your own organization, it is highly likely that management has instituted or is at least acutely aware of this need for employees who work on the phone.

The broker's expertise takes tangible form in assisting with the packaging of the product, especially in the area of overcoming or qualifying specific weaknesses of the offering, such as high delinquency rate or a preponderance of VA loans. This expertise continues through the various stages of an offering, from knowledge of who are the real players and who are merely curious or using the process to gauge the market, through the negotiation process with its many potential legal and practical pitfalls, to the actual closing and transfer phase.

One wouldn't embark on a trek through the jungle without a guide; not if he or she expected to emerge from the jungle alive. So it is in today's secondary market dealings. One is much better served by taking advantage of the capabilities of a guide, in this case, the mortgage servicing broker.

What actual steps does the broker take as the sale process unfolds? They fall into three phases:

- Premarketing
- Marketing

- Closing the deal

These three steps take from one month to six months. How they are handled will determine price and whether the transaction will indeed close.

The balance of this chapter addresses the first two phases.

Premarketing

Premarketing encompasses four functions:
- Organizing and creating the offering package. We have already discussed how important this document is to meeting the "maximized" objectives of the seller. The broker will assist the seller in preparing the offering, again ensuring that positive aspects of the deal are emphasized and negative points strategically positioned.
- Educating the sales force on the offering's content and establishing sales strategies appropriate to the challenge. This means presenting a detailed discussion of the positives and negatives of the package, and establishing a uniform position for all salespeople to take in overcoming objections to the sale.
- Purging the database to target prospective buyers. In addition, the broker ensures that each salesperson assesses specific needs of certain accounts and knows which are prime for the type of package being offered.
- Setting the bid date. Most packages are distributed within a 2- to 3-day period, followed by 10 to 12 days of follow-up before an established date and time by which all bids must be received by the brokerage firm. This bid date is important, because it must permit enough time for salespeople to actively and efficiently market the product.

Part of the sales strategizing before a package is sent out involves determination of true market value, or pricing. Most often, sellers determine a minimum price they require for the package. To some extent, this price is negotiated between the brokerage firm and the seller based on their joint understanding of current market conditions. It is not uncommon for incentives to be built in for the broker, based on exceeding a minimum price for the offering. The existence of these incentive clauses logically are passed on to the salespeople to motivate them.

Managers often discuss potential pricing with salespeople prior to setting specific goals with the seller. Because salespeople are constantly in touch with accounts from all over the country, they are the best source of information about economic nuances that exist in various regions of the country. This has an obvious impact on where the package is likely to get the best reception and result in the highest bids.

The competitive environment is a critical point feature of the brokerage sales process, even within the brokerage firm. Salespeople conduct all of their evaluation, follow-up, and bid submission in complete secrecy. The only information shared among the salestream is information that will ultimately clarify and issues connected with the package so that everyone is selling exactly the same product.

This policy serves all concerned parties: the seller, the buyer, and the broker. Fair and equitable competition spawns productivity and results in meeting the seller's maximized objectives. Prospective buyers know that they are bidding on equal terms with others for the product and that the deal is unlikely to run aground before closure due to the focus and attention to detail on the part of the broker. And the broker stands only to profit by optimizing the results.

There's an old saying in the financial industry: "A good deal is a deal that's good for everyone." As simple as that sounds, it has been proven time and again throughout business history. In the case of brokering mortgage servicing, the good deal most frequently results from honesty in presentation, integrity in dealings, and a good, competitive environment.

In the brokering of mortgage servicing, today's buyer is tomorrow's seller. A firm's future squarely hinges on a reputation for good, honest, aggressive marketing and an ability to optimize results. In other words, it lives or dies on its ability to establish repeat business.

Marketing

During the ten to twelve days of marketing a product, salespeople follow a predictable and proven regimen of activity:

- *Evaluating the network.* As already mentioned, a brokerage firm begins its search for a buyer by performing a targeted purge of its database. Potential buyer profile information is fed in and a large printout of prospects results. The package is sent first to this list, which can number several hundred or more.

- *Targeting prospects.* While the network evaluation and mailing is being performed, individual salespeople actively search their own account files to select prime targets. Prime targets are institutions that have purchased similar packages in the past, have expressed interest in reviewing a package with the characteristics of the one being offered, or accounts the salesperson knows have incorporated the purchase of servicing into their strategic plan.

- *Following up on the mailing.* If the servicing offering never reaches its destination or if it does not come to the attention of the proper individual, it might as well not have been sent. Many possible reasons exist for materials not reaching the appropriate person at the expected time. Sometimes the postal service fails to deliver; other times a package ends up on a busy secretary's desk or buried under a pile of mail in an executive's in-basket. Therefore, the salesperson must follow up with every account to which an offering has been sent, to make sure the right person has received and examined it.

- *Answering questions.* Once prospective buyers have had a chance to review an offering, they nearly always have questions. Speed and accuracy are the keys during this phase. A possible sale breaks down here if the prospect's questions are not clearly understood and expeditiously answered. While nearly two weeks may seem like a reasonable time frame for a prospect to study an offering, determine its desirability, and submit a bid, unclear information and unanswered questions can bring the process to a screeching halt. Salespeople spend a substantial part of their day contacting prospects to ascertain their questions and concerns, or responding to calls for more information from their accounts. Brokering mortgage servicing is a service business, and efficient service is universally measured by speed of response and accuracy of information.

- *Shortening the list.* During the final few days before the bid date is reached, salespeople prepare their lists of the real players, called the short list, composed of the top five to ten prospects. They determine who goes on the list from responses to the offering as well as from their specific account knowledge. From now until the bids are received, salespeople focus almost exclusively on this short list, speaking to those on it several times a day if necessary to finalize details and answer questions.

Salespeople are often consulted by their prospects about pricing. What offer do they think will get it? What caveats, assurances, or guarantees is the seller likely to agree to that can impact on price? Other than stressing the competitive nature of every deal, a salesperson is extremely aware of the need to fairly and honestly answer these questions, or *not* answer them, as the case may be.

Remember two things:
- The brokerage firm has been hired by the seller and represents the interests of the seller in all dealings regarding that offering.
- Prospective buyers will probably be sellers one day and will expect the same loyalty and integrity when they are on the other side of the equation.

- *Receiving the bids.* Bids are received from prospective buyers at some preset time on the bid date. They are received in complete confidentiality by the salespeople and presented to the management of the brokerage firm. When all bids are in, management possibly will review them privately with the salespeople. Then, at the appointed time, management will conduct the auction with the seller.

All bids are submitted for consideration to the seller. They are then discussed with the seller to determine which meets the maximized objectives. Though one bid is accepted, alternate bids are identified in the event that the deal falls through during the closing stage. Management then informs the salespeople of the results of the auction.

For one member of the salestream, this is a moment of triumph and very real satisfaction. He or she has the pleasure of notifying the successful bidder that it has been awarded the package. Other salespeople have satisfaction as well. Presuming the accepted bid met or exceeded the established minimum, they have played a vital role in the process by maintaining confidentiality, marketing aggressively, and contributing to a healthy competitiveness. All salespeople involved in the deal must contact every account that submitted a bid and present the results.

4

Economic Analysis

Over the past several years, in tandem with the development of the secondary mortgage market and mortgage-backed securities market, mortgage servicing has gained recognition as an attractive financial investment. The trading of mortgage servicing rights has become increasingly liquid, dispelling the long-held belief that servicing mortgages is simply a back-office function performed by a cost center. In fact, excluding "boutique" mortgage banks that specialize in originations, mortgage servicing is the primary asset of a mortgage bank and a "major business line" of thrifts and commercial banks.

Servicing mortgages is a business. As such, it is significantly different from investing in mortgage-backed securities or their derivatives. With the latter, once you make your initial investment, you receive a passive (albeit uncertain) stream of income. With the former, however, you are required not only to make an initial investment but also to perform an array of activities at an additional cost, in order to produce an income stream.

This chapter discusses the elements that affect the economic value of servicing portfolios. In doing so, it provides analytical methods appropriate for this complex task. Finally, it discusses the dynamics of the marketplace and the divergence or balance between price and economic value.

Evaluating Mortgage Servicing

Valuing mortgage servicing requires a sophisticated financial model that incorporates an array of variables. However, the value of servicing may be summarized as the present value of the combined income stream provided by contractual service fees, ancillary income, payment float, and escrow values, less the present value of an expense stream comprised not only of direct operational costs such as personnel and data processing, but also of costs associated with advancing funds, default costs, interest paid on escrow, and so forth.

Even if one assumes that, with the exception of defaults, the life of the underlying mortgages extends to their contractual maturity, none of the elements of either the income or expense stream are certain. Inflation, actual level and cost of defaults, and a variety of operational risks affect servicing costs. Depth of portfolio penetration in terms of optional insurance (accidental death, disability, mortgage life, etc.) and the level of delinquencies and collection of late fees determine actual ancillary revenues; changes in real estate/school taxation levels, investor requirements pertaining to the handling of escrow balances, potential changes to federal/state regulatory requirements regarding the payment of interest on these escrow balances to the mortgagor, and available/allowable investment opportunities for these funds will impact the servicer's escrow revenues. Changes in federal, state, and local tax codes (the 1986 Tax Reform Act, for example) also affect the servicing investment.

Of course, very few mortgages actually extend to their contractual maturity. Even more than the uncertainties described above, prepayment levels (in technical terms, the exercising of the call options granted to mortgagors by their ability to prepay the loans) represent a significant risk to the actual level and duration of a servicer's net income stream. Because of prepayment risk and the other above-mentioned uncertainties, it is not possible to determine an absolute economic value for a given servicing portfolio. Instead, the goal in analyzing servicing should be to construct several internally consistent scenarios from which a most likely economic value range can be established.

Present Value Analysis

When a company originates mortgages and then sells them into the secondary market retaining the servicing rights, or purchases servicing on a bulk or flow basis, it is, in essence, investing in an expected future stream of cash flows. The financial question that must be answered in making this investment decision is, "What am I willing to pay today for cash flows that I expect to receive on a monthly basis over an estimated time period?" Present or discounted cash flow analysis is accepted broadly now as the proper financial technique to use in making this decision.

Present value analysis reduces future cash flows to their equivalent value today, according to the principle that a dollar received today is worth more than one received tomorrow, because the dollar today can be invested immediately to earn a return. Present value analysis is the opposite of calculating the value at some future point in time of a cash investment made today. Start by determining the income and expense streams associated with servicing activities over the life of a portfolio. Then discount each of these expected cash flows by the rate of return offered by similar investment alternatives and according to when these cash flows will occur. This rate of return generally is referred to as the *discount rate* or *opportunity cost* of capital. It represents the return forgone by investing in a particular servicing portfolio rather than in some other project.

The income and expense streams forecast for servicing activities are not certain, which brings up another important financial principle—a safe dollar is worth more than a risky one. Because not all investments are equally risky, the discount rate selected should reflect the expected return from alternative investments with a similar level of risk. The following examples illustrate the concept of present value and the impact of selecting different discount rates.

As tables 4.1 and 4.2 demonstrate, the choice of a discount rate has a significant impact on the value of the servicing asset. A firm that has a required after-tax return of 10 percent will discount the expected future cash flows from a given portfolio less severely than one using 12 percent as the discount rate. The former firm will assign a higher value to the portfolio, all other things being equal.

Analysis Preparation

Unless a servicing portfolio is composed entirely of similar product (such as FNMA Laser I, thirty-year fixed, single family, 10.50 percent note rate, two-year-old, geographically concentrated, conventional mortgages), the first step in evaluating its economic worth is to stratify the portfolio into components with similar characteristics. Analyze these components sep-

Table 4.1   Present Value Analysis of Hypothetical After-Tax Cash
Flows Forecast Over a Five-Year Period (discount
factor 12 percent)

Year	Net After-Tax Cash Flows	Present Value Discount Factor	Present Value of Cash Flows
1	$1,000,000	0.8929[*]	$892,900
2	900,000	0.7972	717,480
3	800,000	0.7118	569,440
4	700,000	0.6355	444,850
5	600,000	0.5674	340,440
			$2,965,110

[*]Discount factor $= \dfrac{1}{(1+i)^n}$

i = 12% (.12) required return

n = Time period in which cash flow will occur relative to present (year 0)

Table 4.2   Present Value Analysis of Hypothetical After-Tax Cash
Flows Forecast Over a Five-Year Period (discount
factor 10 percent)

Year	Net After-Tax Cash Flows	Present Value Discount Factor	Present Value of Cash Flows
1	$1,000,000	0.9091	$909,100
2	900,000	0.8264	743,760
3	800,000	0.7513	601,040
4	700,000	0.6830	478,100
5	600,000	0.6209	372,540
			$3,104,540

arately and then combine the respective values to determine the overall economic value of a portfolio, rather than simply evaluating the portfolio in its entirety. Failure to perform this stratification will invariably result in over- or underestimating the economic value of a portfolio, because the unique characteristics of different types of servicing have a direct impact on the value of that segment of servicing.

Step 1: Investor Stratification

The first necessary stratification separates the portfolio into investor components:

- GNMA I
- GNMA II
- FNMA Laser I
- FNMA Laser II
- FNMA MBS/MRS
- FHLMC regular
- FHLMC ARC (accelerated remittance cycle)
- Private investor(s)

Each of these investor/agency types has specific characteristics that affect the value of servicing. These characteristics include the following:

- different investor remittance dates for the payment of principal and interest
- varying requirements as to whether these payments must be advanced for delinquent loans
- specific guidelines regarding payoffs—when they are remitted to the investor and how much interest is due the investor for the payoff month
- different servicer custodial requirements

In addition, the mortgage note type generally is distinguished along investor lines, with government loans (FHA/VA) being serviced for GNMA and conventional loans serviced for FNMA, FHLMC, and private investors. These note types have different prepayment risks as well as possible foreclosure costs.

Step 2: Note Type Stratification

Sometimes the mix of note types (FHA, VA, conventional with private mortgage insurance, conventional without private mortgage insurance) does not correspond precisely to the investor mix. In these instances, you need to create subsets within the investor components to reflect the different note types. Make a primary distinction in the prepayment risk between government and conventional note types. Because government loans are assumable and conventional loans generally are not, government loans historically have experienced a lower prepayment rate. In addition, borrowers who qualify for FHA/VA loans usually have a lower income level, and their mortgages have a higher loan-to-value ratio, making it less likely that they will be able to take advantage of a falling interest rate environment by refinancing at a lower rate.

Foreclosure costs for conventional loans will vary by state and by investor, according to whether the state is "judicial" or "power-of-sale," and the process, therefore, takes more or less time to complete, and according to the specific agreement with the investor—whether the investor has recourse to the servicer or must assume all reasonable costs. FHA and VA loan programs have specific guidelines regarding the agencies' coverage of foreclosure costs, which generally increase the servicer's exposure in the event of a foreclosure over that of a conventional loan. This exposure will be discussed in detail later.

Step 3: Loan Type Stratification

The next step in the stratification process is to separate servicing by loan type: fixed, ARM (adjustable rate mortgage), GPM (graduated payment mortgage), buydown, etc. Just as with the stratification by note type, this segmentation is important because of the different risks of prepayment associated with these product types. Much research and information is available regarding the prepayment characteristics of fixed-rate product. This information is available less readily and less reliably for ARM, GPM, and other non-vanilla products; however, it is certain that these latter loans carry with them a higher and more volatile prepayment risk. They should, therefore, be separated from fixed-rate product. Furthermore, the activities related to servicing ARM, GPM, and other non-fixed rate products generally are more complex and time-consuming, which translates to higher costs for servicing them. Include these higher costs in the analysis of these servicing components only; do not spread them over the entire portfolio.

Step 4: Geographic Stratification

Some portfolios have a highly concentrated geographic distribution; others are dispersed. In the latter instance, a stratification should be made by geographic region so that varying prepayment risks, delinquency rates, foreclosure risks and potential costs, etc. can be accurately captured for each region.

Step 5: Original Term Stratification

Next, separate the components into original maturity groupings—30-year, 25-year, 20-year, 15-year, etc. This stratification enables you to more accurately pinpoint the relative age of different components. Portfolio aging or seasoning is important to ascertain, because prepayment risk is lower in the earlier years of a portfolio's life. Also, there is simply a different prepayment risk for 30-year versus 15-year loans (with the shorter term product exhibiting higher prepayment rates).

Step 6: Age Stratification

Once you have segregated your components along the line of original maturity, further stratify these components by their relative age. The Public Securities Association (PSA) developed a prepayment curve based on historical FHA loan data, for use in standardizing the pricing of collateralized mortgage obligations (CMOs). As this curve demonstrates, loans undergo a seasoning period during the first thirty months of their life, during which time they are less likely to prepay. When this period is over, even if the interest rate environment remains stable, a higher level of prepayments will still occur due to factors such as employment changes, deaths in the family, desire to "move up," and so forth.

Step 7: Property Type Stratification

Always perform a separate analysis for residential-single-family, multi-family, and commercial mortgages. Not only do multifamily and commercial mortgage servicing often have specific features such as prepayment lockout periods, prepayment penalties, and balloon payments, but the costs associated with servicing these loans are higher because of increased inspection requirements, etc. In addition, their higher loan balances increase the servicer's exposure in the event of a foreclosure or bankruptcy.

Step 8: Note Rate Range Stratification

Prepayment risk varies not only by note and loan type, relative age, and geographic region, but also by the level of the note rate relative to the current note rate, as well as the level of the current note rate relative to what is projected at the lowest level to which that rate could decline. If the current note rate for conventional, 30-year, fixed-rate loans is 10.50 percent, for example, the probability of a similar loan with a note rate of 11.50 percent prepaying should rates fall further will·be much greater than that for a loan with a note rate of 9.50 percent. On the other hand, if the current note rate is 9.50 percent, and it is highly unlikely that rates will drop by more than another .50 percent, the prepayment risk of a 9.00 percent note rate loan and a 10.00 percent loan will not vary significantly. As a rule of thumb, borrowers generally exercise their right to prepay and refinance when the difference between their note rate and the current available rate is 1.50 to 2.00 percent or greater.

Dividing a servicing component into note rate bands is important, because excess servicing fees usually are associated with loans carrying higher note rates. While these loans bring in higher fee income, it is likely that this income stream will not last as long as that associated with lower-note-rate ranges, because the probability of prepayment is greater. To capture the greater uncertainty of receiving excess servicing fees for an extended period of time, the servicer must isolate them from servicing with lower note rates.

Evaluation Variables: Determining Values

Once you have stratified a servicing portfolio into a set of components with like characteristics, it is time to determine the actual values to use in evaluating each segment. A portfolio evaluation assumptions worksheet, such as the one shown in table 4.3, is helpful during this process. For ease of use, this worksheet should be designed to correspond with the order in which the variables will be input into the evaluation model. The following discussion of these variables starts with the more objective inputs and ends with the most subjective ones and will, therefore, not always follow the order shown in table 4.3.

Original Term (Months)

Each computer model has a unique design, but there should be a means to indicate the original term of each portfolio segment being evaluated. In the case of balloon loans, you normally would indicate the term being used to determine the monthly principal and interest payments, rather than the term to balloon, but the model documentation should be consulted for treatment of balloon loans.

Weighted Average Remaining Term (Months)

This variable impacts the evaluation in several ways, depending on the particular model being used:
1. Along with the prepayment rate assumption, it determines how long the servicing net income stream will continue for each servicing component.
2. It can be used together with original term to determine the relative age of the component and to vary the prepayment speed for new/unseasoned servicing components.
3. Some models use this value, along with the note rate and average loan size, to compute the principal and interest payment automatically.

As with original term, you should be careful in your treatment of balloon loans. Some models have separate inputs for the remaining term used to calculate loan amortization and the actual term to balloon payoff, while others do not.

Beginning Number of Loans

This variable is straightforward. The number of loans simply should be as of the same date as that for all other pertinent information concerning the portfolio.

Table 4.3   Portfolio Evaluation Assumptions

	Component 1	Component 2
Original Term (months)		
Remaining Term (months)		
Months to Balloon		
Beginning Number of Loans		
Average Loan Size (or Current UPB)		
Principal and Interest Payment		
Tax and Insurance Payment		
T&I Growth Rate		
Weighted Average Note Rate		
Prepayment Table (PSA, CPR, or user defined)		
Prepayment Rate (% PSA or CPR)		
Income Tax Rate (Federal / State / Local)		
Pre-Tax Discount Rate		
Post-Tax Discount Rate		
Amortization Method = FASB/SYD/SL/FASB91/DDB		
Number of Years to Amortize Purchase Price		
Net Servicing Fee Rate		
Late Fee Rate		
Late Fee Collection Rate		
Late Fee Calculated on P&I or Total Payments?		
Annual Ancillary Income (per loan)		
Inflation Factor for Ancillary Income (optional)		
Days Float for P&I Payments		
Days Float on Payoffs		
Reserve Requirements on P&I Payments		
Earnings Rate on Float		
Average Escrow Balance (as % of UPB)		
Escrow Reserve Requirement		
Earnings Rate on Escrow Balances		
Interest Rate Paid on Escrow Balances		
Escrow Balance Growth Rate		

Table 4.3 Portfolio Evaluation Assumptions (continued)

	Component 1	Component 2
One-Time Transfer/Conversion Cost Per Loan	_____	_____
Annual Servicing Cost Per Loan (on-time loans)	_____	_____
Servicing Cost Per Loan Inflation Factor	_____	_____
Payoff Cost Per Loan	_____	_____
Payoff Cost Inflation Factor	_____	_____
Days Uncollected Interest Paid to Investor on Payoffs	_____	_____
15–30-day Delinquency Rate	_____	_____
added cost to service per delinquent loan	_____	_____
31–60-day Delinquency Rate	_____	_____
added cost to service per delinquent loan	_____	_____
61–90-day Delinquency Rate	_____	_____
added cost to service per delinquent loan	_____	_____
91–120-day Delinquency Rate	_____	_____
added cost to service per delinquent loan	_____	_____
Delinquencies are Current or Peak?	_____	_____
Apply Inflation Rate to delinquent loan costs?	_____	_____
Cost of Funds - Advances Required on Interest	_____	_____
Cost of Funds - Advances Required on Principal	_____	_____
Foreclosure Rate	_____	_____
Foreclosure Rate Is Current or Peak?	_____	_____
Foreclosure Cost Per Loan	_____	_____
Apply Inflation Rate to Foreclosure Costs?	_____	_____
Number of Months Required to Foreclose on Loan	_____	_____
P&I Advances Required on Foreclosures?	_____	_____

Average Loan Size (or Unpaid Principal Balance)

Depending on the computer model, you should input either the average loan size or the total unpaid principal balance for each portfolio segment.

Income Tax Rate

The income tax rate is used in conjunction with net earnings before taxes to determine the tax liability for each time period. This particular expense is by no means a minor one and should accurately reflect a given institution's combined tax bracket for federal, state, and local taxes. If an institution knows its tax bracket will be changing over time —such as in the case of a loss carryforward for three years followed by a normal tax rate thereafter, or with the implementation of new tax legislation—this should be captured, if possible, in the evaluation by creating a time series that reflects how the tax rate changes over time. Obviously, the tax rate varies from institution to institution for structural reasons—location of company (level of local tax rates), type of legal entity (the tax code for thrifts varies from that for commercial banks or mortgage banks), and past, present, and future anticipated operational performance (loss carry-forwards, etc.).

Weighted Average Note Rate

Unless the analysis is being performed on a loan-by-loan basis, or by note rate, the weighted average note rate for loans in each component should be used. As previously mentioned, portfolios should be stratified by note rate range.

The weighted average note rate is straightforward for fixed-rate loans, but what about for ARMs? Even if the model being used allows the inputting of a time series for note rates, to show their change over time the analyst will still have to integrate information concerning period and life rate caps, margins, and projections concerning changes in the underlying index for ARM loans. This is a very complex and subjective task. If this sort of modeling is being performed for ARM components, it is critical that assumptions for other variables be consistent—changes in principal and interest payments, prepayment probability, and servicing fees (if applicable).

Principal and Interest Payments

As mentioned in the Note Type Stratification section, some models automatically calculate this variable, based on other inputs. Others require that you provide it on a per-loan or total-beginning-balance basis. Be sure that the model is decreasing the level of total principal and interest payments over time based on loan prepayment and default assumptions. This will result, of course, in earnings from float on these payments declining over time.

Weighted Average Net Servicing Fee

As one might expect, the value of servicing is very sensitive to this parameter. Always be certain that the servicing fee indicated is net of any guarantor fees due the agency. These fees are not part of the servicer's income stream, and their inclusion would result in overestimating the value of the servicing asset.

For ARM components, determine whether the servicing fee can change at the roll date. It is relatively common for the servicing fee to be lower during the initial (or teaser) period of an ARM and then to increase at the first roll date. In some instances, the fee can continue to change (within certain ranges agreed upon with the investor) at each roll date. If the servicing fee will or can change, this should be incorporated in the analysis.

Late Fees

In evaluating servicing portfolios, earnings from late fees always should reflect actual levels of collections. The late fee assumption, together with the delinquency rate and principal and interest or total payment, determines the level of income received for handling late payments. Distinctions in this fee must be made for state or agency limits (2 percent on total payments for GNMA servicing, 2 percent for New York loans serviced by mortgage banks, etc.). In addition, the actual level of late fee collection must be incorporated. While an institution's policy may be to assess a 5 percent late fee on payments fifteen or more days past due, if the rate of collection on these fees is only 75 percent, then the actual income received will be less than that due the servicer.

Other Ancillary Income

In addition to the supplementary (or ancillary) income provided by late fees, estimate commissions received from collecting optional insurance premiums (mortgage life, accidental death, disability, etc.), assumption fees, and miscellaneous charges to the borrower. Usually this is done on a dollars-per-year-per-loan basis. Normally insurance premiums are locked in at the time the policy is written so that commissions on existing policies will not change over time until the mortgage pays off. An institution may, however, anticipate stepping up its effort to solicit optional insurance. If so, this increase in revenues should be estimated and included in the evaluation.

Days Float on Principal and Interest Payments

The servicing agreement with each investor includes explicit wording concerning the remittance schedule for principal and interest payments. Under the FHLMC regular remittance program, for example, payments are due the investor on the first Tuesday of the month following a payment's due date. The servicer, therefore, has use of these funds for up to thirty-three days before they must be remitted. For FNMA Laser I servicing, however, the servicer must remit such payments to FNMA whenever collections exceed $2,500; essentially no float is available from this type of servicing.

The float-days assumption for a given servicing component should hinge on the actual investor remittance schedule, the pattern of payment collection, and the number of days it takes for checks to clear (funds become available). Payments are dispersed both before and after the due date, and an institution must analyze what the payment pattern is or is likely to be for a given portfolio component.

If an institution is analyzing its own portfolio, research also should be conducted regarding the average number of days that elapse from the time a payment is received to the time the funds become available. For portfolios being reviewed for purchase, estimate this figure based on the geographic location of loans relative to the servicer, use of lock-boxes, and so forth.

Finally, the float-days assumption can vary depending on the mechanics of the evaluation model itself. Some evaluation models do not have a separate variable to calculate the impact of late payments on float. In this instance, a "net" float days figure must be input. For other models, delinquency and foreclosure assumptions are referenced automatically to determine the percentage of on-time (or performing) loans, and the float-days assumption is applied only to these loans.

Days Float on Payoffs

While early payoffs negatively impact the servicing income stream going forward, some earnings may be associated with float on these payoffs that should be reflected in the evaluation. Review investor requirements to determine how many days the servicer can hold a payoff balance before it must be remitted to the investor. For example, similar to the treatment of normal principal and interest payments, FNMA Laser I servicing payoffs must be remitted immediately. For FHLMC servicing, the payoff must be remitted within five business days of the payoff date. For GNMA, FNMA SRS, and FNMA MBS/MRS servicing, however, payoffs are remitted together with the normal monthly remittance. The opportunity to earn income from payoff float thus varies significantly, depending on the investor type.

Reserve Requirements for P&I Payments and Early Payoffs

After estimating float days for both P&I payments and early payoffs, reserve requirements for the treatment of these payments must also be determined in order to arrive at the level of average available principal and interest balances and payoff balances on which the servicer can earn income. Some investors explicitly require that these funds be held in demand deposit accounts, which are reserved at 12 percent, while others do not specify.

Even if the servicer could hold the funds in accounts reservable at 0 or 3 percent, if they are being held in transactions accounts reserved at 12 percent, and this is unlikely to be changed over the foreseeable future, then the 12 percent requirement should be reflected in the analysis. Obviously, a servicer should review its handling of these payments periodically to determine whether these funds are being handled as efficiently as possible. If not, appropriate changes should be made.

Earnings Rate on P&I and Early Payoff Float

The final input in the determination of income from principal and interest, as well as early payoff float, is the anticipated earnings rate on these balances. Depending on the type of institution, as well as varying forecasts, this rate will differ. A thrift or commercial bank, for example, can utilize these balances effectively as part of its pool of funds available for use in extending loans. The earnings potential for these funds can be very high. Mortgage banks, however, may only be able to earn income on these balances indirectly, through the use of compensating balances.

Basically, the mortgage bank would deposit these funds in custodial accounts at a financial institution that is providing it with warehouse funding. A specific agreement is drawn up regarding the use of these compensating balances to "buy down" the cost of borrowing funds to finance loans the company has made and is holding in "warehouse" prior to their sale into the secondary market. A portion of these balances might also be used by the bank at which they are deposited to compensate the bank for various account activity charges. The precise earnings rate available to a mortgage bank will vary both according to its strength in negotiating a deal with a warehouse bank, as well as the general interest rate environment.

In early May 1990, the FDIC ruled that federal deposit insurance on P&I accounts will be limited to $100,000 per investor or mortgage security holder, effective October 27, 1990. In light of this, secondary market agencies are reviewing their custodial account guidelines, and it seems likely that deposits will be removed from weak or smaller banks. This will affect the value of P&I custodial account balances directly at both thrift and mortgage banking firms. Weaker thrifts that will be required to place these deposits in highly rated institutions will lose an inexpensive source of funds. Also, as the number of institutions qualified to hold these deposits shrinks, the remaining players will be able to negotiate compensating balance arrangements that are less favorable to the thrifts and mortgage banks.

Average Escrow Balances

To the extent a servicer collects monthly installments from the borrower to cover anticipated taxes, insurance premiums, and other charges on the real estate securing the loan, and coordinates the disbursement of these funds, the servicer has another source of income—earnings from average escrow balances. The level of average escrow balances varies due to a number of factors:

- number of loans escrowed
- frequency of disbursements (quarterly payment of taxes will result in a lower average balance than an annual payment)
- amount of cushion the servicer builds into the payment to ensure that enough funds will be collected to meet the various obligations

The frequency of disbursements will vary according to the policy of local tax authorities and insurance carriers. Historical information regarding monthly average escrow balances over the past twelve months is the best source from which to estimate average balances going forward. When this is not available, estimates can be made establishing "factors" for each state (or county) based on items 2 and 3 above. These factors can then be used in conjunction with total monthly tax and insurance payments calculated by state to estimate average escrow balances.

As of the time this chapter goes to press, much uncertainty exists regarding potential regulatory changes to the handling of escrow balances. These changes could have a significant impact on the level of average escrow balances. The Real Estate Settlement Procedures Act (RESPA) contains a section on escrow accounting (Section 10) that states that a maximum of two months' cushion will be allowed. While RESPA was first enacted in 1974 and amended in 1976, the Department of Housing and Urban Development (HUD) has never issued formal regulations to implement the provision of this section.

In May 1988, HUD issued proposed regulations that did not appear to require major changes from current industry practice. However, in December 1988, a draft copy of HUD's final RESPA regulations became available and included a much more restrictive interpretation of Section 10. It stated that no cushion whatsoever would be allowed unless written into the mortgage instruments, with a maximum of two months' cushion permitted. Aggregate accounting also would be required so that, in determining this cushion, funds collected for later disbursement to satisfy a school tax obligation would have to be applied in satisfying an earlier real estate tax obligation, for instance. Where no cushion is allowed, the escrow balance for a borrower would be required to drop to $0 once during the year. Furthermore, this change in escrow accounting would be enforced on a retroactive basis, so that adjustments would be required to properly handle escrow accounting for existing mortgages.

Estimates of the impact of these potential changes vary according to the current escrow policy of individual organizations, but a decline in average escrow balances of 25 to 50 percent is possible.

During the latter half of 1989 and early 1990, HUD put the enforcement of this part of RESPA on hold indefinitely. However, the attorneys general from seven states recently have revived the issue. The attorneys general have asked HUD to enforce RESPA Section 10 to prevent escrow overcharging. They contend that HUD has the power to enforce the escrow limits of RESPA.

Escrow Balance Growth Rate

Tax obligations and insurance premiums generally increase each year, and the average annual increase should be estimated and incorporated in the evaluation.

Escrow Reserve Requirements

Just as for float on principal and interest payments, reserve requirements on escrow balances must be determined and included in the evaluation to arrive at available average escrow balances.

Escrow Earnings Rate

Comments regarding earnings on float from principal and interest payments also are applicable for earnings on escrow balances. Some models do not have a separate variable for interest paid on escrow—interest that must be paid to borrowers when escrow payments are held in their behalf. When a separate variable does not exist, the level of interest payment should be netted from the earnings rate.

Interest Paid on Escrow

The geographic distribution of loans in a given servicing component and state legislative requirements for the payment of interest to borrowers on escrow balances held should be utilized in determining a weighted average rate of interest paid on escrow. As indicated above, some models will treat this as a separate expense, while others will simply net down interest income earned on average escrow balances.

One-Time Transfer/Conversion Costs

When buying servicing on a bulk basis, or for that matter on a flow basis, in addition to the funds actually paid to the seller, the buyer initially incurs numerous other expenses. Estimates for such expenses should be included in the cash flow analysis that the buyer performs in determining the economic value of the servicing to his organization. These expenses can include the following:

- tape transfer of loan information and other data processing related activities
- physical transfer of loan documents
- notification of transfer to mortgagors
- issuance of coupon books
- assignments

Those transfer costs to be borne by the seller should not be included.

Annual Servicing Cost Per Loan

As with several previously discussed variables, the costs included under this category depend on how many separate variables are used in a given model to capture the costs associated with servicing loans. Many models treat separately the routine expenses incurred in servicing on-time (performing) loans, the additional costs of servicing delinquent loans, direct foreclosure costs, costs incurred at the time of a payoff, and the cost of having to advance funds to the investor in the case of delinquent loans or loans in foreclosure. Even if these expenses must be combined in the analysis, it is wise to research and estimate them separately first. This helps ensure that no significant cost factor is inadvertently omitted and that the combined amount accurately reflects the cost structure of a given organization. This discussion assumes that each of these cost categories is handled separately in the analysis.

If the analysis involves evaluating the current economic value of an existing portfolio, then using the fully loaded costs associated with performing the various activities necessary to service performing loans is appropriate. However, if the evaluation concerns adding servicing to a portfolio, it is essential to estimate the incremental costs that will be incurred rather than spread fixed costs over these additional loans and include variable costs as well. By definition, fixed costs will not change with the addition of a new block of servicing. Including such costs in the analysis results in a value lower than what the additional servicing is actually worth to an organization. This, in turn, could lead to the wrong investment decision—not pursuing a servicing opportunity at all, or bidding too low in an auction for servicing and thereby failing to win the servicing in question.

Incremental costs that should be estimated on a per loan, annual basis include the following:

- data processing
- postage
- forms/coupon books and other supplies
- telephone charges
- custodial costs
- expansion of facilities and increase in utilities
- purchase of additional equipment
- additions to personnel (loan set-up, loan administration, customer service, escrow accounting, optional insurance area, investor accounting, collections area)

These costs can vary widely from institution to institution because of such factors as these:

- different types of loans being serviced
- location of servicing operation and varying labor and facility costs
- location of properties relative to servicing operation (long distance telephone charges, lock-box charges, etc.)
- efficiency of the servicing operations

Structural differences in servicing costs is one of the primary reasons that the economic value of servicing is unique for each organization.

Servicing Cost Per Loan Inflation Factor

The evaluation of servicing encompasses many years over which it is logical to assume that costs will rise due to personnel cost-of-living and merit raises, increases in data processing, supply and telephone costs, and so forth. An annual inflation factor should be incorporated into the analysis based on prior experience as well as anticipated levels of inflation. On the other hand, if an organization has definite plans to make operational changes or invest in equipment that will result in cost savings, the anticipated reductions should be included in the analysis from the point in time at which they are projected to start.

Payoff Costs Per Loan

When a loan pays off early, not only is the servicer's income and expense stream impacted going forward, the servicer also incurs certain expenses at the time of the payoff. There are two types of payoff expenses:

- the cost of processing a payoff which, in general, consists of the staffing costs associated with the number of hours this process takes
- the payment of interest to the investor for the payoff month, which was not collected from the borrower

A processing cost is incurred for all payoffs. The interest cost, however, varies according to investor requirements specific to the type of servicing and the note rate of the underlying loan. For FNMA Laser I and FHLMC servicing, interest due the investor is calculated for the number of days up to but not including the date of payoff. The servicer, therefore, does not incur any interest expense on payoffs for this type of servicing. For FNMA MBS, FNMA MRS, GNMA I, and GNMA II servicing, interest must be passed through to the investor for the entire month in which the payoff occurs regardless of the payoff date. Depending on the payoff date then, the servicer may have to pass through anywhere from one to thirty days of interest which it did not collect.

Under the FNMA Summary servicing program, a half-month's interest must be passed through to the investor. In this case, the servicer actually earns interest income on payoffs occurring in the second half of the month. If payoffs are distributed evenly during the month, then the interest income received on some loans offsets the interest expense incurred for others.

Delinquency Rate

Almost all portfolios have a certain percentage of mortgagors delinquent in making scheduled payments. Most models require that an expected delinquency rate be input separately from the foreclosure rate, to handle their distinct costs accurately.

In determining a delinquency rate for a specific servicing component, there are several considerations to be made:

- What is the current delinquency experience for the servicing component?
- Is the servicing new or seasoned?
- Are adverse economic factors that are expected to change in the future currently affecting the delinquency rate?

If a portfolio segment is seasoned and the servicer believes its current delinquency experience will continue, this rate should be incorporated in the analysis.

While newer servicing usually will have a fairly low delinquency rate, it would not be appropriate to assume that this favorable rate will continue once the portfolio has seasoned and delinquency problems have had time to surface. For new servicing, use either (1) the experience of similar but seasoned servicing components in the organization's portfolio, or (2) delinquency rates typical for the specific loan type and geographic region.

The Mortgage Bankers Association (MBA) provides a detailed survey of delinquency trends on a quarterly basis. The delinquency rate anticipated for newer portfolios, once they have seasoned, should not be applied immediately. This should be the peak delinquency rate; lower but gradually increasing rates should be applied until the portfolio is fully seasoned.

For seasoned portfolios, the current delinquency experience may be high due to adverse economic trends, such as that experienced recently in the "oil patch" states, for instance. If there are signs that these trends will improve, the higher delinquency rates used in the early period(s) of the analysis should be followed by lower, historical averages.

Some models require that the total delinquency rate, one to three-plus months, and the average days delinquent be input. Other models allow a more detailed analysis in which the different categories of delinquencies are each input separately.

Costs to Service Delinquent Loans

The delinquency rate impacts late-fee income according to the level of delinquencies assumed, the late-fee rate, and the expected percentage of late-fee collections. On the cost side are expenses associated with servicing delinquent loans beyond the normal servicing costs. An organization should analyze its collections area to determine what additional costs are incurred in handling loans that are 30 days, 60 days, and 90 days past due. Based on this analysis, the additional costs should be incorporated into the servicing evaluation according to the level of delinquencies assumed for each delinquency period.

Failure to make this distinction in servicing costs causes a highly delinquent servicing component to appear more valuable than a low-delinquency segment. The reason for this error is simple: if servicing costs are assumed to be the same for all loans, whether on-time or delinquent, the net income stream calculated for more delinquent portfolios will be higher than that for those that are less delinquent. This occurs because expenses are estimated to be the same, while the more delinquent portfolio is generating higher income from late fees.

Foreclosure Rate

Estimation of going foreclosure rates fits well with most of the points already made about the determination of a delinquency rate for a portfolio segment. You must weigh recent foreclosure experience of the portfolio segment against the relative age of the component, type of loans, economic conditions anticipated for the geographic region in which the loans are located, and so forth. Similar to delinquency rates, the probability of foreclosures varies with the aging of the portfolio. FHA statistics for 1988 show a gradually increasing foreclosure rate through the fourth to fifth year of a portfolio's life, after which the rate drops off significantly. A similar pattern should be anticipated for most portfolios, unless significant economic factors come into play. As loans season, the borrowers' income generally is increasing, and their equity in the property also is being built up, making it increasingly less likely that they will default on their investment.

The analyst should use all available information to determine as accurately as possible the maximum foreclosure rate likely for a given portfolio; however, applying this rate as constant will result in an undervaluing of the servicing. The best model allows for the entry of a time series whereby the foreclosure rate may be varied.

Foreclosure Costs per Foreclosed Loan

Foreclosure costs vary significantly depending on the type of servicing, the underlying loan type, and location of the property and state legislation regulating the foreclosure process. Loans sold "with recourse" to investors have much higher foreclosure costs than those with no recourse. When an FHA loan is foreclosed, the servicer loses two months' interest and is reimbursed for subsequent payments at the FHA "debenture" rate, which is virtually always lower than the loan's underlying note rate. VA foreclosure costs, especially from no-bids, actually have caused some servicers to go under.

For several types of conventional loan servicing, such as FNMA Laser I, FNMA Summary, FHLMC, and some private investor arrangements, the agency/investor agrees to reimburse the servicer for all reasonable costs, or all reasonable costs above a certain threshold. Servicers carefully examine what their actual out-of-pocket costs have been for processing foreclosures under these arrangements and often place limits on reimbursable lawyer's fees and other expenses that add to the servicer's true foreclosure costs. An accurate analysis includes these actual costs.

VA No-Bids

The VA loan guarantee program is financed by public funds and was created in 1944 as a benefit for eligible veterans of World War II who might not otherwise have been able to purchase homes. VA borrowers pay a funding fee of 1.25 percent of the loan amount; in exchange, they obtain a controlled (government-administered) interest rate, pay a minimal downpayment, and obtain a loan that is "guaranteed," obliging the VA to repay a specific percentage of the loan should the borrower default.

VA no-bids are foreclosures at which the VA declines to purchase the property, based on a calculation that determines whether paying the full cash guaranty to the lender will cost the VA less than purchasing the property at the current loan amount and disposing of it later.

Initially, the VA seldom exercised its option to leave the lender with the foreclosed property and pay only the guaranteed portion of the loan. The VA's soaring costs have led to a much more thorough analysis on its part, and VA no-bids rose from approximately 3 percent in 1984 to 24 percent in 1988. Because the VA has revised its net value calculation to incorporate an estimate of the government's cost of funds for holding a foreclosed property, the incidence of VA no-bids probably will increase by an additional 10 percent.

Servicers increasingly have been using the option to buy down the indebtedness on a foreclosed property so that the net value will be higher than the unguaranteed portion of the debt, rather than experience a VA no-bid. The VA then acquires the property rather than paying the guaranty.

The critical factor in determining whether pursuing the buydown option is more cost-effective than taking in the property as real estate owned ("REO") is whether the servicer anticipates that the property can be sold for enough that the loss would be less than the amount required to buy it down.

During the second quarter of fiscal year 1990, the VA reported that 12 percent of VA foreclosures were no-bids and an additional 6.5 percent were buydowns. VA no-bids and buydowns have impacted seriously the profitability of organizations servicing VA loans. Recent estimates of VA buydown costs range from $10,000 to $13,000 per loan, while no-bid losses average $20,000 to $25,000.

To properly estimate the costs of foreclosing on VA loans, the servicer should examine its recent experience, determine the location of VA loans being evaluated and the level of no-bids experienced in those regions, and carefully review current loan-to-value ratios. The servicer must determine what percentage of VA foreclosures are likely to be no-bids and buydowns and then weigh foreclosure costs accordingly.

Cost of Advancing Funds on Delinquent Loans

One sometimes forgotten expense in the evaluation of servicing is the cost of having to advance funds to investors on delinquent loans and loans in foreclosure. When required to advance interest and/or principal payments to the investor, the servicer either incurs direct costs to borrow the necessary funds or reduces the funds available on which to earn income. Whichever perspective one employs, this can be a significant expense and should not be overlooked.

FNMA Laser I servicing does not require such advances; only payments that are actually collected are passed through to the investor. For FNMA Summary and FHLMC servicing, scheduled interest must be passed through to the investor, regardless of whether it is collected. FNMA MBS, FNMA MRS, and GNMA I and II servicing all require that both scheduled interest and principal be passed through on delinquent loans and loans in foreclosure. Consult the specific agreements for private investors to determine what type of advances, if any, are required.

Unless circumstances specific to an organization make the cost of advancing funds different from the rate at which the firm can earn income on principal and interest and escrow balances, these rates should be assumed to be the same in the analysis.

Foreclosure Completion Time

Many servicing evaluation models include a variable to indicate how many months generally are required to complete the foreclosure process. This estimate varies according to the loan type and whether the loans are in states that are "judicial" or "power-of-sale." In the former case, the foreclosure process can be extremely lengthy, because it involves a foreclosure by court action in which the lender files suit against the borrower, and the court supervises virtually the entire process.

In states that permit foreclosures by the exercising of the *power-of-sale*, also known as *foreclosure by advertisement*, if the original mortgage contract contains a power-of-sale clause, the mortgagee has the right to sell the property if the borrower defaults. State laws specify lender requirements for notifying the mortgagor and advertising the sale. The power-of-sale foreclosure not only take less time, but it also entails much less legal expense.

The minimum time for completing a foreclosure, defined as the period from the day the organization turns the account over to its lawyers until the day it receives the sale proceeds or deed, is approximately four months. When foreclosure by court action is necessary and statutory redemption periods must be added, the process can extend up to two-and-one-half years. Statutory redemption periods are time periods (after the default) established by state legislation during which the borrower has the right to pay the outstanding balance (plus costs) and recover the property.

The months-to-foreclosure assumption used should be determined based on those characteristics and affects the actual number of loans assumed to be foreclosed during the servicing's expected life. This in turn will determine, together with assumptions used for other foreclosure-related variables, actual foreclosure expenses, curtailment of servicing income, and interest expense associated with advancing funds.

Purchase Price Amortization

To the extent that all or part (in the case of excess servicing) of the value of servicing has or will be capitalized on the servicer's balance sheet, a portion of this value must be amortized each year. The Federal Accounting Standards Board (FASB) requires that this amortization be carried out using the interest method defined under FASB 65. This method involves projecting the positive pretax income over the expected life of the portfolio and then apportioning the amortization according to the percentage of total positive pretax income a given period is projected to have. This is an accelerated method of amortization and reflects the decreasing value of the servicing over time.

In practice, a number of amortization methods are accepted, because they are not deemed to be materially different from the interest method. Sum-of-the-years' digits, declining balances, and even straight-line over a short time period are still used by some organizations. Generally, the amortization occurs over a 10- to 15-year period for 30-year loans and a 5- to 7-year period for 15-year loans. The determination of the number of years depends on both the contractual life of the loans and prepayment assumptions.

Accelerating the amortization of the purchase premium or excess servicing capitalized will decrease GAAP income. Amortizing faster rather than slower enhances the value of an organization's servicing investment. The amortization expense is not a cash expense, yet it reduces taxable income and thereby lowers the firm's tax liability, so that the firm's cash flows are actually increased. For this reason, the amortization of the purchase price represents what is known as a *tax-shield benefit*.

This benefit should be estimated in the analysis according to the particular circumstances of each organization. The amortization method used in the servicing analysis should be the same as that used in practice by the company's accounting area, and the income tax bracket of the firm will affect the level of benefit it receives from this amortization.

Prepayment Rates

Prepayment rate assumptions are by far the most subjective ones used in the analysis of servicing. Yet these assumptions, along with the discount rate/required return utilized, affect the value of servicing the most significantly. Loan type, note rate, relative age, geographic location, and, of course, expected changes in the interest rate environment all have bearing on the likely prepayment rate a given portfolio segment will experience.

For portfolios that are not yet seasoned, the prepayment assumption used should not be a constant one. In general, prepayment rates should follow the shape of the PSA prepayment curve or a seasoning curve developed by the institution itself. The level of prepayments assumed may not fall precisely on this curve, but the rates should generally correspond to the shape of the curve.

Discount Rate/Required Return

A great deal has been written on how an organization should go about determining its discount rate and required return. In practice, a variety of approaches are used. Some organizations use their cost of capital as determined by averaging, according to the firm's debt/equity ratio, the expected return of shareholders and its cost of debt. Some buyers of servicing use the "net cash out" approach and deduct the portfolio's escrow balances to be received from the cash to be paid to the seller, in order to determine how much equity will be used to fund the purchase. On the debt side, financing specific to the transaction may be employed. The discount rate used should reflect the risk of the servicing investment and the return offered by alternative investments with a similar risk profile.

As demonstrated in the examples explaining present value analysis, the lower the discount rate used, the higher the value of the servicing because the future cash flows are less steeply discounted. Different return requirements among organizations, together with their varying cost structures and projections of prepays, are the primary reasons that servicing has a different economic value to each institution.

Sample Portfolio Evaluation

This section evaluates a hypothetical $80 million FHLMC ARC (accelerated remittance cycle) servicing portfolio offering. ABC Mortgage Company ("ABC"), based in Raleigh, North Carolina, is interested in adding this servicing to its current portfolio of $500 million composed of conventional, residential servicing concentrated in the southeastern United States. ABC has performed the following evaluation to determine what the economic value of this servicing is to its organization.

Portfolio Characteristics

The portfolio consists of FHLMC ARC, thirty-year fixed rate, conventional loans located in North Carolina. All loans in this portfolio are assumed to have the same characteristics (loan size, note rate, servicing fee, and so forth) and were sold without recourse. The essential details of the portfolio are provided in table 4.4.

Evaluation Assumptions

Based on the loan characteristics of the servicing portfolio, ABC Mortgage Company constructed the set of evaluation inputs shown in table 4.5.

ABC Mortgage Company's evaluation inputs include the objective loan characteristics of the portfolio and reflect the organization's cost structure, tax bracket, required return, and its most-likely projections regarding prepayment rates, available earnings rates on float and escrow balances, cost of funds on advances, and servicing cost inflation rates.

Currently, ABC is offering fixed rate mortgages at 10 percent with two origination points. In selecting a prepayment rate of 175 percent PSA experience, ABC decided that it was likely that interest rates would continue to fall over the coming months before leveling off, possibly bringing the current note rate to as low as 8.50 to 9.00 percent. ABC's prepayment assumption was conservative due to the massive refinancing wave it experienced in 1986.

This prepayment rate is used in conjunction with the PSA curve. Because the portfolio is only six months old, the full impact of this assumption does not occur until the beginning of the third year of the analysis, when the portfolio is thirty months old and is seasoned. At that time, the annual conditional prepayment rate is assumed to be 10.50 percent.

Based on its debt/equity ratio and returns available from alternative investments with a similar level of risk, ABC's senior financial executives decided that the required rate of return should be 11 percent, after taxes. Given its combined federal and state tax bracket of 36 percent, this translates into a 17.20 percent pretax discount rate.

ABC's outside auditors require the company to use the method prescribed in FASB 65 to amortize the purchase price. ABC normally uses a twelve-year amortization period for new, thrity-year, conventional fixed-rate product.

For late fees, ABC charges 4 percent of the total monthly payment, the maximum permitted in North Carolina. Based on a review of the delinquency rate of its current portfolio and actual late-fee collections, ABC has determined that it generally collects about 75 percent of the late fees it charges. ABC decided to assume this collection rate in its evaluation, because the loans in the FHLMC portfolio being evaluated have similar characteristics to its existing portfolio.

The FHLMC portfolio has not been solicited for optional insurance. ABC has plans to solicit the portfolio should it win the auction and estimates that ancillary income from the insurance policy premium commissions spread over the new portfolio will be approximately $8.50 per loan.

Regarding float days on principal and interest, ABC's model will apply this calculation only on performing loans—those loans that have a current status. ABC's experience has been that it benefits from approximately eleven days of float, on average, from on-time principal and interest payments for FHLMC ARC servicing which requires a remittance within three business days after the fifteenth of each month.

Payoffs on loans serviced for FHLMC must be made within five business days, and ABC has therefore assumed four days of float on the payoff balances. Also, ABC is required to pass through to FHLMC interest only on the number of days up to but not including the payoff date. This means ABC does not have to remit any interest which it has not actually received as part of the payoff balance.

Based on the average tax and insurance constant of $92.31 per loan and the fact that taxes are paid annually in North Carolina, ABC estimated that the average escrow balances would be approximately .75 percent of

---

Table 4.4   FHLMC ARC Portfolio: Essential Details

Date of Information	July 31
Product Type	30-Year Fixed
Note Type	Conv. w/o PMI
Principal Balance	$80,000,000
Number of Loans	1,000
Average Loan Size	$80,000
Weighted Average Net Servicing Fee	0.375%
Weighted Average Note Rate	10.50%
Weighted Average Original Term (months)	360
Weighted Average Remaining Term (months)	354
Current Escrow Balance	$369,055.38
Tax and Insurance Constant	$92,310.00
Principal and Interest Constant	$733,579.26
Geographic Location	North Carolina

Delinquencies

	Number of Loans	Percentage of Loans
30 days	4	0.40
60 days	2	0.20
90 days	0	0.00
Net Delinquencies	6	0.60
Foreclosures	0	0.00
Total Delinquencies	6	0.60

Additional Information

Seller's Servicing System: CPI
Tax Service, TransAmerica
All files and records are on hardcopy.
Weighted Average LTV: 80%
Loans are 100% without recourse.
Loans are 100% FHLMC whole loans, under accelerated remittance cycle.
Loans are 100% single-family, owner occupied.
Loans are 100% self-originated.
Loans have not been solicited for insurance.
Offering represents approximately 10% of the seller's portfolio.

Source: Cohane Rafferty Securities, Inc.

Table 4.5   ABC Mortgage Company: FHLMC Portfolio Evaluation
Assumptions

		Segment 1
1.	Original Term (months)	360
2.	a) Wtd. Avg. Remaining Term	354
	b) Months to Balloon (if applicable)	N/A
3.	Beginning Number of Loans	1,000
4.	Average Loan Size (or Unpaid Principal Balance)	$80,000
5.	Income Tax Rate	36%
6.	Wtd. Avg. Note Rate	10.50%
7.	P&I Payments	$733.58
8.	Wtd. Avg. Net Servicing Fee	.375%
9.	a) Late Fee Rate	4%
	b) Late Fee Collection Rate	75%
	c) Late Fee Calculation on P&I or Total Payment	Total
10.	a) Other Ancillary Income Per Loan	$8.50
	b) Inflation Factor (Optional)	None
11.	Days Float on P&I	11
12.	Days Float on Payoffs	4
13.	Reserve Requirements for P&I Payments and Early Payoffs	12%
14.	Earnings Rate on P&I and Early Payoff Float	8%
15.	Average Escrow Balances	.75%
16.	Escrow Balance Growth Rate	5%
17.	Escrow Reserve Requirements	12%
18.	Escrow Earnings Rate	8%
19.	Interest Paid on Escrow	0%
20.	One-Time Transfer/Conversion Costs	$10 per loan

Table 4.5   ABC Mortgage Company FHLMC Portfolio Evaluation
Assumptions (continued)

21.	Annual Servicing Cost Per Loan	$65
22.	Servicing Cost Per Loan Inflation Factor	5%
23.	Payoff Costs Per Loan	
	a) Processing costs	$20
	b) Days of uncollected interest paid to investor	0
24.	Peak Delinquency Rate and Additional Cost to Service	
	30-day	2.05% – $150
	60-day	.35% – $200
	90+ day	.36% – $250
25.	Foreclosure Rate	.36% peak
26.	Foreclosure Costs Per Foreclosed Loan	$500
27.	Cost of Advancing Funds on Delinquent Loans	8%
28.	Advances on P&I or Interest Only	Interest
29.	Months Required to Complete a Loan Foreclosure	10
30.	Amortization of Purchase Price FASB65	12 Years
31.	Prepayment Rate	175% PSA
32.	After-Tax Discount Rate	11%

Source: Cohane Rafferty Securities, Inc.

the unpaid principal balance during the first year of the analysis. Taxes and insurance have risen approximately 5 percent per year in the past, and this pattern is assumed to continue.

ABC's P&I payments, payoff balances, and escrow balances are kept on deposit in custodial accounts at XYZ Bank. In accordance with its agreement with XYZ, ABC earns income indirectly via a reduced rate on its warehouse borrowings. Historically, ABC has earned, on average, approximately 8 percent on these compensating balances and expects this trend to continue. For advances on the interest portion of delinquent P&I payments, ABC assumed that its cost of funds would be the same as its earnings rate.

ABC estimates its incremental servicing cost for on-time loans at $65 per loan. Additionally, approximately $10,000 will be expensed in the first year before the final transfer is completed, which translates into a $10-per-loan conversion cost. Finally, a cost analysis of payoff related activities has revealed that it costs ABC around $20 per payoff to perform these activities.

Because the FHLMC portfolio is quite new, it is not surprising that its current delinquency experience is only .60 percent and that no loans are in foreclosure. ABC knows it is unrealistic to assume that this level can be maintained once the portfolio has seasoned. ABC's seasoned portfolio has a delinquency and foreclosure experience that is in line with the average delinquency experience for North Carolina conventional loans reported in the MBA's quarterly delinquency survey for the first quarter of 1990.

ABC decides it is accurate to assume that the FHLMC portfolio will perform similarly, and, therefore, these averages were input as the peak, or maximum rates, that the portfolio would experience over its life. ABC employs normalizing curves in its model to determine the shape of delinquency and foreclosure experience curve over time. It assumes that delinquencies will rise in a relatively linear manner over the first thirty months of a portfolio's life and then level off. The total U.S. thirty-year 1988 HUD/FHA foreclosure rates indicating foreclosure experience of mortgages insured since 1970 have been utilized to estimate how foreclosure rates will change as the portfolio ages.

ABC's cost accountant also has been busy analyzing the additional costs incurred by its collections area in servicing delinquent loans. Based on this cost study, ABC estimated that it costs an additional $150 per year per delinquent loan to service loans that are 30- to 59-days delinquent, $200 per year for each loan that is 60- to 89-days delinquent, and $250 per year for each loan that is 90+ days delinquent. While FHLMC reimburses ABC for all reasonable costs associated with a foreclosure, ABC's experience has been that its own out-of-pocket costs average approximately $500 per foreclosed loan. Finally, ABC's foreclosure process has been averaging about ten months for North Carolina conventional loans.

Evaluation Reports

After inputting the assumptions into the evaluation model and performing a present value analysis of the resulting cash flows, ABC found that the value of the $80 million FHLMC ARC servicing portfolio, based on the combined impact of these assumptions (including its 11 percent after-tax required return), was 1.494 percent of the unpaid principal balance, or $1,195,381. See table 4.6 for a summary of these calculations.

If these assumptions prove to be correct, the portfolio will have a mean loan life of just over 113 months, or 9.5 years, with a six-year payback period. Of the 1,000 loans in the original portfolio, only 42 will go to their full term, and 17 will be foreclosed on. The majority of the loans, 941, will prepay at various points over the life of the portfolio. Table 4.7 shows detailed cash flows for each year of the analysis.

This evaluation represents a conservative scenario constructed by a hypothetical ABC Mortgage Company to determine the portfolio's economic value to this institution. The portfolio's economic value is sensitive to changes in any of the primary assumptions. The following section provides an analysis of price sensitivity to changes in various assumptions, using the FHLMC ARC portfolio evaluation inputs in table 4.5 as the base case.

Sensitivity Analysis

A comprehensive set of sensitivity analyses have been performed on ABC Mortgage Company's initial evaluation of the $80 million FHLMC ARC servicing portfolio. These analyses are summarized in table 4.8. Unless otherwise indicated, only the variable that is the subject of a particular price-sensitivity analysis has been changed from the base case shown in table 4.5.

The level of price sensitivity to changes in a particular variable will differ depending on the value of other variables that are part of the analysis. For instance, the price sensitivity of the FHLMC ARC servicing to a one-basis-point (1/100th of a percent, bp) change in the servicing fee drops from about 4 bps to about 3.5 bps portfolio when the prepayment assumption is increased from 175 percent PSA experience to 243 percent PSA.

The goal in analyzing servicing is to construct internally consistent scenarios from which a most-likely economic value range can be estab-

---

Table 4.6   FHLMC ARC Portfolio: Summary Calculations

Segment Code Name	FHLMC
Segment Description	30-year fixed
Starting Principal($1,000)	$80,000
Purchase Price Dollars	$1,195,381
Purchase Price Percent	1.494%
Post-Tax Return	11.00%
Years to Payback	6.06
Total Operating Revenue	$3,560,999
Total Operating Expense	$1,099,151
Total Purchase Amortization	$1,195,381
Total Net Income Pre-Tax	$1,266,466
Total Taxes	$455,928
Total Net Income Post-Tax	$810,538
Total Cash Flow Post-Tax	$2,005,919
Mean Loan Life (Months)	113.4
Prepay Acceleration Factor (PSA)	175%
Number of Loans Prepaying	941.1
Number Loans Going to Full Term	41.8
Number of Loans Foreclosed	17.2

Source: Cohane Rafferty Securities, Inc.

lished. While discrete variables are the subject of the sensitivity analyses provided, in most instances the analyst would change several variables to construct a more aggressive or more conservative scenario than that provided in ABC's initial evaluation.

Many of the sensitivity analyses provided are self-explanatory. Several, however, require some additional comments. The impact on value of changes in prepayment speeds is not linear (table 4.8, item 2). While a change from 107 to 124 percent PSA experience results in a decrease in value of 7 bps, a change of similar magnitude from 226 to 243 percent PSA results in a drop in value of only 4 bps. Figures 4.1 through 4.3 help explain the reason behind this declining price sensitivity.

Figure 4.1 plots the remaining principal balance over the life of the portfolio at four different PSAs (107 percent, 124 percent, 226 percent, and 243 percent). Figure 4.2 clarifies these varying principal amortization patterns by presenting the differential of the remaining principal for the low and high sets of prepayment speeds. The difference between the remaining principal curves resulting from the 107 percent and 124 percent PSA assumptions is much greater than that for the two higher prepayment speeds (226 percent and 243 percent).

Figure 4.3 translates this difference into dollar terms by showing the differential of undiscounted net operating revenues (income before purchase price amortization and taxes) between the low and high sets of prepayment assumptions. The dollar impact on servicing value is greater when changes are made at the lower end of the prepayment scale, because changes at this end have a much greater impact on the pattern of principal balance amortization over time.

Price sensitivity to one-percentage-point changes in the after-tax discount rate (holding the tax rate constant at 36 percent) is not linear either, as can been seen from the sensitivity analysis provided under table 4.8, item 3. If the after-tax discount rate increases by a constant percentage, the price sensitivity does become approximately linear, within the range of the analysis shown. In other words, if the required return is increased from 7 to 7.70 percent, or if it is raised from 10.25 to 11.27 percent (both 10 percent increases), the resulting change in price will be the same—a drop of approximately 7.3 bps.

Table 4.8, item 8 presents the price sensitivity of changes in the method of purchase price amortization. The more accelerated the amortization method, the higher the economic value of the servicing. This is because

Figure 4.1 Remaining Principal

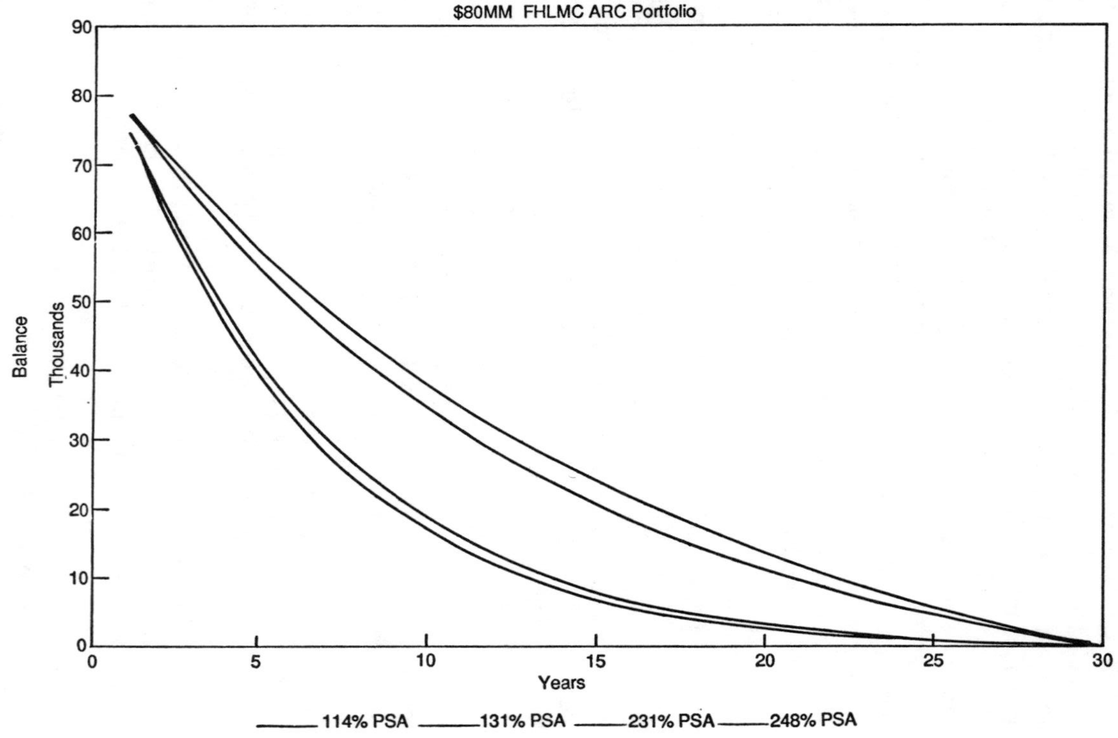

$80MM FHLMC ARC Portfolio
Balance
Thousands
90
80
70
60
50
40
30
20
10
0
0
5
10
15
20
25
30
Years
114% PSA
131% PSA
231% PSA
248% PSA

Figure 4.2 Difference in Remaining Principal

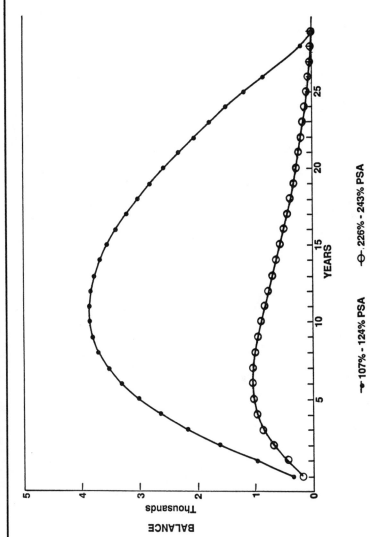

BALANCE Thousands

YEARS

—•— 107% - 124% PSA   —⊖— 226% - 243% PSA

Figure 4.3 Net Operating Revenue Differentials

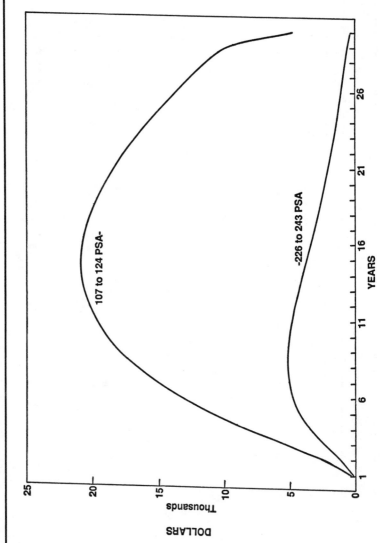

the amortization expense, while a noncash item, lowers taxable income. Decreasing an organization's tax liability has a positive impact on cash flows. As shown, the sum-of-the-years' digits method is slightly more accelerated than the FASB 65 method. Both methods are much more accelerated than the straight-line method.

Two factors impact the decreasing price sensitivity (table 4.8, item 9) as the amortization period is extended:

- Using the FASB 65 method, the amortization is in proportion to the ratio of the positive pretax income in a given year to the total before-tax income over the amortization period. When one changes from a relatively short amortization period such as 7 years to a longer period such as 12 years, the percentage of the purchase price amortized in the early years drops significantly, because the pretax positive income in years 8 through 12 is still at a reasonable level. However, as amortization extends further, the income levels for the later periods drop off dramatically so that the reapportioning of the purchase price is not as material.

- Discounting of the cash flows affects price sensitivity. As the amortization is spread over more years, the tax shields in the later years are of a decreasing value, because they are more highly discounted.

Table 4.8, items 15 and 16, shows matrices of price sensitivity to changes in average loan size at specific servicing cost levels and sensitivity to changes in servicing costs for portfolios with varying average loan sizes. The basic messages from the first matrix are that the higher an institution's servicing cost, the more sensitive servicing value is to differences in average loan size, and that this sensitivity diminishes as one moves toward the high end of the average-loan-size scale.

The second matrix confirms what one would expect normally: the value of portfolios with relatively low average loan sizes is much more sensitive to changes in servicing cost assumptions than that of portfolios with high loan balances. The reason for this is that servicing income is based on a percentage of the principal balance (and is therefore quite sensitive to average loan size), while servicing cost is calculated on a per-loan basis and remains essentially the same whether a $20,000 loan or a $120,000 loan is being serviced.

Table 4.8, items 17 and 18, shows the interrelationship of average escrow balance and interest paid on escrow assumptions when sensitizing

Table 4.7   FHLMC ARC Portfolio: Summary of Cash Flows

Time Period	Principal Outstanding ($1,000)	Average Number of Loans	Service Fee	Ancillary Income	Late Fee Income	Float Earnings	Escrow Earnings	Operating Revenue	Servicing & Acqu. Cost	Prepay Servicing Cost
Year 1	76,090	983	293,203	8,343	3,524	20,622	42,365	368,058	75,356	794
Year 2	69,148	921	273,032	7,806	7,240	21,597	41,494	351,170	64,294	1,703
Year 3	61,480	831	245,114	7,041	8,499	20,656	39,245	320,555	60,891	2,088
Year 4	54,619	744	217,995	6,306	7,664	18,494	36,902	287,360	57,223	1,962
Year 5	48,482	666	193,735	5,648	6,903	16,560	34,704	257,550	53,775	1,844
Year 6	42,991	596	171,995	5,058	6,220	14,822	32,633	230,728	50,535	1,733
Year 7	38,079	533	152,477	4,528	5,606	13,243	30,674	206,527	47,490	1,628
Year 8	33,686	477	135,017	4,053	5,054	11,829	28,833	184,787	44,629	1,530
Year 9	29,757	427	119,401	3,629	4,558	10,564	27,104	165,257	41,940	1,438
Year 10	26,242	382	105,420	3,248	4,112	9,428	25,477	147,685	39,413	1,352
Year 11	23,099	342	92,903	2,908	3,711	8,408	23,944	131,874	37,039	1,270
Year 12	20,289	306	81,705	2,603	3,350	7,493	22,503	117,653	34,807	1,194
Year 13	17,776	274	71,689	2,329	3,025	6,673	21,148	104,864	32,710	1,122
Year 14	15,529	245	62,732	2,085	2,733	5,939	19,874	93,363	30,739	1,054
Year 15	13,521	220	54,725	1,866	2,469	5,283	18,677	83,020	28,887	991
Year 16	11,726	197	47,568	1,670	2,232	4,695	17,552	73,717	27,147	931
Year 17	10,122	176	41,171	1,495	2,019	4,169	16,494	65,348	25,511	875
Year 18	8,689	157	35,454	1,338	1,827	3,699	15,501	57,819	23,974	822

Time Period	Principal Outstanding ($1,000)	Average Number of Loans	Service Fee	Ancillary Income	Late Fee Income	Float Earnings	Escrow Earnings	Operating Revenue	Servicing & Acqu. Cost	Prepay Servicing Cost
Year 19	7,408	141	30,346	1,197	1,654	3,278	14,567	51,043	22,530	773
Year 20	6,264	126	25,784	1,072	1,497	2,902	13,689	44,944	21,172	726
Year 21	5,243	113	21,709	959	1,356	2,565	12,865	39,455	19,897	682
Year 23	3,518	90	14,823	768	1,115	1,995	11,362	30,063	17,571	603
Year 24	2,792	81	11,925	688	1,011	1,754	10,677	26,055	16,513	566
Year 25	2,144	72	9,340	615	918	1,539	10,034	22,446	15,518	532
Year 26	1,567	65	7,035	551	834	1,346	9,430	19,195	14,583	500
Year 27	1,053	58	4,980	493	757	1,174	8,862	16,266	13,704	470
Year 28	595	52	3,149	441	688	1,020	8,328	13,627	12,878	442
Year 29	187	47	1,519	395	626	883	7,826	11,249	12,103	415
Year 30	—	43	205	182	292	394	3,735	4,807	5,775	3,706
TOTAL	—	320	2,544,224	80,171	92,725	225,291	618,588	3,560,999	967,300	34,386

Source: Cohane Rafferty Securities, Inc.

Table 4.7   FHLMC ARC Portfolio: Summary of Cash Flows (*continued*)

Time Period	Cost of Advances	Cost of Delin-quency	Cost of Fore-closure	Operating Expense	Amortized Purchase Price	Net Income Pre-Tax	Income Tax	Net Income Post-Tax	Cash Flow Post-Tax	Discounted Cash Flow Post-Tax
Year 1	1,460	1,959	1,091	80,661	165,491	121,905	43,886	78,019	243,511	231,300
Year 2	2,616	3,770	1,983	74,366	159,392	117,412	42,268	75,144	234,535	200,744
Year 3	2,704	4,379	1,903	71,966	143,145	105,444	37,960	67,484	210,629	162,439
Year 4	2,272	4,116	1,482	67,055	126,858	93,447	33,641	59,806	186,664	129,693
Year 5	1,874	3,868	1,032	62,393	112,377	82,780	29,801	52,979	165,357	103,501
Year 6	1,556	3,635	689	58,148	99,377	73,204	26,353	46,850	146,227	82,461
Year 7	1,343	3,416	547	54,424	87,585	64,518	23,226	41,291	128,876	65,476
Year 8	1,153	3,210	407	50,929	77,079	56,779	20,440	36,338	113,417	51,911
Year 9	982	3,016	265	47,641	67,726	49,889	17,960	31,929	99,655	41,093
Year 10	844	2,835	172	44,616	59,351	43,719	15,739	27,980	87,331	32,443
Year 11	733	2,664	126	41,832	51,849	38,193	13,750	24,444	76,292	25,534
Year 12	640	2,503	99	39,243	45,151	33,259	11,973	21,286	66,437	20,033
Year 13	559	2,353	84	36,828	—	68,036	24,493	43,543	43,543	11,829
Year 14	488	2,211	75	34,567	—	58,796	21,167	37,629	37,629	9,209
Year 15	425	2,078	67	32,447	—	50,573	18,206	32,367	32,367	7,137
Year 16	369	1,952	60	30,459	—	43,258	15,573	27,685	27,685	5,500
Year 17	319	1,835	54	28,593	—	36,755	13,232	23,523	23,523	4,210
Year 18	274	1,724	48	26,843	—	30,975	11,151	19,824	19,824	3,197
Year 19	235	1,620	44	25,201	—	25,842	9,303	16,539	16,539	2,403

Time Period	Cost of Advances	Cost of Delin- quency	Cost of Fore- closure	Operating Expense	Amortized Purchase Price	Net Income Pre-Tax	Income Tax	Net Income Post-Tax	Cash Flow Post-Tax	Discounted Cash Flow Post-Tax
Year 20	199	1,523	39	23,659	—	21,285	7,663	13,623	13,623	1,783
Year 21	167	1,431	35	22,212	—	17,243	6,207	11,035	11,035	1,301
Year 22	139	1,345	31	20,854	—	13,659	4,917	8,742	8,742	929
Year 23	114	1,264	28	19,579	—	10,483	3,774	6,709	6,709	642
Year 24	92	1,188	25	18,383	—	7,673	2,762	4,911	4,911	424
Year 25	72	1,116	21	17,259	—	5,187	1,867	3,320	3,320	258
Year 26	54	1,049	17	16,202	—	2,993	1,077	1,915	1,915	134
Year 27	38	986	12	15,210	—	1,056	380	676	676	43
Year 28	24	926	8	14,278	—	(651)	(234)	(417)	(417)	(23)
Year 29	11	870	5	13,404	—	(2,155)	(776)	(1,379)	(1,379)	(70)
Year 30	2	415	1	9,899	—	(5,092)	(1,833)	(3,259)	(3,259)	(154)
TOTAL	21,756	65,257	10,452	1,099,151	1,195,381	1,266,466	455,928	810,538	2,005,919	1,195,381

Source: Cohane Rafferty Securities, Inc.

Table 4.8   Sensitivity of FHLMC ARC Portfolio Servicing Value
to Changes in Specific Parameters

1. Servicing Fee

Change in Parameter	Impact on Value
+/! bp[*]	+/! 4 bps[*]

2. Prepayment Rate

PSA Experience Increased	Impact on Value
From 107% to 124%	!7.0 bps
From 124% to 141%	!6.5 bps
From 141% to 158%	!5.9 bps
From 158% to 175%	!5.5 bps
From 175% to 192%	!5.1 bps
From 192% to 209%	!4.7 bps
From 209% to 226%	!4.4 bps
From 226% to 243%	!4.0 bps

3. After-Tax Discount Rate

Discount Rate Increased	Impact on Value
From 7% to 8%	!10.3 bps
From 8% to 9%	! 9.3 bps
From 9% to 10%	!8.3 bps
From 10% to 11%	! 7.6 bps
From 11% to 12%	!6.8 bps
From 12% to 13%	!6.3 bps
From 13% to 14%	!5.7 bps
From 14% to 15%	!5.3 bps

[*] bp(s) = basis point(s); each bp is 1/100th of 1 percent

Table 4.8 Sensitivity of FHLMC ARC Portfolio Servicing Value to Changes in Specific Parameters (continued)

Change In Parameter	Impact on Value
4. Days P&I Float	
+/! 1 day	+/! .9 bps
5. Days Float On Payoffs	
+/! 1 day	+/! .7 bps
6. Ancillary Income	
$1/loan/year	+/! .5 bps
7. Tax Rate	
+/!1%	+/! 1.0 to 1.1 bps

8. Amortization of Purchase Price (over 12-year period)

SYD vs FASB	+1.8 bps
SYD vs SL	+7.3 bps

SYD = Sum of the Years Digits
FASB = FASB Positive Cash Flows
SL = Straight Line

9. FASB 65 Method

Amortization Period Increased	Impact on Value
From 12 Years to 15 Years	!2.2 bps
From 15 Years to 20 Years	!2.0 bps
From 20 Years to 25 Years	!.7 bps
From 25 Years to 30 Years	0 bps

10. P&I Float and Payoff Reserve Fraction

Change In Parameter	Impact on Value
3% vs 12%	+1.3 bps

Table 4.8 Sensitivity of FHLMC ARC Portfolio Servicing Value to Changes in Specific Parameters (continued)

Change In Parameter	Impact on Value

11. Escrow Reserve Fraction

    3% vs 12%   +2.9 bps

12. Transfer Costs Year 1

    +/! $5 per loan   +/! .5 to .6 bps

13. Uncollected Interest Passed Through to Investor on Payoff

    +/! 5 days   +/! 5.2 to 5.3 bps

14. Payoff Costs Per Loan

    +/! $5 per loan   +/! .3 bps

15. Average Loan Size

Average Loan Size Increased	Cost Per Loan Per Year (bp change)					
	$35	**$50**	**$65**	**$80**	**$95**	**$110**
From 100,000 to 120,000	3.2	4.6	5.8	7.2	8.5	9.9
From 80,000 to 100,000	4.8	6.7	8.8	10.7	12.8	14.7
From 60,000 to 80,000	8.0	11.3	14.6	18.0	21.2	24.6
From 40,000 to 60,000	16.0	22.7	29.2	35.8	42.5	49.2
From 20,000 to 40,000	47.9	67.8	89.1	113.7	127.4	147.2

Table 4.8 Sensitivity of FHLMC ARC Portfolio Servicing Value to Changes in Specific Parameters (continued)

16. Cost Per Loan Per Year

Servicing Cost Decreased	Average Loan Size (bp change)					
	$20,000	40,000	60,000	80,000	100,000	120,000
From 50 to 35	39.7	19.9	13.2	9.9	8.0	6.6
From 65 to 50	41.0	19.8	13.3	10.0	7.9	6.7
From 80 to 65	44.5	19.9	13.3	9.9	8.0	6.6
From 95 to 80	33.7	19.9	13.2	10.0	7.9	6.6
From 110 to 95	39.8	20.0	13.3	9.9	8.0	6.6

17. Average Escrow Balance

Average Escrow Balance as Percentage of UPB Increased	Interest Paid On Escrow (bp change)					
	0%	1%	2%	3%	4%	5%
From 1.00% to 1.25%	9.3	8.0	6.6	5.3	4.0	2.7
From .75% to 1.00%	9.3	7.9	6.7	5.3	4.0	2.6
From .50% to .75%	9.3	8.0	6.6	5.4	4.0	2.7
From .25% to .50%	9.2	8.0	6.7	5.3	4.0	2.7

18. Interest Paid On Escrow

Interest Paid on Escrow Decreased	Average Escrow Balance as Percentage of UPB (bp change)				
	1.25%	1.00%	.75%	.50%	.25%
From 1% to 0%	6.6	5.3	3.9	2.6	1.4
From 2% to 1%	6.6	5.2	4.0	2.6	1.3
From 3% to 2%	6.6	5.3	3.9	2.7	1.3
From 4% to 3%	6.6	5.3	4.0	2.6	1.3
From 5% to 4%	6.6	5.3	3.9	2.6	1.3

Table 4.8   Sensitivity of FHLMC ARC Portfolio Servicing Value
                 to Changes in Specific Parameters (continued)

19. Foreclosure Costs

	Maximum Rate of Foreclosure (bp change)			
	.25%	.50%	.75%	1.00%
$500 increase	!.5	!1.1	!1.5	!2.1

20. Rate of Foreclosure

	Foreclosure Cost Per Foreclosed Loan (bp change)				
	$500	$1,000	$1,500	$2,000	$2,500
Maximum rate increased .25%	!1.0	!1.6	!2.1	!2.5	!3.1

21. Delinquency Rate when no additional costs to service delinquent loans assumed

Delinquency Rate	Advances Required (bp change)		
	A/A	S/A	S/S
+1%[*]	1.3	.9	.9

22. Delinquency Rate using additional costs shown in ABC Initial Evaluation ($150 additional cost 30-day; $200 additional 60-day; $250 additional 90-day)

Delinquency Rate	Impact on Value
+1%[*]	.1 bp

23. Delinquency Rate using additional costs shown in ABC Initial Evaluation and decreasing collection rate on late fees to 65% from 75%

+1%[*]	.09 bps

24. Delinquency Rate using higher additional costs and 75% collection on Late Fees ($200 additional cost 30-day; $250 additional 60-day; $300 additional 90-day)

+1%[*]	!.4 bps

[*] Increase distributed as follows: .70% 30-day; .20% 60-day; .10% 90-day

Source: Cohane Rafferty Securities, Inc.

price to either of these variables. Basically, the less interest a servicer must pay the borrower on escrow balances, the more sensitive price is to different levels of escrow balances, because the servicer is able to earn more income on these balances. Likewise, the higher the average escrow balances, the greater the price sensitivity to changes in levels of interest paid on escrow. This matrix also can be used to determine the price sensitivity of changes in the earnings rate on escrow.

When servicing costs for delinquent loans are not distinguished from those for current loans, the higher the delinquency rate the greater the economic value the portfolio will appear to be due to additional late-fee revenues. Table 4.8, item 21, shows this pattern for the FHLMC ARC servicing portfolio, while also indicating how the assumption of advances of interest and/or principal on delinquent loans tempers the price sensitivity. Loans serviced on an actual/actual basis would have no expense stream netting against the increased late fees, while those serviced under a schedule/actual or schedule/schedule agreement would have a cost associated with advancing payments on delinquent loans.

Table 4.8, item 22, indicates that even using the additional costs to service delinquent loans assumed by ABC Mortgage Company would still result in a modest rise in price when delinquency rates are increased. While it may be true in the case of ABC Mortgage Company that late fees more than cover the cost to service delinquent loans, these analyses point out the importance of analyzing collections area costs carefully. A variety of factors must be examined in determining pricing sensitivity to changes in delinquency rates:

- collection rate for late fees
- distribution of delinquencies (30-day versus 90-day)
- additional costs associated with servicing loans delinquent over varying time periods

For example, if a 75 percent late-fee collection rate is assumed, but the additional cost to service 30-day, 60-day, and 90-day delinquent loans is raised to $200, $250, and $300, respectively, the value of the portfolio will decrease as the delinquency rate assumption is increased (table 4.8, item 24).

Market Value versus Economic Value

This chapter has focused on evaluating servicing portfolios from an economic perspective. The economic value of a given portfolio will vary from institution to institution, and even at the institutional level the economic value will normally be expressed in terms of a range of possible scenarios rather than a single value. The market value of a portfolio, on the other hand, is quite simply the highest bid received from a large universe of prequalified servicing buyers as a result of an aggressive marketing effort that maximizes competition.

Some portfolios will be more marketable/liquid than others for a variety of reasons:

- investor type
- portfolio size
- geographic location of loans
- low note rate ranges
- age
- recourse/nonrecourse issues

The total number of bids received as the result of a competitive auction process constitutes the market value range of the portfolio as of the time of the auction. When attractive mortgage servicing portfolios are offered for sale in a competitive auction, the distribution of bids often form a bell-shaped curve. Normally, a few very aggressive bidders fill the high end of the curve and several conservative, or bottom-fishing, bidders submit bids that fall at the low end. Most bids are concentrated in a 20- to 30-bps band around the mean bid-price received. Of course, a variety of supply and demand, regulatory, and legislative issues come into play in determining the market value of a portfolio as of a given time.

From the buyers' perspective, if the market environment is somewhat depressed, they may be able to increase their potential return by bidding on and winning a portfolio for a price below its economic value to their organization. On the other hand, valid reasons sometimes exist for an institution to bid somewhat higher than the economic value of the portfolio per se to the institution. This is especially true with regional portfolios that local buyers find attractive, because they may be able to add to their customer base and benefit from building additional customer relationships.

From the seller's perspective, the ideal situation, obviously, is to sell a portfolio component for more than what it is worth economically to the selling institution. Sometimes, however, time-sensitive income or cash needs of the selling institution, or the required sale by an agency, in combination with weak marketplace dynamics, force the seller to accept an offer that is lower than its economic value to the organization.

During the second and third quarters of 1989, for instance, the market for mortgage servicing portfolios developed into a buyers' market, with prices dropping for a variety of reasons:

- Pending thrift legislation and uncertainty over the treatment of purchased and retained servicing for core capital and risk-based capital requirements caused many buyers to go to the sideline. Even with the August 1989 passage of legislation that recognized the value of purchased servicing in meeting core capital requirements, the precise limits and means of calculating fair market value was uncertain and subject to a formal interpretation by the FDIC.

- Uncertainty regarding the interpretation and enforcement of RESPA Section 10, limitation on escrow accounts (discussed earlier), and the impact of this treatment on the value of mortgage servicing portfolios provided another catalyst for the development of a wait-and-see posture on the part of buyers.

- The development of a falling interest rate environment, the perception that this environment would remain in place over the near-term due to a slowdown in the U.S. economy, and cautious easing of the nation's money supply by the Federal Reserve to avoid a recession resulted in the forecast of increasing prepayment risks on the part of most servicers. The net result was that active buyers began to define more narrowly the coupon ranges on which they were willing to bid, and to discount their prices on loans in this range based on their increased probability of prepayment.

- Anticipation of market prices falling further due to both the falling interest rate environment and knowledge that the supply of product would be increasing due to asset sales by the FDIC, as well as by FNMA and GNMA, was another reason there were fewer buyers in the marketplace.

- Thrifts and banks were increasing the supply of product as they looked to the sale of servicing as a means to raise additional equity.

It is essential that players in the mortgage servicing business understand thoroughly how to evaluate the economic value of components of their existing portfolios and of portfolios they are considering for purchase. This requires not only the use of a sophisticated evaluation model but also the development of assumptions appropriate to the particular institution, as well as staying abreast of current and potential changes in the external environment that can impact the value of servicing.

Beyond this, to protect and enhance the value of their servicing assets, institutions must stay attuned to the changing dynamics of the marketplace and actively manage their portfolios to take advantage, where possible, of these dynamics.

5

Bidding and Closing

The process by which a mortgage servicing package is distributed, reviewed by prospective buyers, negotiated, and purchased is known as bidding and closing the sale. Up to the point at which the package is sent to a list of prospective buyers, the creation of that package has been a joint effort between the seller and the broker.

The broker has reviewed the data and structured the package in the clearest, most understandable, and most attractive form for sale. The broker then has distributed the package to a prequalified list of prospects from his or her own database. The bidding process officially has begun.

At this point the seller's job is complete (until the bids are submitted and final terms of the sale are negotiated). For the broker, it is another story. Bidding, negotiating, and closing the sale are the heart of the mortgage servicing transaction. The success of this transaction—from the seller's, the broker's, and the buyer's perspective—hinges on the broker's experience and expertise.

This chapter examines the bidding process:

- types of transactions
- the auction
- when and how a buyer should bid
- timing the bid
- the broker's role

It also discusses negotiating and closing the sale, bid submission, caveats, timing of the closure, the purchase and sale agreement, and troubleshooting, and it provides a model mortgage servicing purchase and sale agreement and a model bid notification letter.

Types of Transactions

Mortgage servicing transactions traditionally have taken one of four possible forms:

Private Sale

A private sale is a direct sale between a seller and a buyer without the intervention of a broker. The seller contacts several prospective buyers, probably banks with whom he or she has conducted some type of business in the past. During the days before the mortgage portfolio played as important a part in a bank's financial plans as it does today, the private sale was the standard for this type of transaction.

Private sales still occur, but they are rarer now because most banks see an added value in using the communications network and capabilities of a broker. The odds of most banks getting higher prices for their portfolios are greater when they use reputable brokers. The bidding process is to some extent a numbers game. If a seller has 5–10 contacts while a broker has 200–300, the broker is likely to get more bids and thus a higher price. There is a definite correlation between the number of bids and the high bid received. By using a broker, the seller also avoids the time-consuming process of answering questions about the package from many different prospects. By going though the broker, the seller has the two-pronged expectation of making more money on the sale while letting the broker handle all the administrative follow-up involved with the bidding process.

In spite of all this, there are still direct deals done. Some companies still prefer to take a somewhat lower price in exchange for dealing exclusively with someone with whom they have dealt before. However, as earnings pressure increases, these relationships tend to become less important.

Broker Sale

In a broker sale, the seller may give the package to several brokers, operating under the belief that the more brokers involved the more exposure the purchase will receive and thus attain a higher bid. This is seldom the case. More often than not packages distributed by several brokers become unruly and confusing for everyone involved. Moreover, because no one broker has an exclusive right to represent the portfolio in question and therefore a guaranteed sale, none of them will put 100 percent of his efforts and resources into it.

Brokers package a product based on their own systems and marketing philosophies. A package may appear confusing to a prospective buyer who receives two or three packages from different brokers for the same deal. Prospective buyers may opt to disregard the package altogether to avoid the confusion, waiting instead for the next offering that comes along, one that they can clearly understand.

Exclusive with One Broker

The key to a smooth, successful mortgage servicing transaction is focusing control in one place. Sellers who select a single broker to market a package surrender control to that broker. They trust the broker to package the product correctly and attractively, to distribute the package to the most likely buyers, and to represent the seller's best interest during the bidding process.

As the secondary market for servicing has grown and developed, many executives are under increasing pressure to convert this asset into cash. Add to that the fact of lower origination income over the past few years and you readily see that a portfolio sale is now a major part of the bank's annual business plan and must be optimized. The broker offers the best alternative to the achievement of these goals.

The Auction

Auction is the term applied to the culmination of the bidding process; it occurs on the day and at the hour when bidding on a package closes. A mortgage portfolio servicing auction involves many of the same elements as an art or antique auction:

- The product is displayed.
- Questions are answered to clarify any uncertain information about the product.
- Buyers reconcile the balance between their needs and what they can spend.
- Buyers determine and submit their bids.

Motives are similar in that different prospective buyers attach different values to the product. Buyers usually know their limits and attempt to bid as low as possible, depending on their perceived value of the product, their judgment concerning the competition and what they might bid, and their previous experience in buying mortgage servicing through the auction process.

At an art or antique auction, the item is awarded to the highest bidder. This is not always the case in the auction of a servicing portfolio because of certain caveats in a bid letter (a subject discussed later in this chapter).

Bidding

The bidding process occurs from the time a package is distributed until a buyer has been awarded the sale. Prospective buyers receive the package and undertake an analysis to see how it fits their needs and objectives. They measure this value to them. Based on that estimated value, they also project what they can afford to bid.

Prospective buyers also need to ascertain how competitive the bidding is likely to be. For example, if they value a package at 210 basis points, they must measure what they can afford to pay versus what they estimate others will bid. They may decide that this package will sell between 200 and 205 basis points. If they value it highly enough, they may opt for the top end of this estimated spread and go with a 205 bid. Conversely, they may feel that it is worth the gamble of bidding 200 basis points, hoping to win the auction and realize more value from the sale.

When a broker is involved, prospective buyers tap into that resource for as much information as they can get before reaching a decision. They call and ask what the broker expects the package to sell for. In most cases, the broker responds with an anticipated range, which prospective buyers can then compare with their own estimates.

Brokers' reputations hinge on few things more than the honesty and integrity with which they handle these questions during the bidding process. While the broker truly represents the seller and must attempt to get the best possible price for the package, it is equally true that today's buyer is tomorrow's seller. Brokers who expect to build a reputable following deal honestly with everyone. As a result, prospective buyers who call with questions know that the answers they receive are being shared with other prospects. In other words, the broker should not provide an edge to any one buyer.

What besides a prospective buyer's own ability to evaluate a package and correctly assess its market value dictates a winning bid? The answer lies in the caveats attached to the package.

Caveats equal basis points. In other words, caveats equal money. There are seven important variables to take into account when bidding a servicing portfolio. Any and all can become critical factors in submitting a winning bid and therefore in the true value of the package to the prospective buyer. The basis for these caveats can be found in information provided in the package. And they all are based on timing. In the bidding on a servicing portfolio, timing is everything (see Exhibit 5.1).

1. *Bid price.* The buyer decides on a bid price that meets his or her needs, objectives, and limit (i.e., discount rule).

2. *Payment terms.* What is the percentage payment schedule as described in the package? The key here is how this payment schedule fits the buyer's financial needs.

3. *Transfer date.* This refers to the actual date on which the buyer can take possession of the loans in the package. Again, how does this timing affect the buyer's financial projections?

4. *Tax service.* Are all the loans in portfolio on a tax service? If not, and you want to put them on a tax service, who will incur this cost?

5. *Indemnification.* Some buyers build an indemnification clause into their bid which simply says that the seller will indemnify the buyer against foreclosure risk for a specific period of time (e.g., one year, two years, five years, etc.). Of all potentially hidden items that could prove costly to the buyer, costs of foreclosure are probably the highest. You will see indemnification clauses beyond normal reps and warranties only in GNMA and Recourse portfolios.

6. *Bid expiration date.* The old saying "Time is money" applies here. Buyers often will build in an expiration date to the bid they submit. This serves two functions:

    ■ It forces the seller to act on the bid submitted, resulting in an advantage to the buyers who have undoubtedly favored themselves with their offers.

- It avoids a protracted negotiation period during which everyone's assets are tied up pending outcome.
7. *Payment of delinquent loans.* Is the buyer paying for only correct loans or is he or she paying for 30s, 60s, or 90s as well?

Experienced bidders, knowing that timing is everything, consider every package in light of these factors before finally submitting their bid. When the competitive bids are all considered, which bid is most attractive often is determined based on both the caveats and the price.

It's then up to the sellers, using the negotiation expertise of the broker, to determine which bid makes the most sense to them.

Negotiating

With the submission of the competitive bids, one would think that the deal virtually is complete. The broker faxes the top three or four bids to the seller who makes her or his choice and informs the broker of that choice, and the broker notifies the winning bidder. However, with the acceptance of the bid the final negotiation process begins, and the reality is that the deal can easily fall apart at this juncture.

Problems that occur during the negotiating phase are almost always caused by the caveats. It would be impossible to present all the variables that can come into play during the negotiating of the sale, but there are several rules that apply to both seller and buyer. If observed, these rules facilitate the process greatly and can result in a quick, smooth, profitable transaction.

1. *Know what you want to achieve.* Both seller and buyer have established goals for this transaction before it ever comes to fruition. If both parties adhere to these objectives without becoming greedy, then their differences usually can be resolved through negotiation.

2. *Be flexible.* As with any negotiation, flexibility is a must for both parties. Remember that in a competitive bid auction, everything is negotiable. An inflexible seller may think that if one bid falls through other interested parties are waiting in the wings. This may be the case, which is why the broker submitted the top three or four bids for the seller's consideration. However, as often as not, the alternate bidders quickly move on to other business, considering this particular bid lost. They may not be there after all.

3. *Use the broker as a buffer.* As in other phases of the transaction, both buyer and seller should depend on the experience and expertise of the broker to act as interlocutor, especially in negotiating potentially sticky points. Brokers have dealt with virtually every possible scenario in negotiating these sales. They probably can offer a compromise position that will satisfy both sides.

4. *Don't let the "rabbits" kill you.* Many good deals have gone wrong because both buyer and seller got caught up in negotiating small points and lost sight of their larger objectives. In transacting a servicing portfolio sale, it's the "elephants," such as the bid price or the more critical caveats like indemnification, that really can hurt you, not the "rabbits."

Closing the Sale

The final step in the transaction is the purchase and sale agreement, the document that is sent to both parties by the broker. It stipulates all aspects of the agreed sale, the timing of events, and the payment schedule (see Exhibit 5.2).

Once the terms of the sale have been agreed upon, both seller and buyer should move quickly to effect the completion of due diligence, transfer, and payment. From the seller's point of view, the marketplace is constantly changing and a better package might come to the attention of the buyer. Also, the buyer's financial condition could change drastically, or interest rates might suddenly change, affecting the desirability of the package.

For the buyer, moving quickly averts the possibility that a new player comes into the picture with a higher bid, even after the bid has been tacitly accepted. Until the purchase and sale agreement is signed and the loans and money are transferred, it still is possible for things to go wrong. Buyers also want to perform due diligence as quickly as possible to ensure that the product is exactly as presented. If the data is accurate, they can save considerable time.

Exhibit 5.1
Offer

RE: Exclusive Servicing Offering No.

Gentlemen:

We have reviewed the information you provided us concerning the above captioned servicing offering. We represent that our mortgage banking subsidiary is an approved (FNMA, FHLMC, GNMA, Private) Seller/Servicer in good standing, with the requisite financial resources necessary to complete this transaction.

This letter will serve to notify you of our ("Purchaser") offer to purchase from Seller the servicing rights to the portfolio, aggregating approximately $ _____ million, covered by the attached offering memorandum of Cohane Rafferty Securities, Inc., on the terms and conditions expressed in this letter.

1. *PURCHASE PRICE:* The Purchase Price for the Servicing shall be the result of multiplying _____, by the unpaid balance of all loans which are not (i.e., 30, 60, 90) days or more past due, in litigation, bankruptcy, or in foreclosure, as of the Sale Date. The Sale Date will be as set forth in a mutually acceptable Loan Servicing Purchase and Sale Agreement (the "Agreement").

The payment of the Purchase Price will be as follows:

a) Upon written acceptance by Seller of Purchaser's bid, Purchaser will deposit, within 48 hours, five percent (5%) of the estimated Purchase Price, in a mutually agreed upon escrow or trust account.

b) 15% of the Purchase Price shall be paid to Seller upon the signing of the Purchase and Sale Agreement.

c) 80% of the Purchase Price shall be paid to Seller on the Transfer Date upon satisfaction of the terms and conditions set forth in this agreement.

2. In the event that the sale does not take place because of a reason which is not the fault of the Purchaser, or because all of the contingencies herein stated are not met, then such deposit and interest earned to that date will be returned to the Purchaser.

3. The Transfer Date will be the date the Purchaser assumes the actual servicing of the Portfolio in accordance with the terms of Investor's

approval or consents required to be obtained in connection with the transfer of the Servicing. The Transfer Date may be on, or subsequent to, the Sale Date.

4. Prior to the Transfer Date, Seller will continue to service the Loans in accordance with all applicable Investor's regulations, requirements and procedures.

5. This offer to purchase the Servicing is subject to the following conditions:

a) The reasonable determination by Purchaser, through an on-site due diligence review, that the books, records and accounts of Seller with respect to each Pool are in order and verification by Purchaser that the information provided as part of the Offering Package is substantially correct. This examination is to be completed within (30) thirty days of acceptance by Seller of Purchaser's bid.

b) The delivery by Seller to Purchaser of Investor's written approval of transfer of Servicer rights and responsibilities.

c) Execution by Purchaser and Seller of a Loan Servicing Purchase and Sale Agreement mutually acceptable to both parties (not to be unreasonably withheld) and which will contain, among other provisions, the Seller's agreement to hold purchaser harmless, by Loan repurchase or otherwise, for any and all expenses and costs, including Purchaser's attorney's fees, resulting from Seller's improper or inadequate origination, and servicing performed prior to the delivery date, or liability from any governmental or judicial order.

d) The approval and acceptance by Purchaser and Seller of documentation which may be required to effectuate the transfer of the Servicing rights by Seller to Purchaser.

e) Seller shall transfer to Purchaser on the Transfer Date, in immediately available funds, all Loan escrow monies and unearned fees, and the P&I balances collected by the Seller as of the Transfer Date.

f) Seller's representation that it has the sole right and authority to sell the Servicing and is not contractually obligated to sell the Servicing to any other party.

g) Seller's agreeing to pay the costs of securing Investor's approval and transfer fees due them, if any, and bearing the costs of custodial transfer and preparing and recording assignments of mortgage and/or notes, as required. Blanket assignments may be used where permitted.

h) Seller will be responsible for fees due Cohane Rafferty Securities, Inc.

Upon acceptance, this letter will constitute a binding agreement between the parties for the Purchaser and Sale of the subject Servicing Portfolio.

Sincerely,

PURCHASER: _____

BY: _____

DATE: _____

TITLE: _____

Accepted:

SELLER: _____

BY: _____

DATE: _____

TITLE: _____

Exhibit 5.2
Mortgage Servicing Purchase and Sale Agreement

This Mortgage Servicing Purchase and Sale Agreement (the "Agreement") is dated as of the _____ day of _____, 19____, by and between _____, a federally chartered savings bank (the "Purchaser"), and _____, a _____ located at _____ (the "Seller").

WITNESSETH:

WHEREAS, Purchaser desires to assume and Seller desires to transfer to Purchaser certain responsibilities of Seller as the servicer of certain mortgages transferred to FNMA under the FNMA MBS (the "Program"), and Purchaser and Seller desire Purchaser to administer and service certain mortgage loans transferred to the Association, in accordance with the terms and conditions hereof;

NOW THEREFORE, in consideration of the mutual covenants made herein and for other good and valuable considerations, the receipt and sufficiency of which are hereby acknowledged, the parties hereto agree to as follow:

Article I
Definitions

As used herein, the following capitalized terms shall have the meaning specified in the Article I.

1.1 **"Adjustment Date":** The fifth Business Day after the Transfer Date.

1.2 **"Agreement":** As defined in the first paragraph hereof.

1.3 **"Assignment Agreement":** The agreement between Seller and Purchaser, in the form required and to be approved by the Association, to transfer the Servicing to Purchaser.

1.4 **"Association":** FNMA, or any successor thereto.

1.5 **"Business Day":** Any day other than a Saturday, Sunday or a day on which banking institutions in _____ or _____ are authorized or obligated by law or executive order to close.

1.6 **"Custodian":** The financial institution or other person (including the Association) designated to hold certain documents relating to the

Mortgages pursuant to the Guide; or, if no such person is designated, the Seller and after the Sale Date the Purchaser.

1.7 **"Delinquent Mortgage":** A Mortgage that is two monthly payments or more past due or otherwise in default under the terms of the Mortgage; is the subject of litigations, investigations, legal process or proceeding; as to which enforcement proceedings must be or have been brought by Seller as required by the Guide or other applicable Requirements; the obligator on which is in bankruptcy or other insolvency proceedings; has been transferred to a receiver or is the subject of an assignment for the benefit of creditors; the collateral securing which has been abandoned or sold by the Mortgagor; is being foreclosed upon or repossessed; with respect to which Seller has accepted a voluntary deed in lieu of foreclosure or has arranged a preforeclosure sale; is the subject of a pending insurance claim or pending or threatened condemnation proceeding; or that the Association may require or permit to be repurchased by Seller.

1.8 **"FHA":** The Federal Housing Administration or any successor thereto.

1.9 **"Guide":** The Association's FNMA or other similar or successor guide establishing requirements applicable to the Servicing, the Mortgages and MBSs.

1.10 **"Interim Servicing Agreement":** The Interim Servicing Agreement between the parties hereto dated the date hereof in the form of Exhibit E attached hereto which provides for servicing of the Mortgages and certain other duties relating to the Servicing to be performed by Seller between the Sale Date and the Transfer Date on the terms and conditions provided therein.

1.11 **"Letter Agreement":** The letter agreement dated _____, between Seller and Purchaser relating to the Transfer and assumption of the Servicing.

1.12 **"MBSs":** The mortgage-backed securities or participation certificates issued by FNMA representing the Mortgages or an interest in the Mortgages.

1.13 **"Mortgages":** The _____ mortgage loans described in Exhibit A attached hereto having an outstanding aggregate principal balance of $_____ as of _____, 19____.

1.14 **"Mortgagor":** With respect to a Mortgage, the obligator on the promissory note or other evidence of indebtedness relating to such Mortgage.

1.15 **"Pool":** A group of Mortgages represented by an MBS.

1.16 **"Prior Services":** All persons who have had the obligations, responsibilities and duties of the servicer or seller of any of the Mortgages prior to Seller. For purposes of the representations in Articles IV and V hereof, references to the Seller shall include, where appropriate, any Prior Services and the originator of each Mortgage.

1.17 **"Purchase Price":** As defined in Paragraph 3.1 hereof.

1.18 **"Purchase Price Percentage":** As defined in Paragraph 3.1 hereof.

1.19 **"Purchaser":** As defined in the first paragraph hereof, or any assignee or successor thereto.

1.20 **"Related Escrows Accounts":** Mortgage escrow funds, impound accounts and loan trust funds held by Seller (including the Principal and Interest Custodial Account and the Tax and Insurance Custodial Accounts, for the payment of taxes, special assessments, hazard, flood and mortgage insurance premiums, postponed improvements, ground rents and similar items and to buy down the Mortgagor's monthly debt service) pursuant to the terms of the Mortgages and other applicable Requirements, or any disbursement or draft account into which such funds are deposited.

1.21 **"Requirements":** All contractual and federal, state or local legal and regulatory requirements (including laws, rules, regulation, statutes and ordinances), any other requirement of any government or agency or instrumentality thereof or of the Association, (including the Guide) any guidelines, or any judicial or administrative order, award, judgment, writ, injunction or decree.

1.22 **"Sale Documents":** This Agreement, the Interim Servicing Agreement, the Assignment Agreement and all other instruments, agreements and documents necessary to effect the transfer of the Servicing and other transactions contemplated hereby.

1.23 **"Sale Date":** The date of this Agreement or such later date as may be mutually agreed to in writing by Seller and Purchaser and approved by the Association.

1.24 **"Seller":** As defined in the first paragraph of this Agreement.

1.25 **"Servicing":** All obligations of Seller under the Servicing Agreement and the Guide as the seller or servicer of the Mortgages [and as issuer of the MBSs] and for the administration of the Mortgages pursuant to all applicable Requirements, and all rights of Seller as servicer of the Mortgages [and issuer of the MBSs], including Seller's rights in and to the Related Escrow Accounts and the Mortgages, to payments under any buy-down arrangement relating to any mortgage, to any fees, payments or other amount payable to or retainable by the servicer of the mortgages, to any rights with respect to the proceeds of foreclosure or other exercise of a remedy with respect to a Mortgage, to any other recovery with respect to any Mortgage, and to any insurance or guaranty of a Mortgage or the property securing a Mortgage or otherwise relating to or insuring against any loss with regard to a Mortgage and any claim against any closing attorney, tax service or other person relating to or arising out of such person's performance of or failure to perform services relating to the origination and servicing of the Mortgages.

1.26 **"Servicing Agreements":** The agreements between Seller and the Association pursuant to which Seller is currently servicing the Mortgages.

1.27 **"Transfer Date":** _____, or such later date as may be mutually agreed to in writing by Seller and Purchaser and, if required, approved by the Association.

1.28**"VA":** The Veterans Administration or any successor thereto.

Article II
Transfer and Assumption

2.1 **"Transfer of Responsibilities as Servicer":** Subject to and upon the terms and conditions of this Agreement, as of the Sale Date Seller (i) sells, transfers, assigns, and delivers to Purchaser, and purchaser will accept the transfer of and assume from Seller, responsibility for the Servicing, including responsibility for servicing and administering the Mortgages; and (ii) assigns and transfers to Purchaser all right, title and interest of Seller in and to the Servicing, including all Related Escrow Accounts and all of Seller's right to receive all fees and other amounts accrued or paid on or with respect to the Servicing on and after the Sale Date, including all servicing fees, late charges and other similar service or handling fees or charges accrued or paid on and after the Sale Date, and other fees, charges or other amounts payable or retainable in respect of the Servicing accrued, paid or retainable after the Sale Date; and (iii) assigns, transfers and delivers to Purchaser all files, documents and records relating to the Servicing. Purchase shall not, however, assume the Servicing with respect to any Delinquent Mortgage that has been repurchased by Seller pursuant to Section 8.7 or any Mortgage prepaid prior to the Sale Date and in either case no longer included in a Pool.

2.2 **"Substitution of Purchaser":** On the Sale Date, purchaser shall be substituted for Seller as the servicer of the Mortgages as provided in the Guide. Seller and Purchaser shall enter into the Interim Servicing Agreements. On the Transfer Date, the Interim Servicing Agreement shall terminate and Purchaser shall assume, and Seller shall cease, all responsibility related to the Servicing except as specifically provided in the Interim Servicing Agreement or herein. Purchaser will assume responsibility for the Servicing only to the extent required by the Assignment Agreement and the Guide, and Purchaser does not assume any other responsibility with respect thereto.

2.3 **"Obligations of Seller":** Seller covenants and agrees that from the date hereof until the Sale Date Seller shall timely and fully pay, perform and discharge all its duties, liabilities and obligations relating to the Servicing, the MBSs, the Pools, the Mortgages and the Related Escrow Accounts.

2.4 **"Obligations of Purchaser":** Seller and Purchaser agree that the Servicing and all MBSs, Mortgages, Related Escrow Accounts and Pools with respect to which responsibilities are to be transferred as provided herein must satisfy the requirements set forth herein, and that Purchaser shall have no obligation to assume any responsibility with respect to any thereof that do not satisfy such requirements.

2.5 **"Cooperation":** To the extent practical, the parties hereto shall cooperate with and assist each other, as requested, in carrying out the transactions contemplated hereby, in obtaining all required approvals and consents, in furnishing information and preparing and filing documents to obtain the Association's approval of the transactions contemplated hereby and in executing and delivering all documents, instruments or copies thereof reasonably deemed necessary by the other party hereto.

2.6 **"Assignment of Mortgages":** Seller shall prepare and execute or cause to be executed assignments, meeting all applicable Requirements, from Seller to Purchaser of the mortgage or deed of trust for each of the Mortgages as required by the Guide and all other applicable Requirements and shall deliver copy of such executed assignments to Purchaser with evidence satisfactory to Purchaser that each such assignment has been submitted, together with any applicable fees and charges.

Article III
Consideration

3.1 **"Purchase Price"**: In full consideration for the sale of the Servicing and other obligations of Seller as provided herein, and upon the terms and conditions and subject to the provisions of the Agreement, Purchaser shall pay to Seller the purchase price (the "Purchase Price") of (____) percent (___) (the "Purchase Price Percentage") of the aggregate unpaid principal balance of all Mortgages as of the Sale Date excluding (i) Mortgages that are, at any time from the Sale Date through and including the Transfer Date, Delinquent Mortgages, and (ii) Mortgages with respect to which, on or after the date of the Letter Agreement, the Mortgagor has given notice that the Mortgage is to be prepaid by prepayment has not been made prior to the Sale Date.

3.2 **"Payment"**: The Purchase price shall be paid as follows:

(a) 10% of the Purchase Price shall be paid to the Seller on the Sale Date, provided that Seller has performed all of its obligations hereunder required to be performed prior to such date.

(b) 90% of the Purchase Price shall be paid by the Purchaser to the Seller on the Transfer date provided that Seller has performed all of its obligations hereunder and under the Interim Servicing Agreement required to be performed prior to such date. Purchaser shall be entitled to credit against such payment (i) $2,500.00 for each Mortgage that was a Delinquent Mortgage as of the Transfer Date and (ii) any unpaid obligations of Seller hereunder or under the Interim Servicing Agreement.

For purposes of Section 3.2(b) and (c), the term Delinquent Mortgage shall have the meaning specified in the definition except that the reference to two monthly payments or more past due shall be amended to be three monthly payments or more past due.

3.3 "Other Costs":

(a) Seller shall bear the entire cost of securing the Association's approval of the transfer of Servicing from Seller to Purchaser, including all transfer fees due to the Association and all other costs associated with such transfer.

(b) Seller shall, at its sole cost and expense, ship to Purchaser and insure all loan files, insurance files, tax records and collection records or other documents required to be delivered by Seller to Purchaser.

(c) After giving effect all expenses of such collection and all advances made by Purchaser as service with respect to such Mortgage, Purchaser shall reimburse Seller for any advances of principal, interest, insurance premiums, taxes ground rents and other similar amounts made or expenses incurred by Seller in its capacity as servicer of the Mortgages.

Article IV
Seller's Representations and Warranties

As an inducement to Purchaser to enter into this Agreement, Seller represents and warrants to Purchaser (it being acknowledged that each such representation and warranty relates to material matters upon which Purchaser relied) as of the Sale Date and the Transfer Date, as follows:

4.1 **"Due Incorporation and Good Standing":** Seller is a corporation duly organized, validly existing and in good standing under the laws for the State of _____. Seller was, at all times relevant, properly licensed and qualified to transact business in all appropriate jurisdictions to conduct all activities necessary with respect to origination sale and servicing of the Mortgage [and the issuance and administration of the MBSs].

4.2 **"Authority and Capacity":** Seller has all requisite corporate power, authority and capacity to enter into the Sale Documents and to perform the obligations required of it thereunder and to carry out the transactions contemplated hereby. The execution and delivery of the Sale Documents and the consummation of the transaction contemplated hereby have each been duly and validly authorized by all necessary corporate action. The Sale Documents constitute valid and legally binding agreements of Seller enforceable in accordance with their respective terms, and no offset, counterclaim or defense exists to the full performance of the Sale Documents.

4.3 **"No Violations"**: The execution, delivery and performance of the Sale Documents by Seller, Seller's compliance with the terms thereof and consummation of the transactions contemplated hereby will not violate, conflict with, result in a breach of, constitute a default under, be prohibited by or require any approval under its certificate of incorporation, bylaws, or any instrument or agreement to which it is a party or by which it is bound or which affects the Mortgages, the MBSs, the Servicing or Related Escrow Accounts, or any other Requirements applicable to it or to the Mortgages, the MBSs, the Servicing or the Related Escrow Accounts, except for any consents or approvals required that have been obtained prior to the Sale Date.

4.4 **"Compliance with Requirements"**: Seller has complied with all its obligations under all contracts to which it is a party and with all Requirements applicable to Seller or its property or applicable to and which might affect the Servicing, the MBSs, the Mortgages or the Related Escrow Accounts. The originator of each Mortgage had the authority under applicable laws to make the mortgage loan represented thereby at the interest rate provided therein and was, if applicable, eligible at all relevant times to originate mortgages insured or guaranteed by the FHA or VA, eligible for purchase by FHLMC or FNMA and/or eligible for inclusion in a GNMA Pool.

4.5 **"Filing of Reports"**: For each Mortgage, Seller has filed or will file through the month following the Transfer Date, all required reports, including reports to the Association and all governmental agencies having jurisdiction over the Servicing, the Mortgages, the MBSs, the Pools and the Related Escrow Accounts and all reports required to be made pursuant to the Internal Revenue Code of 1986, as amended, and the regulations thereunder. Seller shall provide to each Mortgagor a "year-end statement" for the period ended on the Transfer Date.

4.6 **"Title to the Servicing"**: Subject only to the interest of the Association (to which Seller has assigned all by nominal title to the Mortgages under the Program) and the rights of Purchaser. Seller is the lawful owner of the Mortgages and the Mortgages are and will continue to be free and clear of all liens, encumbrances, charges and/or rights of others, and Seller will warrant and defend nominal title thereto. Seller is the lawful owner of the Servicing, is the lawful holder of the Related

Escrow Accounts, is the sole servicer of the Mortgage and has the sole right and authority to transfer the Servicing as contemplated hereby. The transfer of the Servicing, including the Related Escrow Accounts, in accordance with the terms and conditions hereof shall vest in Purchaser all rights to the Servicing (including the servicing fees and the Related Escrow Accounts) free and clear of any and all claims, charges, defenses, offsets and encumbrances of any kind or nature whatsoever, including those of Seller, any Prior Servicers or the originator of any Mortgage or any lender with a security interest in any Mortgage or the Servicing.

4.7 **"Related Escrow Accounts":** All Related Escrow Accounts have been established and continuously maintained, and all disbursements therefrom have been made, in accordance with applicable Requirements. Seller shall assign any buy-down arrangements relating to the Mortgages to Purchaser effective on the Sale Date.

4.8 **"Litigation":** There is no litigation, proceeding or governmental investigation pending or threatened (and Seller does not know of any basis for any such litigation, proceeding or governmental investigation pending or threatened).

4.9 **"Compliance with Requirements":** Each Mortgage complies in all respects with all applicable Requirements, including the Guide. Seller has performed all obligations to be performed under all applicable Requirements with respect to or that may affect the MBSs, the Mortgages, the Servicing or the Related Escrow Accounts, and no event has occurred and is continuing that, but for the passage of time or the giving of notice or both, would constitute an event of default, breach or violation of any Requirement. Seller has serviced the Mortgage and has kept and maintained complete and accurate books, records and accounts relating to the Mortgages, the Servicing, the MBSs and the Related Escrow Accounts in accordance with all applicable Requirements and sound and customary practices in the mortgage banking industry. Each Pool of Mortgages has been certified as required by the Association and is eligible for recertification.

4.10 **"Compliance with Insurance and Guaranty":** Seller has complied with all obligations under all applicable insurance or guaranty agreements, including title insurances, hazard insurance, and FHA or VA mortgage insurance or guaranty or private mortgage insurance. Seller has not taken or failed to take any action that might cause the cancellation of or otherwise adversely affect any insurance or guaranty agreements or obligations. All insurance premiums for all insurance policies required to be written in connection with the Mortgages have been paid to insurance companies; all insurance policies or certificates of insurance have been written by licensed agents and delivered to the obligator, are for required amounts, provide the required coverages and comply with all applicable Requirements; and upon transfer of the Servicing such policies are and will continue to be in full force and effect and enforceable against the insurance carriers in accordance with the terms of the respective policies and will not be terminated or otherwise adversely affected by the transfer of the Servicing contemplated hereby. Each insurance carrier is generally recognized as a reputable and sound company, is licensed and authorized to do business in the state where the insured property is located and the Mortgagor rises and meets all requirements of the Association and, if applicable, the FHA or VA or any private mortgage insurer.

4.11 "**Title Insurance**": A fully enforceable title policy, in at least the amount of the Mortgage (even if such amount may increase during the duration of the Mortgage) and that otherwise meets all applicable Requirements, which is paid-up and currently in effect, which has not been modified, has been issued for each Mortgage insuring that the mortgage or deed of trust relating thereto is a valid first lien on the property therein described and that the mortgaged property is free and clear of all encumbrances and liens having priority over the first lien of the mortgage or deed of trust, except for liens for real estate taxes and special assessments not yet due and payable and except for easements and restrictions of record identified in the title policy.

Article V
Representations and Warranties as to Mortgages

As further inducement to Purchaser to enter into this Agreement, Seller represents and warrants to Purchaser (it being acknowledged that each such representation and warranty relates to material matters on which Purchaser relied) as of the Sale Date and Transfer Date, with respect to each Mortgage, as follow:

5.1 "**Mortgage Documents**": Each Mortgage, and the mortgage/deed of trust and promissory note or other evidence of indebtedness and other loan documents relating thereto, are in all respect true, accurate, correct, complete and undisputed. The Mortgage documents are genuine, duly executed by a Mortgagor of legal capacity, and all insertions in any such document are correct.

5.2 **"Unpaid Balance":** The amount of the unpaid balance for each Mortgage which is reflected on Exhibit A is correct as of the date of Exhibit A. Each Mortgage is free of any defenses, setoffs or counterclaims of any nature whatsoever; no settlement, compromise or accommodation or agreement of forbearance has been made with respect to any Mortgage; no special promise or consideration has been made to any obligor, guarantor or insurer other than the FHA, the VA or the Association.

5.3 **"Security Interest":** Each Mortgage covers the property described therein and the collateral is correctly and accurately described and was and is presently in existence and situated at the location described therein and in the Seller's records. The lien granted by the Mortgagor in the property described in the Mortgage is valid first lien on the property described therein and will remain so throughout the term of the Mortgage. There are no encumbrances on the property described in the Mortgage except as listed in the title insurance policy relating thereto. At the time the Mortgage was made the title to the real property secured thereby met applicable title standards of the Association and the FHA or VA or other insurer or guarantor. All filings and recordings necessary to protect Seller's right, title and interest in the Mortgages have been made and all filing fees have been paid.

5.4 **"Validity of Note; Legal Proceedings":** With respect to each Mortgagor, no facts exist that would impair the validity of the promissory note, the mortgage/deed of trust, any other loan document or the collateral. Each of the Mortgages, together with the promissory notes, mortgages/deeds of trust, other instrument evidencing such Mortgage and other loan documents are the bona fide, legal, valid and binding obligations of the Mortgagor, enforceable in accordance with their respective terms under the laws of the state where the real property is located and under the laws of the United States. Transfer of the Mortgage to Purchaser or any subsequent purchaser will not detract from its enforceability. Seller has not committed or omitted to commit any act that would waive, estop or otherwise bar the right to enforce any Mortgage or done any act to impair any escrow, impound or similar account or otherwise impose upon the servicer or owner of the Mortgage responsibility with respect to such escrow, impound or similar accounts in excess of that imposed by the language of the mortgage instruments and the requirements contained in the Guide. The collateral for each Mortgage is neither being foreclosed upon nor being repossessed, has not been abandoned or sold by the Mortgagor nor is the subject of any pending insurance claim or pending or threatened condemnation proceeding; none of the obligors on the Mortgages is in bankruptcy or other insolvency proceeding; and none of the Mortgages is the subject of any litigation, investigation, legal process or proceeding or been transferred to a receiver or is the subject of an assignment for the benefit of creditors, nor have enforcement proceedings been brought or are required to be brought with respect thereto. Seller has not accepted a voluntary deed in lieu of foreclosure or arranged a preforeclosure sale with respect to the collateral for any Mortgage. No Mortgage is otherwise in default under the terms of his Mortgage. Seller has no written or other indication, knowledge or information that would suggest the possibility of commencement of any legal proceeding by a Mortgagor concerning or involving a Mortgage or other circumstances involving the Mortgage, the mortgaged premises or the Mortgagor that could adversely affect the value, marketability or collectibility or a Mortgage. Any right of recession involving a Mortgage under any applicable requirements has expired.

5.5 **"Compliance with Law"**: Each Mortgage has been made in accordance with and pursuant to all applicable Requirements. Each of the Mortgages is and will remain free of usury.

5.6 **"Hazard Insurance"**: Each building or other improvement located on the premises covered by each Mortgage is insured in the manner required by all applicable Requirements (including the Guide) under standard mortgagee clauses against (i) loss or damage by fire and from such other insurable risks and hazards as are set forth in the standard extended coverage form of endorsement, and (ii) such other insurable risks and hazards required by the Association, FHA, VA or other insurer or guarantor.

5.7 **"Tax Identification"**: All tax identification and property descriptions in the Mortgages are legally sufficient. The tax identification for each Mortgage as shown on Seller's records, and as used to pay taxes with respect to such Mortgage, is correct. Tax segregation, as required, has been completed.

5.8 **"Interest on Escrows":** Seller has credited to the account of or paid to the appropriate Mortgagors all interest required to be paid on any Related Escrow Account through the Transfer Date. Evidence reasonably satisfactory to Purchaser of such credit shall be provided to Purchaser upon request.

5.9 **"Payoff Statements":** All prepayment and assumption statements with respect to each Mortgage provided by Seller to Mortgagor or its agents were complete and accurate in all respects.

5.10 **"Escrow Analysis":** With respect to each Mortgage, Seller has within the last twelve months (unless such Mortgage was originated within such twelve month period) in accordance with accepted practice in the mortgage banking industry (i) analyzed the payments for escrow deposits required to be deposited into the Related Escrow Accounts relating thereto, and (ii) with respect to any deficiency discovered at the time of such analysis in the amount of the payments by the Mortgagor required to be made in respect thereof, adjusted the amount of such payments so that, assuming all required payments are timely made, such deficiency will be eliminated on or before the first anniversary of such analysis, all in accordance with the applicable requirements of the Association and other applicable Requirements.

5.11 **"Schedule of Insurance":** All Mortgages for which mortgage/credit life insurance, accidental death, disability, unemployment insurance, or any similar insurance is escrowed for as part of the Mortgagor's monthly payment are identified in Exhibit H attached hereto. All such insurance shall, upon Purchaser's request and to the extent that Seller has the authority to do so and that such action will not result in the violation of any applicable Requirement, not be renewed, and Seller shall take all steps necessary to notify the Mortgagors that their coverage will not be renewed.

5.12 **"Transfers":** Except for any Mortgage secured by real property that is not, as of the Date of the Mortgage Note, the primary residence of the obligor (and is so disclosed to Purchaser prior to the Sale Date), the obligor named in each instrument or document evidencing a Mortgage presently resides at the address set further in Seller's records. For each mortgage there has been no transfer of any interest in the real property securing the Mortgage nor any assumption or attempted assumption of the Mortgage except as disclosed to Purchaser in writing prior to the Sale Date.

5.13 **"Mortgage Pools":** Each Mortgage and each Pool conforms to all the requirements for Mortgages and Pools included in the Program contained in Section 2 of the Guide, including the appropriate requirements concerning type of property, project approval, buy-down provisions, capitalized loans, priority of lien, maximum principal amount, loan-to-value ratio, underwriting guidelines, documentation, amortization schedule, payment schedule, delinquency status, term to maturity, variation in interest rates, seasoning (age of mortgages), mortgage insurance or guaranty, and the minimum number and aggregate principal amount of Mortgages included in each Pool, at the time of the transfer of the Mortgages to the Association [and the issuance of the MBSs representing the Pool in which the Mortgage is included].

Article VI
Representations and Warranties of Purchaser

As an inducement to Seller to enter into this Agreement, Purchaser represents and warrants as follows as of the Sale Date and the Transfer Date:

6.1 **"Due Organization":** Purchaser is federally chartered savings bank duly organized and validly existing under the laws of the United States of America.

6.2 **"Authority and Capacity":** Purchaser has all requisite corporate power, authority and capacity to enter into this Agreement, the Interim Servicing Agreement and the Assignment Agreement, and the consummation of the transactions contemplated hereby and thereby have been duly and validly authorized by all necessary corporate action. This Agreement, the Interim Servicing Agreement and the Assignment Agreement constitute valid and legally binding agreements of Purchaser enforceable in accordance with their respective terms.

6.3 **"Effective Agreement":** The execution, delivery and performance of this Agreement, the Interim Servicing Agreement and the Assignment Agreement by Purchaser, its compliance with the terms hereof and thereof and consummation of the transaction contemplated hereby and thereby will not violate, conflict with, result in a breach of, constitute a default under, be prohibited by or require any approval under the articles of association, bylaws, or any instrument or agreements to which it is a party or by which it is bound or which, to its knowledge, affects the Servicing, or any Requirement applicable to Purchaser or, to its knowledge, to the Servicing, except for approvals and consents that Seller is responsible for obtaining pursuant to Sections 7.1, 7.3 and 7.4 or any other provisions of this Agreement.

6.4 **"Good Standing":** Purchaser is an Association-approved FNMA and a FHA or VA approved sevicer.

Article VII
Covenants

7.1 **"Regulatory Approvals":** Seller shall, at its expense, obtain the approval of the Association for (i) the transfer of the Servicing from Seller to Purchaser pursuant hereto [including the assumption by Seller of certain of Purchaser's obligations with respect to the MBSs, as provided in the Assignment Agreement, (ii) the Interim Servicing Agreement, (iii) the transfer of documents relating to the Mortgages to a Custodian selected by Purchaser, and (iv) the transfer of Related Escrow Accounts to a financial institution selected by Purchaser. Such approval shall be obtained in a timely fashion so that the transactions contemplated hereby may be effected on the Sale Date. Seller shall use its best efforts to secure such approval, including promptly complying with all requirements imposed by the Association with respect to obtaining such approvals.

7.2 **"Notice to Mortgagors":** Seller shall, at Seller's expense, mail to each Mortgagor a letter advising the Mortgagor of the transfer of the Servicing to Purchaser at least 15 days prior to the Transfer Date by certified mail, return receipt requested, that the servicing has been transferred to Purchaser and that on and after the Transfer Date all insurance premium billings for the Mortgages shall be sent to Purchaser. The form and content of the notice shall have Purchaser's prior written approval. Seller shall provide Purchaser with a copy of the certified mail receipt. Seller shall, prior to the Sale Date, obtain the written consent of any of the foregoing persons that have the right to approve the transfer of the Servicing or the assignment of such insurance or guaranty.

7.3 **"Notice to Insurers and Guarantors":** Seller shall, at Seller's expense, notify all applicable insurers, guarantors and/or agents at least 15 days prior to the Transfer Date by certified mail, return receipt requested, that the Servicing has been transferred to Purchaser and that all notices, tax bills and insurance statements and escrow account statements shall be sent, and all payments made, as the case may be, to or as directed by Purchaser from and after the Transfer Date. The form and content of such notice shall have Purchaser's prior written approval. Seller shall, prior to the Sale Date, obtain the consent of any of the foregoing persons that have the right to approve the transfer of the Servicing or the assignment of any such insurance or guaranty.

7.4 **"Delivery of Loan Documents":** Before the transfer date, Seller shall cause its Custodian to deliver to the Custodian selected by Purchaser a complete custodial file for each Mortgage (or, if Seller is the Custodian, Seller shall deliver to Purchaser such documents as Purchaser may reasonably request). Each custodial file so delivered shall contain all documents required by all applicable Requirements to be held by the Custodian. Seller shall deliver to Purchaser on or prior to the Transfer Date all other loan documentation described in Exhibit D for each Mortgage.

7.5 **"Delivery of Servicing Records":** Seller shall deliver to Purchaser on or prior to the Transfer Date all servicing records in Seller's possession related to each mortgage. In the event Seller is unable to provide a Social Security number or taxpayer identification number of each Mortgagor, Seller shall reimburse Purchaser of its reasonable expenses in obtaining such numbers.

7.6 **"Related Escrow Account Balances":** On the five days prior to Transfer, the Seller will transfer in the manner specified by Purchaser (i) to an account designated by Purchaser immediately available funds in the amount of the net escrow and suspense balance and all loss draft balances associated with Mortgages and (ii) all payments received by Seller within five days prior to the Sale Date, which shall be held for delivery to Purchaser and not deposited for collection. Seller shall provide Purchaser with an accounting statement of escrow and suspense balances and loss draft balances sufficient to enable Purchaser to reconcile the amount so transferred with the accounts of the Mortgages.

7.7 **"Prepayments and Assumptions":** Seller shall provide to Purchaser on the Transfer Date copies of all assumption and prepayment statements on the Mortgages within the preceding sixty (60) days. Additionally, Seller shall provide Purchaser prior to the Transfer Date a list of all prepayments and assumptions in process.

7.8 **"Mortgage Payments Received Prior to Transfer Date":** Prior to the Transfer Date, all payments received by Seller on each Mortgage shall be properly applied by Seller to the account of the appropriate Mortgagor and shall be deposited in the appropriate Related Escrow Account.

7.9 **"Mortgage Payments Received After Transfer Date"**: Any payments received by Seller after the Transfer Date on any Mortgage shall forthwith be endorsed over and delivered or otherwise paid to Purchaser; and Seller shall provide with such payment sufficient information to permit appropriate processing of the payment by Purchaser.

7.10 **"Misapplied Payments"**: Misapplied payments shall be processed as follow:

    (i) Both parties shall cooperate in correcting misapplications errors.

    (ii) The party receiving a misapplied payment occurring prior to the Transfer Date shall immediately notify the other party.

    (iii) If a misapplied payment occurring prior to the Transfer Date cannot be identified by either party and said misapplied payment has resulted in a shortage in a Related Escrow Account, Seller shall be liable for the amount of such shortage. Seller shall reimburse Purchaser for the amount of such shortage within five Business Days after receipt of written demand therefore from Purchaser.

    (iv) Any payment made under the provision of this Section 7.11 shall be accompanied by a statement indicating the purpose of the payment, the Mortgagor and property address involved, and the corresponding Seller and/or Purchaser identification number for the Mortgage.

7.11 **"Inspection of Records"**: Purchaser may, through its employees, agents, accountants, counsel, auditors or other representatives (its "Agents"), make or cause to be made such investigations of the Servicing, the origination and servicing of the Mortgages, administration of the MBSs and the Related Escrow Accounts, and any such investigation shall not affect the representations and warranties made by Seller herein, in the Interim Servicing Agreement or the Assignment Agreement or in any instrument, statement or document provided pursuant hereto or thereto. During normal business hours, Purchaser and its Agents shall have full access to the premises of Seller, including all documents relating to the Servicing, the Mortgages, the MBSs and the Related Escrow Accounts, and Seller shall furnish to Purchaser and its Agents such financial and operating data and other information (or copies thereof) as Purchaser and its Agents may from time to time request. Further, Seller shall instruct its auditors, accountants, and counsel to cooperate with Purchaser and its Agents in making available to them all financial and legal information requested and to make copies and extracts thereof as they pertain to the Servicing, the origination and servicing of the mortgages, the administration of the MBS and the Related Escrow Account. Further, Seller shall assist Purchaser in making such independent verifications of information relating to the Servicing, the Mortgages, the MBS or the Related Escrow Accounts as Purchaser may reasonably require (including verification that payments made on the Mortgages by the Mortgagors have been properly applied by Seller). Seller shall make available to Purchaser all records available to Purchaser all records needed to set up its system for servicing Mortgages and performing its other obligations with respect to the Servicing, including master dumps, history ledgers, trial balances and Association reports.

7.12 **"Solicitation of Accounts":** Seller shall not, at any time, directly, solicit a refinancing of any Mortgage or make any other solicitation of a Mortgagor that may result in the prepayment of a Mortgage, nor will it directly assist or be employed by or participate with any other party in soliciting a refinancing of a Mortgage or making any other solicitation of a Mortgagor that may result in making the prepayment of a Mortgage.

7.13 **"Notices":** Any notices, documents or other information received by Seller after the Transfer Date that related to the Servicing, the Mortgages, the Related Escrow Accounts or the MBSs shall be promptly forwarded by Seller to Purchaser.

7.14 **"Statistical and Other Information":** Seller shall compile or prepare and provide to Purchaser such historical and statistical information regarding the Mortgages and other mortgages originated or serviced by Seller, including default, delinquency and prepayment information, as Purchaser may reasonably request.

Article VIII
Conditions Precedent to Obligations of Purchaser

The obligations of Purchaser under this Agreement are subject to the satisfaction of the following conditions:

8.1 **"Certificates of Seller":**

(a) On the Sale Date, Purchaser shall receive from Seller a certificate dated as of the Sale Date of an authorized officer of Seller covering the following matters:

    (i) that the information set forth in Exhibit B with respect to each Mortgage and Related Escrow Account has been delivered to Purchaser and that such information is true and correct;

    (ii) that an accurate copy of all corporate resolutions approving the execution and delivery of the Sale Documents and the consummation of the transactions contemplated hereby, which have not been repealed, amended or modified, is attached to the certificate, together which such other evidence of incumbency and corporate authority as Purchaser may request;

    (iii) that each of Seller's representations and warranties made in Articles IV and V hereof are true and correct as of such date and that all of the terms and conditions of and obligations of Seller under the Sale Documents to be performed or fulfilled by Seller (including the conditions set forth in this Article 8) by such date have been performed and fulfilled;

    (iv) that the information contained in all documents and reports submitted by Seller to the Association is true, complete and correct; and

    (v) such other matters as Purchaser may request.

(b) On the Transfer Date, Purchaser shall receive from Seller the Certificate specified in Section 8.1(a) dated as of the Transfer Date.

8.2 **"Correctness of Representations and Warranties":** The representations and warranties made by Seller in this Agreement, the Interim Servicing Agreement and the Assignment Agreement are true and correct and shall continue to be true and correct on the Sale Date and the Transfer Date.

8.3 **"Compliance with Conditions":** All of the terms, covenants and conditions of and obligations of Seller under this Agreement, the Interim Servicing Agreement and the Assignments Agreement and any other applicable Requirements to be complied with and performed by Seller at or prior to the Sale Date or the Transfer Date shall have been duly complied with and performed by the applicable date.

8.4 **"Regulatory Approval":** The Association shall have approved, on or before Transfer Date, effective on the Sale Date, the transactions specified in 7.1, and Seller shall have fulfilled all applicable requirements for the transfer to be effected.

8.5 **"Legal Opinion":** Seller shall provide an opinion of counsel (which counsel shall be reasonably satisfactory to Purchaser) to Purchaser on the Sale Date. Such opinion shall be in form and substance satisfactory to Purchaser and its counsel and shall provide that:

(i) Seller is a corporation duly organized and validly existing under the laws of its jurisdiction or incorporation and in good standing under the laws of the state of its incorporation and in each other jurisdiction where the conduct of its business or its ownership or leasing or properties requires it to so qualify and has all requisite corporate power to enter into the Sale Documents and to perform the obligations required of it thereunder and to consummate the transactions contemplated hereby.

(ii) The Sale Documents and all other agreements and instruments delivered or prepared by Seller hereunder comply in all respects with all applicable Requirements. The execution and delivery of the Sale Documents and the consummation of the transactions contemplated hereby have been duly and validly authorized by Seller, and the Sale Documents have been duly executed and delivered and are legally valid and binding obligations of Seller enforceable in accordance with their respective terms, except as such reforceability may be limited by (A) applicable bankruptcy, reorganization, insolvency, moratorium and other laws affecting generally creditors' rights or debtors' obligations from time to time in effect and (B) the availability of the remedy of specific performance or injunctive relief or any other equitable remedy.

(iii) All preconditions to the transfer of Servicing contemplated hereby have been fulfilled (including all requirements set forth in the Guide).

(iv) There are no legal actions pending or threatened that would or might affect the Servicing or Seller's ability to transfer the same or to consummate the transactions contemplated hereby or by the other Sale Documents.

(v) The transfer and assignment of Seller's rights with respect to the Servicing and the Mortgages, including all rights to the proceeds of insurance or guaranties of the Mortgages, is legally effective against all persons.

(vi) The execution, delivery and performance of the Sale Documents by Seller, Seller's compliance with the terms thereof and consummation of the transactions contemplated hereby will not violate, conflict with, result in breach of, constitute a default under, be prohibited by or require any approval under its certificate of incorporation, bylaws, or any instrument or agreement to which it is a party or by which it is bound or which affects the Mortgages, the MBSs or the Servicing, or any Requirements applicable to it or to the Mortgages, the MBSs or the Servicing, except of any required consents or approvals that have been obtained prior to the Sale Date.

(vii) To the best of such counsel's knowledge, after due investigation, there is no litigation or other matter required to be described in Exhibit F hereto that is not described as required.

(viii) Such other matters incident to the transaction contemplated hereby as Purchaser may request.

8.6 **"Schedule of Items"**: All items set forth in Exhibit G shall have been prepared, executed, delivered or performed by Seller by the dates indicated in Exhibit G.

8.7 **"Repurchase of Delinquent Mortgages"**: Prior to the Sale Date and the Transfer Date, to the extent required by the Association or permitted by the Guide, Seller shall repurchase or replace any Mortgage that is a Delinquent Mortgage on either such date.

8.8 **"Certification of Pools"**: Seller shall have provided to Purchaser evidence satisfactory to Purchaser that the Pools have been certified and are eligible to be recertified at the Sale Date and Transfer Date.

8.9 **"Excess Funds"**: Prior to the Sale Date, Seller shall have repaid all "excess funds" previously withdrawn from any Related Escrow Account.

Article IX
Conditions Precedent to Obligations of Seller

The obligations of Seller under this Agreement are subject to the satisfaction at or prior to the Sale Date of each of the following conditions.

9.1 **"Correctness of Representations and Warranties":** The representations and warranties made by Purchaser in this Agreement are true and correct.

9.2 **"Compliance with Conditions":** All of the terms, conditions and covenants of this Agreement required to be complied with and performed by Purchaser at or prior to the Sale Date shall have been duly complied with and performed.

9.3 **"Regulatory Approval":** The Association shall have approved, effective on the sale Date on or before Transfer Date, the transfer of the Servicing from Seller to Purchaser pursuant hereto and the provision of servicing by Seller pursuant to the Interim Servicing Agreement.

Article X
Miscellaneous

10.1 **"Cost and Expenses":** Except as otherwise specifically provided herein each party hereto shall pay the expenses incurred by it in connection with the transactions contemplated hereby are consummated.

10.2 **"Indemnification by Seller":** Seller shall indemnify Purchaser and its successors, assigns, employees, servants and agents against, and protect, save and keep harmless each of them from, any and all liabilities, obligations (including obligations based on strict liability in tort of actual or imputed negligence), losses, damages, penalties, actions, suits, deficiencies, claims, causes of action or costs, expenses or disbursement (including reasonable attorney's fees and costs) of whatsoever kind and nature, imposed on, incurred by or asserted against any of such persons before or after the Sale Date that:

(a) in any way relate to or arise from any false, inaccurate, untrue, incomplete or unfulfilled representation, warranty or covenant by Seller in any Sale Document, or in any schedule, statement, certificate or other information furnished by Seller pursuant to this Agreement;

(b) in any way relate to or arise from any misrepresentation or breach of warranty by Seller, or the nonfulfillment of any covenant or condition of Seller contained in any Sale Document or in any schedule, statement, certificate or other information furnished by Seller pursuant hereto;

(c) in any way relate to or arise from any defect in any Mortgage existing as of the Sale Date (including those defects subsequently discovered);

(d) in any way relate to or arise from errors in origination or servicing any of the Mortgages (including misquoted prepayment or assumption statement, misapplied payments, failure to file timely notice of default or failure to pay taxes or other charges including penalties and interest), or any failure by Seller, any Prior Servicer or the originator of any mortgage to comply fully with all applicable Requirements in originating, transferring to the Association or servicing the Mortgages; or

(e) in any way relate to or arise from Seller's failure to permit Purchaser to examine records, to comply with provisions hereof or Purchaser's instructions regarding the transfers of Servicing or to provide accurate information requested by Purchaser regarding the Mortgages or the Servicing.

Seller's indemnification shall include all penalties, claims, costs, expenses and disbursements incurred by any of the persons specified (i) due to the failure by Seller or any Prior Servicer to service and administer the Mortgages prior to the Transfer Date in accordance with all applicable Requirements and sound and customary practices in the mortgage banking industry; (ii) in correcting, repurchasing and/or replacing any Mortgage found to be ineligible under applicable Requirements or otherwise defective; or (iii) otherwise as a result of Purchaser's assumption pursuant to the Assignment Agreement of the duties and obligations formerly incumbent on Seller as seller/servicer of the Mortgages [and issuer of the MBSs]. The provisions of this Section shall survive termination of this Agreement.

10.3 **"Termination"**: Purchaser may terminate this Agreement prior to the Sale Date if (i) any representation or warranty or Seller herein or other information provided by Seller to Purchaser with material respect to the transactions contemplated hereby is false or misleading in any respect or omits to state a material fact; (ii) the Mortgages were not originated or serviced in accordance with sound and customary practices in the mortgage banking industry; (iii) the Mortgages involve greater than normal risk of default delinquency or prepayment; (iv) any information provided to Purchaser by Seller relating to the Servicing, the Mortgages, the MBSs or the Related Escrow Accounts or the Seller's status or condition was misleading or incomplete; (v) Purchaser learns of facts or circumstances that Purchaser in good faith determines will adversely affect the benefit expected to be received by Purchaser from the transactions contemplated hereby; (vi) Seller pursuant to or within the meaning of Title II of the U.S. Code or any similar federal or state law for the relief of debtors commences a voluntary case, consents to the entry of an order for relief against it in an involuntary case, consents to the appointment of a receiver, trustee, assignee, liquidator or similar official under any bankruptcy or insolvency law of Seller or for all or substantially all of its property or makes a general assignment for the benefit of creditors; or (vii) a court of competent jurisdiction enters an order or decree (which remains unstayed in effect for 60 days) under Title II of the U.S. Code or any similar federal or state law for the relief of debtors that is for relief against Seller in an involuntary case, appoints a receiver, trustee, assignee, liquidator or similar official under any bankruptcy or insolvency law of Seller or for all or substantially all of its property or orders the liquidation of Seller. In the event of such termination, Seller shall immediately pay to Purchaser all amounts paid or advanced by Purchaser to Seller hereunder or under the Letter Agreement; the portion of the Purchase Price under the Letter Agreement, held in escrow pursuant to the Letter Agreement shall be immediately released to Purchaser and (except for termination pursuant to clause (v)) Seller shall reimburse Purchaser for its out-of-pocket expenses incurred in connection with the transactions contemplated hereby.

10.4 **"Repurchase of Servicing":** In the event of a breach by Seller of any of its representations and warranties hereunder, Seller shall refund to Purchaser the Purchase price per Mortgage with respect to those Mortgages affected by such breach and reimburse all costs and expenses (including reasonable attorney's fees) incurred by Purchaser as result of such breach.

If the Mortgage is required or permitted to be repurchased from the Association, upon Purchaser's request Seller shall also pay to Purchaser an amount sufficient to repurchase each such Mortgage from the Pool of which such Mortgage is a part. All such amounts shall be paid by Seller to Purchaser within five business days following receipt from Purchaser of written demand from Purchaser pursuant hereto. Upon payment by Seller of the amount specified in the proceeding sentence and repurchase by Purchaser of any such Mortgage to Seller and at Seller's expense shall file such assignments of record and deliver to Seller all documents (including the mortgage note endorsed to Seller without recourse), in Purchaser's possession or control that relate to the repurchase Mortgages.

10.5 **"Agency Authorization":** Seller agrees that it shall from time to time hereafter execute and promptly deliver to Purchaser such documents, assignments, endorsements, applications or other instruments necessary, proper or convenient to effect the transactions contemplated hereby. Seller does hereby irrevocably constitute and appoint Purchaser and its duly authorized officers and employees as Seller's agent and to endorse checks and other instruments or payments with respect to the Mortgages and to execute and deliver, in Seller's name and on its behalf, any such documents, assignments, endorsements, applications or other instruments. Such power of attorney is coupled with an interest and may not be revoked.

10.6 **"Supplementary Information":** From time to time prior to and after the Transfer Date, Seller shall furnish Purchaser such additional information and shall prepare and file such reports as Purchaser may request.

10.7 **"Confidentiality of Information":** Seller and Purchaser and their affiliates shall, and shall cause their respective directors, officers, employees and agents to, hold in strict confidence and not use or disclose to any other person without the prior written consistent of the party hereto all information concerning customers or proprietary business procedures, servicing fees or prices, policies or plans or the other party hereto in connection with the transactions contemplated hereby. No action will be taken by either party or their facilitates to publicize this sale of Servicing in any trade or public media using the other party's name without the prior written approval of the other party, except as required by law.

10.8 **"Broker's Fees":** Seller represents and that it has made no agreement to pay any agent, finder or broker, fees or commission in the nature of a finder's or originator's fee or arising out of or in connection with the subject matter of this Agreement. Seller agrees to indemnify and hold Purchaser harmless from any liability in connection with its agreement with Cohane Rafferty Securities, Inc. and against any such obligation or liability and any expense incurred in investigation or defending (including reasonable attorney's fees and costs) any claim for any such fee by any other person.

10.9 **"Survival of Representations and Warranties"**: Each party hereto covenants and agrees that the representations and warranties in this Agreement, and in any document, schedule or other information delivered or to be delivered pursuant hereto, shall survive the consummation of the transactions contemplated herein.

10.10 **"Notices"**: All notices, requests, demands and other communications required or permitted to be given under this Agreement shall be in writing and shall be deemed to have duly given upon the delivery or mailing thereof, as the case may be, sent by registered or certified mail, return receipt requested, postage prepaid:

(a) If to the Purchaser, to:

_____

_____

_____

_____

(b) If to the Seller, to:

_____

_____

_____

_____

or to such other address as Purchaser or Seller shall have specified in writing to the other.

10.11 **"Waivers"**: Either Purchaser or Seller may, by written agreement, to the other extend the time for the performance of any of the obligations of the other and waive compliance with any of the terms, conditions or covenants required to be complied with by the other hereunder. The waiver by any party hereto of a breach of any provision of this Agreement shall not operate or be construed as a waiver of any other or subsequent breach. No delay, omission or act by a party shall be deemed a waiver of such party's rights, powers or remedies hereunder. No course of dealing between the parties hereto shall operate as a waiver of any provision hereof. The rights and remedies granted are cumulative, may be exercised singly or concurrently, and are not exclusive of any right, power or remedy provided by law.

10.12 **"Entire Agreement; Amendment"**: This Agreement, the Interim Servicing Agreement, the Assignment Agreement, and the schedules, exhibits and certificates required to be delivered hereunder and any amendments hereafter executed and delivered in accordance with the provisions hereof or thereof, and the escrow agreement pursuant to which a portion of the Purchaser Price is held in escrow, constitute the entire agreement between the parties with respect to the sale of the Servicing and the other transactions contemplated hereby and supersede all prior written or oral agreement (or contemporaneous oral agreements) of the parties with respect thereto. This Agreement may be amended only in writing signed by the parties.

10.13 **"Binding Effect; Severability"**: This Agreement shall inure to the benefit of and be binding upon the parties hereto and their successors and assigns. Nothing in this Agreement, express or implied, is intended to confer on any person other than the parties hereto and their successors and assigns any rights, obligations hereunder without Purchaser's prior written consent. Purchaser may assign this Agreement to any person or entity that it controls, is controlled by, or is under common control with. For purposes of this provision, control is conclusively established by ownership of 25 percent of the equity interest of an entity by another entity of person or group of related entities or persons. If any provision hereof shall be invalid, illegal or unenforceable, the validity, legality and enforceability of the remaining provisions shall not be affected or impaired thereby.

10.14 **"Headings; Interpretive Principles"**: Headings of the Articles and Sections in this Agreement are for reference purposes only and shall not be deemed to have substantive effect. As used herein, the term "including" is intended to be illustrative and not exclusive.

10.15 **"Applicable Law"**: This Agreement shall be construed in accordance with the laws of the State of _____.

10.16 **"Incorporation of Exhibits"**: Exhibits A through H attached hereto shall be incorporated herein and shall be understood to be part hereof as though included in the body of this Agreement.

10.17 **"Counterparts"**: This Agreement may be executed in counterparts, each of which, when so executed and delivered, shall be deemed to be an original and all of which, taken together, shall constitute one and the same agreement.

IN WITNESS WHEREOF, each of the undersigned have caused this Agreement to be duly executed on its behalf by one of its duly authorized officers as of the date first above written.

"PURCHASER"
ATTEST _____
By: _____
Its: _____

"SELLER"
ATTEST _____
By: _____
Its: _____

6

Due Diligence and Portfolio Transfer

Webster defines *diligent* as "painstaking," a word that has important implications to a mortgage banker. Once you have won an auction and purchased a mortgage portfolio, you must take pains to ensure that you bought exactly what you think you bought.

Due diligence is the process of verifying all essential details of the portfolio that were represented by the seller. Due diligence is the responsibility of the buyer. It takes place before the actual transfer of loans to the buyer. If due diligence is not performed, or if it is approached in a cursory or haphazard manner, the result can be a loss rather than the gain that was projected when the package was evaluated.

The seller is not likely to willfully mislead or withhold important information from the offering, but when dealing with hundreds of loans it is impossible to present the basic data about every loan in the mortgage servicing portfolio offering. The due diligence process aims at examining this data and at doing so before the deal is finally closed and money has changed hands.

The due diligence process can proceed in various ways, depending on the nature of the portfolio purchased and the buyer's organization. Regardless of the technical method used, the key to due diligence rests with the individuals selected to conduct the examination. To perform due diligence on a $10 million portfolio, you may need only two people who are knowledgeable in the process. However, a $400 million package probably requires a task force, with representation from each internal department of the buyer's organization, and a supervisor to oversee the project and exercise final review of all areas. The due diligence task force should include specialists from investor reporting, collections/foreclosure, customer service, data processing, and other relevant departments.

Before the actual exercise is undertaken, guidelines should be set in place. One or more planning sessions should be held to gather ideas from all servicing managers or supervisors. Determine specific areas for focus during the due diligence before tackling the data. This is a time to brainstorm and be creative.

The due diligence planning session should answer key questions:

- What are the probable problem areas with this portfolio and how can you best identify them?
- Are there any specific data requirements for your computer system that can be addressed and corrected before the transfer?
- What types of questions can you ask the sellers before the due diligence to better evaluate their servicing area?

The basic process due diligence takes in most cases is to back into essential details by creating detailed reports. However, it does not stop at the essential details. The buyer is equally concerned with how the portfolio is being serviced—what management, compliance, procedures, and follow-through of those procedures are being used by the seller. The buyer must examine and understand those things as part of the due diligence process.

What types of problems would you consider major problems and what would be minor? For example, if the WASF is less than represented, you would need to re-evaluate the portfolio because this would have a direct effect on the bid price.

The task force creates a pre-due-diligence questionnaire for the seller. Upon receiving the completed questionnaire from the seller, the task force may alter the on-site due-diligence process, depending on the answers. For example, if 20 percent of the pools are out of balance according to the seller's responses to the questionnaire, the task force may plan to spend more time on a review of the seller's investor reporting department. The due-diligence plan must be flexible, to allow adjustments midstream as its findings dictate.

Finally, as part of the planning process, the task force will create its on-site due-diligence reports. The purpose of these reports is to provide all information the buyer needs prior to transfer of the loans and finalization of the sale. Due diligence is the buyer's last chance to "kick the tires" before taking possession.

Must the due diligence process always be as exacting as this? A possible exception is when the buyer has purchased from the seller previously without difficulty. In that case, the buyer knows how the seller services loans and understands the seller's management, compliance, procedures, and administrative follow-through.

The balance of this chapter provides a skeleton of a detailed report, to demonstrate one approach to due diligence. The task force will want to review this sample report to clarify the logic and sequence of the desired information (and to add other relevant issues specific to an unusual situation). When gathering data to complete the report, the task force should make sure that all reports from which information is taken have the same date as the data supplied during the offering and bidding process.

The due diligence process should include the following areas for verification of detail, procedures, and state and regulatory compliance:

- Essential details
- Investor reporting
- Taxes and insurance
- Analysis
- Delinquence/foreclosure
- Payoffs
- Balloons
- Assumptions
- General questions
- Servicing agreements for private investors
- System requirements

Essential Details

Date of Information   _____
Product Type   _____
Note Type   _____
Principal Balance   _____
Number of Loans   _____
Average Loan Size   _____
Weighted Average Net Servicing Fee   _____
Weighted Average Note Rate   _____
Weighted Average Original Term (months) _____
Weighted Average Remaining Term (months) _____
Current Escrow Balance   _____
Tax and Insurance Constant   _____
Principal and Interest Constant   _____

Delinquencies

	Number of Loans	Percentage of Loans
30 days	_____	_____
60 days	_____	_____
90 days	_____	_____
Net Delinquencies	_____	_____
Foreclosures	_____	_____
Total Delinquencies	_____	_____

Investor Reporting

GNMA Pools

1. Are all the GNMA pools final certified? NO ____ YES ____ If no, provide a list of the pools that are not.
   What is the date of cutoff for GNMA pools?

2. Name and address of custodian(s):

3. Is there a tax ID number on each pool? NO ____ YES ____

4. Are 1099s or 1041/K-1s used for interest income reporting to security holders? NO _____ YES _____

5. Are security holders' names and addresses current? NO ____ YES _____

6. How many manual checks do you produce monthly?

7. Do you have a security register in pool number order?
8. In what order is the security register?
9. Do you have pools where you overremitted to security holders and are awaiting liquidations to recapture? YES _____ NO _____ How many? _____ Dollar amount _____
10. Are there differences between your trial balance and 1710A Section I? YES _____ NO _____
11. Do the 1710 Section III balances equal the security holder balances? YES _____ NO ____

FHLMC Loans

1. Does the 308 and trial balance equal for all groups? YES _____ NO _____
   If no, what is dollar amount? _____
   How many? _____
2. If there are adjustments to line 5 form 330, provide detail for past six months.

FNMA Pools

1. Are there differences between your trial balance and 2010 Section I? YES _____ NO _____ If yes, attach details.
2. Do you have pools where you overremitted to security holders and are awaiting liquidations to recapture? YES _____ NO _____ How many? _____ Dollar amount _____
3. Provide name, address of custodian.

FHA 235, 265, and 246 Loans

1. Number of
   235s _____
   265s _____
   246s _____
2. Describe how billing records are maintained.
3. Describe how recertification records are maintained.

4. Describe how each of the following is handled:
   - Escrow shortages
   - Escrow overages
   - Overpaid assistance on HUD subsidy 235 loans
   - How is overpaid assistance reflected?
   - After three years, how are accounts suspended for termination?
   - Assistance billing for 246 loans

GPMs, Buydowns, ARMs

1. How are the following identified?
   - GPMs
   - Buydowns
   - ARMs
2. How is the borrower notified of payment change for each of the following?
   - GPMs
   - Buydowns
   - ARMs
3. How are the interest rate parameters tracked for ARMs?
   Manually _____ System _____
4. What indexes are used for ARMs?

Bank Account Reconciliation

1. Are all your P&I accounts reconciled monthly?
   YES _____ NO _____ If no, explain.
2. Are there any large, undefined reconciling items?
   YES _____ NO _____ If yes, explain.
3. Are all T&I accounts reconciled monthly?
   YES _____ NO _____ If no, explain.
4. Are there any large, undefined reconciling items?
   YES _____ NO _____ If yes, explain.
5. Are private investor accounts commingled?
   YES _____ NO _____

6. How many bank accounts are there?

_____ _____

7. List bank accounts:

Bank name	Account number	Account type	Bank last balance

Cashiering/Payments

1. Do you use a lockbox? YES _____ NO _____
2. How do you handle exceptions? How many exceptions do you have per month?
3. How do you handle the following:
   - Buydowns
   - Subsidy fund
   - HUD 235, 265, and 246 loans
   - Returned checks
4. What type of billing method is used?
   - ☐ Coupons
   - ☐ Monthly billings
   - ☐ Drafts
   - ☐ Other

General Escrow

1. How many loans are escrowed?
2. How many loans are non-escrowed?

   VA_____
   FHA_____
   Other_____

3. Do you pay interest on escrow? YES _____ NO _____
   When is interest credited to account?
   Provide a list of the following:
   - State requiring interest
   - Interest rate
   - Number of escrowed loans in each state

Taxes and Insurance

Taxes

1. Are all loans on a tax service? YES _____ NO _____
2. Do all loans have contract numbers? YES _____ NO _____
3. How many times a year are taxes paid? _____
4. If taxes are paid in different states, provide a list with the following information:
   - Number of loans
   - State
   - Frequency
   - Method
5. Are all taxes paid directly to county or are they paid separately? (Example: school) In total: _____ Sseparately: _____
6. Are all taxes current? YES _____ NO _____
7. Provide a list of the delinquent taxes by investor. Are they FHLMC/FNMA/GNMA?
8. How many are escrowed for taxes? How many are not escrowed for taxes?
9. Total T&I advance amount outstanding: _____

Hazard Insurance

1. How many loans are not escrowed for hazard insurance?
2. What type of evidence of insurance do you require?

3. Is insurance information maintained on the computer?
   YES _____ NO _____
4. How do you identify the following:
   - Expired policies
   - Multiple policies
   - Binder policies
   - Payment dates
   - Flood insurance or other special required insurance
5. Who is default carrier?
6. What payment method is used?

Mortgage Insurance

1. How do you handle the following?
   - Identify MSP paid in advance
   - MSP with no billing
   - Method of payment of FHA premiums
2. Provide the following lists:
   - All PMO companies used
   - All loans with MSP premiums

Option Insurance

1. List the types of optional insurance offered to companies.
2. If life insurance offered, do you have administrative contracts?
   YES _____ NO _____ What is the average T&I percentage received on premiums?
3. Are funds comingled with tax and hazard insurance funds?
   YES _____ NO _____
4. Are funds reconciled monthly? _____ Quarterly? _____ Annually? _____

Analysis

1. How many times per year do you analyze?

2. When was the last time you analyzed all loans?
3. How are overages handled?
4. How are shortages handled?
5. Where are previous analyses stored?
6. Do you analyze delinquent loans?

Delinquencies/Foreclosure

1. Delinquency Ratios
   30 days_____
   60 days_____
   90 days_____
   Foreclosure_____
   Bankruptcy_____
2. How many loans are on payment plans?   _____
3. Are phone numbers on customer records? YES _____ NO _____
4. How are you recording collection histories?
5. Do you use in-house trustee or attorney?
6. Law firms you have relationships with (foreclosure and bankruptcy).
7. How many of each of the following loan types are involved?
   ARM _____
   FHA 235 _____
   Multi-family _____
   Commercial _____
8. How many different lenders are involved? What are their requirements for reporting delinquency?
9. What is the monitoring system of bankruptcy plan payments?
10. Provide the number of and itemization of Chapter 7, 13, and 11 bankruptcies.
11. What is the stance for collection of the following:
    ■ Delinquent taxes
    ■ Escrow shortages
12. Typical "late charge deferred" limit before starting collection.

Payoffs

1. If private investors, do you keep or split the following:
   Prepayment penalty _____% retained
   Late fees _____% retained
2. What is the P.O. rate for the past six months?
   Number of loans _____
   UPB _____
   States _____
3. What is the disbursement method?
   □ Checks
   □ Wires
4. Do files have copies of notes? YES _____ NO _____
5. Do you have a void or expiration date on you payoff statements?
   YES _____ NO _____
6. Are your files with payoff statements separated from regular files?
   YES _____ NO _____

Balloons

1. Do they have balloon loans?
   YES _____ (No. of loans _____)
   NO _____
2. What is the usual call?
   □ 5 years
   □ 10 years
   □ Other
3. Are balloon dates in your system?
   YES _____ NO _____
4. Do they allow extensions on terms when loan is due?
   YES _____ NO _____

Assumptions

1. How many assumptions have been processed over the past six months?

    FHA/VA _____
    Conventional _____

2. Provide a list of private investors indicating the following:
    - Investor's name
    - Investor's numbers
    - Investor's approval needed
    - Servicer can approve
    - Remittance reporting requirements
    - Due dates
        Actual/Actual _____
        Schedule/Schedule _____
        Other _____
    - Comments

General Questions

1. Do you use microfiche?
2. If yes to question 1, what do you have on fiche? What is retention time?
3. Specify location of each of the following, in loan file or elsewhere:
    - Current history
    - Prior years' histories
    - Last escrow analysis
    - Hazard insurance policies
    - Optional insurance certificates/policies
    - Tax receipts
    - Collection records
    - Collection correspondence
    - Miscellaneous closing documents
    - Appraisals
    - Credit package

4. What type of filing system is used?
   - ☐ Numeric by loan number
   - ☐ Alphabetical

Servicing Agreements for Private Investors

1. Do you have in possession executed servicing agreements and documentation to support any change? YES _____ NO _____ Other _____
2. If you deal with a security holder, do you have a current certificate register? YES _____ NO _____
3. How is cancellation without cause handled? (Verify in agreements.)
4. How are advances on P&I handled? (Verify in agreements.)
5. How long does the servicer have to advance on delinquent loans?
6. Is servicer required to advance on taxes and insurance? (Verify in agreements.)
7. Are any subservicing agreements in place? YES _____ NO _____
8. Are any participation agreements in place? YES _____ NO _____

System Requirements

1. What service bureau is used, if any?

   _____

2. What in-house system is used, if any?
   - ■ Software used _____
   - ■ Hardware used _____
3. Is a manual system used? YES _____ NO _____
4. Can the transfer of the mortgage servicing occur with a tape-to-tape transfer? YES _____ NO _____
5. Get a dump of loan files to determine what exactly is stored.
6. Loan file specifications to match with item 7.
7. Are the adjustment periods set up for ARM files?
8. Get layouts of escrow files and vendor files.

9. What file codes are used for property type, loan type, message/stop codes, etc.?
10. Are the following items on the computer, and how valid is the data?
    - Full mortgagor name(s)
    - Property address
    - Property zip codes
    - Mailing address
    - Legal description
    - Social Security number
    - Phone numbers
11. How do you cross-reference the following?
    - Co-mortgagors with different last name
    - Different loans on the same property
12. How do you identify property types (single family, condo, duplex, etc.) on a loan?

Transfer of Servicing

The transfer of servicing is the final step in the purchase of the mortgage servicing portfolio. The transfer refers to the process of physically taking possession of all files that are part of the portfolio, as well as the assumption of the management and administration of the loans. It is the culmination of all the preparation, negotiation, and due diligence that have gone into the purchase.

Of even greater importance, the transfer is the final opportunity for the buyer to verify the integrity of data in the portfolio. Once the transfer is complete and the buyer has issued final payment, the buyer has very little recourse should some tangible problem arise concerning some aspect of the administration of that portfolio. The transfer is the buyer's final chance to ensure that what was purchased is exactly what is received during the transfer.

To alleviate that tension, an option of a 30-day holdback of 5 to 10 percent of the purchase price is not uncommon following the transfer. During due diligence, specific areas were verified, including to some degree the average maturity and average service fee. However, it was impossible to verify these details in the entire portfolio. After the portfolio is transferred, the buyer can run independent reports to verify all details against the original report, taking into account the time difference between receipt of the original data and the transfer date.

Unfortunately, within the industry the difficulty of a servicing portfolio transfer is too frequently underestimated. This results in confusion, which wastes time and money.

Before the transfer can take place, it is usually the responsibility of the seller to obtain investor approval of the transfer. During the transfer process, buyer and seller have specific responsibilities. The majority of the responsibility lies with the seller; however, the buyer should not rely totally on the seller's providing all the information in an accurate, compatible format. Nor can the buyer count on all the information being correct, whether the transfer is conducted on a system-to-system basis or a manual-to-system basis.

The pre-due-diligence questionnaire and the actual due diligence should provide a good feel for the seller's data integrity and servicing capabilities. Nevertheless, even if the results of both processes were satisfactory, a careful transfer review is still vital.

Buyer's Responsibilities

Much of the buyer's responsibility in the transfer process has to do with proper planning and organization to efficiently handle the increased load created by the newly acquired loans. This planning and organization must occur before, during, and after the actual transfer. The buyer must allow a reasonable time frame for completion of these organizational and administrative preparations.

A transfer project manager should be appointed to oversee all aspects of the transfer. If this person is other than the due diligence project manager, the two should work closely together. The due diligence project manager will know sensitive areas of the portfolio and be able to anticipate those that may become problematic during or after the transfer.

The transfer project manager should have regular meetings with department managers or supervisors to create an activity list, assign responsibility for completing the tasks, and identify the start and end dates of each task. This list should be periodically reviewed by the project manager to determine whether schedules are being met or adjustments need to be made.

Four areas need to be addressed by the buyer during the transfer time:
1. Internal preparation, both from a personnel and logistical point of view, involves computer hardware, physical storage space for the loan files that will be transferred, installation of additional phone lines, WATTS lines, copying equipment, etc., and the hiring and training of new personnel necessary to handle the additional load.

At the time the files are received, each file must be verified as received. Each file should contain all necessary documentation (to be discussed later in this chapter). If any file is missing documents, it is the responsibility of the seller to provide this information.

Special aspects of the loan files, such as payoff files and foreclosure files, should be shipped separately or clearly identified. This is very important, since those files usually need immediate attention following the transfer.

When the transfer occurs, you want as smooth a transition as possible in terms of your physical plant, your computer capabilities, and the knowledgeability and competence of your staff. This type of analysis should have been completed at the time the bid was placed on the portfolio, and by the time the loans actually transfer, all of these things must be in place and in working order.

2. The computer conversion requires special attention. Loan file layouts need to be compared between the buyer's and seller's systems. It is not uncommon that some information viewed as critical by the buyer is omitted from the seller's computer layout. If not all the information the buyer requires is in the seller's file, a management decision has to be made about what needs to be input or left out.

   If the buyer is operating through a servicing bureau, it is wise to coordinate the transfer with that bureau. Find out what type of system the bureau uses, whether that system is compatible with the seller's, and whether the servicing bureau can accommodate the seller's system in the event that it is different. Another probable advantage in consulting with the servicing bureau prior to the transfer is that it can usually warn the buyer of potential problem areas.

3. Verification of the details of the portfolio must be undertaken again during the transfer process. This is usually the responsibility of the investor reporting function. The investor reporting manager should review all transferred investor information and loan data. The overall intent of the verification is to ensure that the seller's ending balances are indeed the beginning balances on the buyer's specific reports to the various investors.

During this balancing procedure, a penny one way or another could lead to a substantial discrepancy. For this reason, any discrepancies with regard to the balancing factors should be researched completely. After the research has been completed, the buyer will be able to define whether those discrepancies result in a material difference.

After the actual transfer and before final payment is made to the seller, trial balances should be run. This should occur before any other transaction is conducted or any data is input into the database. Reports should be run to verify and compare the trial balances as reported by the seller with regard to the unpaid principal balance, the escrow balance, the advance, and any suspense accounts.

All these trial balances should be backed by pull reports or investor reports on the private investor side to verify the unpaid principal balance and the servicing spread. The escrow accounts should reconcile with the total amount of escrow funds on the trial balance. Advances should be verified back to the trial balance so the buyer knows which accounts have outstanding advances and why there was an advance.

A separate list of payoff and foreclosure files should be made, since in most cases the buyer is not paying for loans in foreclosure. These totals would be deducted from the total unpaid principal balance agreed upon by the terms of sale contained in the purchase and sale agreement.

The same is true for any delinquent loans. An immediate list of any loans that are 30, 60, or 90 days past due must be kept as they are transferred, then monitored as time goes on. At the time of final settlement, these loans need to be listed and identified since they will be deducted from the unpaid balance due the seller.

4. Bank notification if the buyer wants a lock box set up could come under any of several of the buyer's administrative areas: investor reporting, finance, administration, or cashiering. The involved banks must be informed of the number of new loans they can expect and whether the buyer is setting up any lock box accounts.

These areas are vital to a well-conducted servicing portfolio transfer. Each has significant impact on the other. Given all the documentation necessary during a transfer, there is always the need for open, frank communications between the buyer and seller. If communications break down, the buyer will have a tough time ensuring that the seller is completing its responsibilities on schedule.

Before the transfer takes place, it is the buyer's responsibility to contact the mortgagors. The buyer sends a letter to let mortgagors know that it is the new servicer and to verify the information sent by the seller concerning the individual loans. The letter should be a letter of introduction as well as a verification of the transfer of mortgage servicing and include the following:

- Effective date after which the mortgagor will be making payment to the new servicer
- Information about future coupons
- New account number or verification of existing account number
- Borrower's monthly payment verification, current interest rate, home phone number, and any business telephone number
- Emphasis on the fact that there will be no change in the original terms and conditions of the loan
- Notification of any company policies that are important to communicate, such as to business hours, when payments are due, late penalties, escrow analysis time, etc.

The following checklist summarizes the buyer's responsibilities relating to the transfer process:

- Restructure servicing department
- Outline job responsibilities
- Redesign file room
- Add file room shelving
- Add furniture
- Add personnel
- Create training plan for new employees
- Write and send welcome letter to new borrowers
- Review master PMI policies

- Revise departmental handbooks
- Notify PMI companies of servicer change
- Order coupon books
- Mail coupon books
- Determine when next tax payments will be due
- Identify and purchase system hardware upgrade requirements
- Schedule program conversions
- Verify program conversions
- Order additional letterhead and forms
- Order labels for new files
- Schedule transfer downtown
- Add required phone and WATTS lines
- Set up lock box specifications with bank
- Set up new bank accounts where necessary
- Receive delinquency, foreclosure, and bankruptcy lists
- Receive current council list from seller
- Receive all files from seller
- Review specific loan files
- Verify all stop codes
- Determine advances needed to wire to seller
- Balance all cash accounts after wire and transfer
- Input investor starting balances as required by system
- Calculate purchase price

Seller's Responsibilities

From the responsibilities of the buyer during the transfer process, you get a sense of the volume of work required of the seller. Most of the buyer's preparation and verification derives from information received from the seller. The seller has a substantial job in providing all necessary information. The seller's responsibility also includes critical communications with the mortgagors. It is the responsibility of the seller to send a letter of transfer notification to the mortgagors. Copies of all correspondence should be placed in the respective loan files. The letter must contain key information:

- Effective date of the transfer
- New servicer's name, address, regular phone number, and WATTS line number
- Person and department mortgagors can contact at the new servicer's company
- Instructions concerning interim payments until the mortgagor has received verification of the loan transfer to the new company
- Advice that there are no changes in the terms of the loan
- Information regarding optional insurance, disability, life insurance, and other insurances if applicable.

The timing of both this letter and that of the buyer is extremely important since neither party wants its letter to reach the customer at the wrong time. For example, if the buyer's letter preceded the seller's, the customer would understandably be confused and concerned.

The seller has additional communications responsibilities beyond the mortgagors:

- The hazard insurance carrier or agent has to be notified of the new mortgage company through a corrected mortgagee clause.
- If the loan is on a tax service, the tax service must be notified of the transfer and the identity of the new servicer.
- If there is PMI or FHA insurance on the loans, proper notification should be sent to those companies.

It is also extremely important that the buyer and seller work out time frames with regard to payment of escrow items. It is the responsibility of the seller to bring current any escrow items outstanding or due by the time of the transfer. This includes FHA or PMI insurance from the previous month's collections. If the seller's system can't provide this information, the buyer may want to negotiate for the seller to pay any escrow items due 15 to 30 days after the transfer date. This will assure the buyer that there will be no time lapse in escrow payments during the time the transfer takes place.

The following checklist summarizes the seller's responsibilities relating to the transfer process:

- Notify investor for transfer approval
- Write and send termination letters to mortgagors
- Notify homeowner's insurance companies
- Notify life/disability insurance companies
- Notify PMI companies and FHA
- Notify tax service
- Notify law firms
- Notify bank of ACH cancellation
- Notify lock box bank
- Pay final insurance premiums
- Update bankruptcy files
- Update delinquent files
- Merge any files to be shipped
- Arrange for shipment of files
- Send year-to-date interest statement to borrowers
- Send final remittance to investors
- Wire transfer of principal and interest to new servicer
- Wire transfer of tax and insurance to new servicer

Files

The buyer may receive as many as four files on some loans within a servicing portfolio:

- *Loan file.* All administrative and legal documentation on the loan, including all correspondence to all parties concerning this transfer and change of servicer.
- *Collections file.* A separate file outside of the loan file for collections. The buyer should be sure all collection files have been transferred and consider purging them to the loan file.
- *Foreclosure/bankruptcy file.* Any write-ups that have been completed with regard to the foreclosure process should be included in the file.

Any court documents, agreements, filings, payoff-pending information, or assumption information should be included in the file.

- *Insurance files.* Information regarding insurance claims, modifications, or inspection reports, including FHA or PMI insurance data.

Conclusion

The transfer process is the last chance the buyer has to control the accuracy of the transaction and therefore the precise amount of the funds it wires to the seller. If something is not quite right with the transfer, if some information is missing, this is the time at which the purchaser must address this with the seller and arrange for some kind of monetary holdback until all conditions have been met.

Nevertheless, the seller's responsibility does not end with the transfer. The seller must forward to the new servicer any information about the loan sold that the seller receives after the transfer. The seller should be helpful regarding any inquiries on servicing from previous customers and direct them courteously to the new servicer. The new servicer's responsibility is to be as knowledgeable about the portfolio as was the old servicer and to respond immediately to new customers' concerns.

8

Hedging

The world is non-linear.

Clement III

The uncertainty an investor in mortgage servicing must address is prepayments. A servicing portfolio's return is dictated largely by the prepayment level experienced by the mortgages that comprise the servicing portfolio. As interest rates and prepayment rates have become more volatile over the past few years, the need to properly manage prepayment risk has increased. The characteristics of principal-only stripped-mortgage backed securities (PO SMBS or PO) make them an ideal hedge instrument for servicing.

The PO's expected return profile is just as sensitive to interest rates and prepayments as that of servicing, but in an opposite manner: servicing becomes more (less) valuable as prepayments fall (rise). A PO becomes more (less) valuable as prepayments rise (fall). This chapter provides a comprehensive guide to properly executing this profitable and prudent hedging strategy. It discusses the dynamics of servicing and POs and provides a review of the necessary analytics and analytical models. Examples of specific strategies illustrate the effectiveness of POs as a hedge instrument. The chapter concludes with sections that address the benefits and risks of this strategy as a portfolio investment.

Dynamics of Servicing

Prepayment Risk

To understand the dynamics of servicing, you need a knowledge of the prepayment risk embedded in a servicing portfolio. Servicing fee income is both a function of the underlying servicing fee rate and the outstanding notional principal balance of the portfolio. Given a specific servicing fee, the greater the outstanding balance, the greater the servicing fees earned. This balance declines on a monthly basis, however, due to a combination of normal amortization and unscheduled prepayments.

Normal amortization can be calculated with certainty. Prepayments are by definition unscheduled. All the uncertainty underlying the return of a servicing portfolio lies in the prepayments.

The mortgagor's right as specified in the mortgage contract to prepay the mortgage, typically without penalty, any time prior to maturity, constitutes a valuable option (an *American call option*) that the mortgagee has sold the mortgagor. The mortgagee receives an option writer's fee that is included in the note rate of the mortgage.

An investor in a servicing portfolio is short a portfolio these "sold" options. To gain insight into prepayments, you must thoroughly examine the value of these options.

Prepayment Subclasses

All mortgage prepayments are defined by three basic subclasses:

- *Economic refinancing* is the most important subclass in determining the prepayments of the premium portion of a servicing portfolio.
- *Residential mobility* is the major determinant of prepayments of the discount portion of a servicing portfolio.
- *Defaults and foreclosures*, although not usually significant contributors to overall prepayments of a servicing portfolio, can have a significant effect in economically depressed areas.

The Economic Refinancing Subclass

The owner of a premium mortgage's decision to refinance is normally an economically based one. The mortgagor will compare the rate on the note held to the interest rate available in the market. If the prevailing note rate is lower than the mortgagor's note rate, exercising the refinancing option will lower a mortgagor's total interest expense over the life of the mortgage. The amount of interest savings is a function of the outstanding principal. The larger the principal balance at the time of refinancing, the greater the economic incentive to refinance. Typically, as a mortgage ages and the principal balance has been paid down, the economic incentive declines as the economic value of interest payment savings declines.

Refinancing is not cost-free. The mortgagor must take refinancing expenses into account. Points of between 2 and 3 percent of the refinanced mortgage principal must be paid up front. Appraisal fees, legal fees, and other costs of closing must be incurred. There are also transaction/opportunity costs to refinancing, plus the time and trouble involved in preparing a new mortgage application. For an economically rational refinancing to occur on a premium mortgage, the present value of interest expense savings must be greater than the costs involved. Mathematically, the intrinsic option value of refinancing is defined this way:

$$IOV_r = \sum_{n=1}^{t} \frac{(I_c - I_r) \times P_n}{(1 + I_r)^n} - (P_r \times C_1) - C_2 - C_3$$

IOV_r = Intrinsic option value of refinancing
I_c = Current monthly note rate expressed as a percentage
I_r = Current monthly refinancing rate available alternative note rate expressed as a percentage
P_n = Unpaid principal balance in period n
P_r = Amount of principal to be refinanced
C_1 = Points of new mortgage expressed as a percentage
C_2 = Closing costs appraisal, legal, etc.
C_3 = Transaction/opportunity costs time and trouble
t = Term of mortgage to be refinanced in months
If $IOV_r = 0$, an economically rational refinancing will occur.

The Residential Mobility Subclass

People move for a variety of different reasons. A number of demographic variables are known determinants of prepayments of this subclass:

- Employment Status/Income
- Birth
- Marriage

- Divorce/Breakup
- Death

The employment status/income variable is the most important. As the mortgagor's salary and station in life increases substantially, he or she may pay off the mortgage of one home and purchase a more desirable home. Additionally, a promotion or job change can result in relocation of the mortgagor and prepayment of the mortgage upon sale of the property.

Prevailing note rates affect residential mobility. As interest rates rise, the mortgagor is less likely to move, because of the additional interest expense involved in purchasing another home. For mortgages that are not assumable, typically conventional mortgages, a change of residence always results in a prepayment. This prepayment may be economically rational or irrational. For assumable mortgages (FHA/VA), a prepayment does not necessarily occur with a change in residence. If the seller's note rate is below the current market rate, the new mortgagor can reduce overall interest expense by assuming the mortgage. A number of factors determine whether a mortgage will eventually be assumed:

- The lower the note rate compared to the current market rate, the more likely the mortgage will be assumed.
- The new home buyer is more likely to assume the mortgage if the principal amount assumed covers a significant portion of the purchase price.
- Housing price inflation and scheduled amortization of principal reduce the likelihood that any particular mortgage will be assumed.

The Defaults/Foreclosure Subclass

A default arises when a mortgagor is unable or unwilling to continue making monthly mortgage payments. Normally, defaults occur when the outstanding principal balance of the mortgage exceeds the current market value of the home. Defaults are therefore most likely to occur in economically depressed areas of the country, where the property values have declined significantly. Because normal amortization reduces the outstanding principal balance, the likelihood of default declines as the mortgage ages.

Typical Prepayment Profiles

The discount mortgages prepay at a fairly level rate, reflecting mostly the effects of the residential mobility subclass. As the mortgage note rate increases through the currently available note rate and becomes increasingly premium, rational economic refinancings occur with a rapidly, exponentially rising rate, as the IOVR is increasing exponentially, frequency. The prepayments then level off again at a high steady rate.

There are three specific zones of a prepayment profile:

- *Base zone*: a minimum level of prepayments, typically economically irrational refinancing for discount mortgages, driven by the residential mobility subclass.

- *Acceleration zone*: a prepayment zone above the current note rate where the level of prepayments increases exponentially, as the IOV_r increases exponentially due to the compounded savings of future interest payments. These refinancings are economically rational.

- *Burnout zone*: a prepayment zone well above current coupon where prepayments do not continue to accelerate. The lack of full refinancing in this zone is not economically rational. There appears to be a significant economic benefit to refinance. Several explanations could make IOV_r in this portion of the curve:

  - The mortgagor could be ignorant to currently available refinancing opportunities.
  - The transaction cost/opportunity cost of filing a new mortgage application may be too high.
  - The principal balance to be refinanced may be low.
  - The mortgagor may be a poor credit risk and therefore unable obtain a new mortgage easily.
  - The mortgagor may be moving in the near future and therefore unlikely to realize the interest payment savings over time.

Performance Dynamics

Keeping the prepayment profiles in mind, the expected return of a servicing portfolio in various interest rate environments can be examined. Rather than specific mortgage note rates, we examine the spread of servicing portfolio. The *spread* is defined as the mortgagor's note rate of the servicing portfolio minus the currently available (current) mortgage note rate:

SPREAD = (Servicing Portfolio Note Rate – Available Note Rate)

As interest rates rise (fall), the spread falls (rises). Using the basic shape of a typical refinancing profile, you can estimate prepayments in various interest rate environments. (We discuss prepayment modeling later in this chapter.)

Example

A servicing portfolio with 10.50 percent WAC will prepay like a servicing portfolio with a 9.50 percent WAC servicing portfolio if interest rates rise (the spread decreases) 100 basis points. If interest rates fall (the spread increases) 100 basis points, the portfolio will prepay like a 11.50 percent WAC servicing portfolio. The sample servicing portfolio is listed in table 8.1.

The expected return profile displayed in table 8.2 of servicing is quite volatile. The returns range from 18.17 to –2.06 percent. This is an analysis of a single servicing portfolio assumed to be held as an investment for the entire remaining term. This type of analysis amplifies the volatility of a servicing portfolio return, because decreased costs due to more efficient operations and the addition of servicing to a portfolio are not taken into account. However, to properly hedge the prepayment risk of a servicing portfolio, or a portion thereof, this type of analysis must be performed.

The volatility of the returns of the servicing is due entirely to the uncertainty of prepayments. As the level of prepayments rises and refinancing options are exercised, the principal balance of the servicing portfolio declines as prepayments drive the balance down, resulting in the expected return of the servicing portfolio declining.

Table 8.1   Sample Servicing Portfolio

Listing of Servicing Portfolio Parameters

Servicing Type	FNMA
Recourse Pool	NO
Reporting Description	MBS
Beginning Servicing Month	1
Beginning Servicing Year	1989

Essential Details of Underlying Mortgages

Current Balance Outstanding	$100,000,000
Weighted Average Coupon	10.580%
Weighted Average Maturity	335
Original Maturity	360
Beginning Escrow Balance	0
Average Escrow Payment	200
Weighted Average Servicing Fee	0.330%
Agency Guarantor Fee	0.250%
Average Certificate Pass-Through	10.250%(includes guarantor fee)
Beginning Number of Loans	1,375
Payment Delay	31
Insurance Payment Frequency	Semiannual
Insurance Payment Month	12
Tax Payment Frequency	Semiannual
Tax Payment Month	12

Payment Float Assumptions

Payment Float Rate	8.00%
Date Payment Received	5
Date Prepayment Received	25

Escrow Payment Assumptions

Escrow Float Rate	8.00%
Escrow Inflation Rate	4.00%

Table 8.1 Sample Servicing Portfolio (continued)

Expense Assumptions

Expense Inflation Rate	4.00%
Closing and Transfer Expenses	$13,750.00
Monthly Cost Per Current Loan	$5.00
Percent of Loans Delinquent	3.00%
Monthly Cost Per Foreclosure	$500.00
Variable Expense Payment	0.00%

Miscellaneous Income Assumptions

Percent of Loans Paid Late	2.40%
Late Payment Fee	2.00%

The Need to Hedge Prepayment Risk

An investor in servicing has an economic risk: the price value of servicing that has been booked. Recouping the initial investment of servicing is not guaranteed. This type of investment should be hedged.

Table 8.2 Servicing Portfolio Dynamics

Interest Rate Environment	Servicing PSA (%)	Servicing Yield (%)	Servicing Duration	Servicing WAL
+ 300 bps	129	18.17	3.91	9.54
+ 200 bps	145	17.45	3.90	8.84
+ 100 bps	159	16.81	3.91	8.28
Current	198	15.00	3.71	6.99
− 100 bps	295	10.37	3.14	4.89
− 200 bps	399	5.19	2.65	3.60
− 300 bps	536	−2.06	2.15	2.60

All rates of return in this chapter are Before Tax CBE yields. Formulas for calculations are provided in the notes at the end of this chapter.

Prepayments constitute the uncertainty and volatility of a servicing portfolio's expected return. This uncertainty is due to the fact that a mortgagor has the option, not the obligation, to prepay a mortgage. The obvious solution to removing prepayment risk would be to repurchase the individual "sold" call options from each mortgagor whose mortgage constitutes a portion of the notional principal balance of a servicing portfolio. This solution is neither practical nor possible because the option is embedded within each individual mortgage contract and it is unlikely that most mortgagors would be willing to sell this valuable option.

Principal-Only Stripped Mortgage-Backed Securities

The best way to hedge a servicing portfolio is to participate in mortgage prepayments. Principal-Only Stripped Mortgage-Backed Securities (PO or PO SMBS) enable the investor in servicing do this.

What Is a PO?

A PO (principal only) is stripped mortgage-backed security. It is a derivative of a mortgage-backed security (MBS). An investor in an MBS receives monthly payments that consist of scheduled principal amortization, unscheduled prepayments, and interest minus servicing and guarantor fees. A PO is created when the scheduled principal amortization and unscheduled prepayments are "stripped" and sold separately from the interest payment—Interest-Only (IO SMBS) portion. POs are priced on a cash flow basis. The monthly cash flows are calculated at an expected prepayment speed. These cash flows are then discounted at a current yield. This pricing methodology results in a discount price less than par.

Purchasing POs

Many POs are available. They trade in a very active secondary market. The typical minimum size, although smaller sizes can be negotiated with a dealer, is a $1 million par amount round lot. The purchase price is calculated by par amount, factored appropriately, multiplied by the quoted price as a percentage.

Example

Par Amount	$1,000,000
Factor	0.81941041
Price	57 – 28

$1,000,000 × 0.81941041 × .57875 = $474,233.77 (cash price and beginning book value).

The PO's return profile mirrors the refinancing profile of the underlying mortgages (figure 8.1). The PO benefits from prepayments in a manner that exactly offsets the way servicing is harmed by prepayments. This benefit arises because we are able to purchase prepayments at a discount. When the cash flows from the PO are accelerated by increased prepayments, the discount accretes rapidly, resulting in a rapidly rising yield. By purchasing a PO to combine with servicing as a portfolio investment, one can achieve a stable interest rate with an insensitive rate of return. This stable rate of return typically represents a rate that is 300–400 basis points greater than similar duration Treasury securities.

Dynamics of Principal-Only Stripped Mortgage-Backed Securities

The two major determinants of a PO's value as a hedging instrument are the discount price and prepayment sensitivity. Given similar parameters (see table 8.3) and refinancing profile as our sample servicing portfolio, the PO's expected return profile in different interest rate environments is calculated and provided in table 8.4. The expected return profile mirrors the refinancing profile and is exactly offsetting to that of the sample servicing portfolio.

Interest Rate Model

The interest rate model forms the basic foundation for all analytics involved in constructing a hedge ratio. The interest rate model must focus on eventually generating long-term mortgage rates. The interest rate model and prepayment models are intertwined. The key results or inputs that the interest rate model provides for the prepayment model are mortgage rate volatility, and maximum and minimum mortgage rates. A

Table 8.3   Sample Principal-Only SMBS Parameters

Collateral WAC	10.580%
Collateral Servicing Fee	0.330%
Agency Guarantor Fee	0.250%
Collateral Pass-Through	10.000%
Weighted Average Maturity	335
Original Maturity	360
Trading Factor	0.81941041
Price of PO	57.875%

Table 8.4   PO SMBS Dynamics

Interest Rate Environment	PO SMBS PSA	PO SMBS Yield	PO SMBS Duration	PO SMBS WAL
+300 bps	129%	6.97%	4.98	9.61
+200 bps	145%	7.62%	4.91	8.91
+100 bps	159%	8.21%	4.89	8.35
Current	198%	9.95%	4.51	7.06
−100 bps	295%	14.64%	3.60	4.96
−200 bps	399%	20.14%	2.93	3.67
−300 bps	536%	28.07%	2.30	2.67

basic macroeconomic interest rate model should include the following basic factors.

Factors Determining Real Interest Rates (r)

$S + T = I + G$

$S + T + dM = I + G + dL$

S = Saving, especially by households

I = Investment, especially by firms

T = Government taxes

G = Government spending

The national income and flow of funds accounts showed that supplies and demands for goods must add up ($S + T = I + G$) and so must supplies and demands for funds ($S + T + dM = I + G + dL$).

Factors Determining Inflation (p) and Nominal Interest Rate (R)*

L = The demand for money by households and firms.

M = The supply of money as determined by interactions among the Federal Reserve, commercial banks, non-bank depository institutions, households, firms, and governments.

$R = r + p$ = Inflationary expectations. The equilibrium nominal interest rate (R) is approximately the sum of the expected real rate of return (r) and the expected rate of inflation (p)

E = Exports. Must be included to account for foreign sector influences.

I = Imports. Must be included to account for foreign sector influences.

To analyze ARMs and ARM servicing, the interest rate model must simulate the behavior of underlying index. In the case of Treasury-indexed ARMs, the corresponding treasury rates must be simulated. For cost of funds ARMs, the cost of funds index must be simulated. A popular methodology that involves simulating all possible interest rate paths is the Monte Carlo simulation. A Monte Carlo simulation randomly estimates forward interest rates depending on a series of path constraints defined within the model.

Prepayment Models

A prepayment model is an investor's most important analytical tool in examining servicing and/or PO needs. Estimating prepayments is both a science and art. No current consensus exists on a standard prepayment model. A discussion of the most popular prepayment models follows.

Historical Prepayment Model

The historical prepayment model is based on the idea that past prepayments can be used to project future prepayments. This methodology utilizes the 3-, 6-, 12-month average, or prepayments over the life as proxy for future prepayments.

Using a historical average is a very good estimator for prepayments if interest rates remain stable. This type of prepayment model is not recommended when interest rates are changing or are forecast to change in the near future. However, historical data and historical prepayment levels are used for more sophisticated modeling techniques. From historical data path dependencies, minimum prepayment rates, maximum prepayment rates, and basic prepayment behavior are determined.

Mathematical Prepayment Models

Mathematical prepayment models can utilize historical data or be based on a completely stochastic process. The most popular mathematical prepayment model is a regression model in which past data is analyzed using linear or multiple linear regression. Then the coefficients found are used as estimators for future prepayments.

A stochastic prepayment model utilizes an interest rate model that generates a random interest rate pattern. The interest rate pattern can be historically based or arbitrarily defined. The random interest rates generated utilize prior path dependency studies to estimate prepayments along those interest rate paths. The prepayment rates are averaged on a probability weighted basis to arrive at a single average prepayment speed estimate.

A six-month historical average auto-regressive prepayment model has been accurate in the recent past because interest rates and prepayment rates have exhibited a steady rising or falling trend. Stochastic prepayment models are by far the most sophisticated. Modified versions of these models are gaining wide acceptance today; we discuss these models later.

Market Expectations/Implied Prepayment Model

The implied prepayment model is a somewhat simplified approach to estimating prepayment speeds. Given the current market price and current market yield, prepayment speed is estimated. The prepayment speed is the market's current average expectation value of long-term prepayment rates. This prepayment rate is valid until the price changes. Therefore, this model is used only for estimating prepayment speeds on a given day.

Options-Based Prepayment Model

Options-based prepayment models are modified versions of the stochastic prepayment model. The modification is that the IOV_r intrinsic option-value of refinancing is explicitly included in the model. Options-based models are gaining popularity because of the increased volatility of interest rates. The volatility of interest rates is addressed when the IOV_r refinancing option is calculated, while no accurate interest rate forecast is necessary. Only an implied forward interest rate volatility can be calculated. This model like all other models requires a study of historical data to define its basic parameters.

Servicing Evaluation Model

A servicing evaluation model is essential to the construction of a servicing–PO hedge. The net monthly cash flows of a servicing portfolio before and after tax are required for further analysis.

Principal-Only Stripped Mortgage-Backed Security Model

A principal-only stripped mortgage-backed security model is required to evaluate the hedge instrument. The net monthly cash flows of a PO before and after tax are required for further analysis. This model is a monthly mortgage amortization with prepayments. The amortization is normally simple interest with no prepayment penalties. The cash flows generated by the pools of mortgages are "stripped" such that the PO can be created. The interest payment, servicing fee, and guarantor fee are "stripped" away so that the PO investor receives the scheduled principal amortization and unscheduled prepayments.

A caution must be issued here: All POs are not created equal. The POs used in this chapter as hedging tools for servicing are POs from CMO/REMICS with only a PO tranche and an IO tranche. POs from CMO/REMICS (MBS Collateral or PO Collateral) with PACs, TACs, etc., sometimes referred to as Super POs, do have the potential as hedging tools, but the information required to evaluate them is much greater than for a standard agency PO.

The major benefit of POs from alternative structures is that they typically are purchased at a deeper discount than "standard" POs. To evaluate alternative PO structures the actual collateral, and PAC, TAC etc., schedules must be known. Each of these structures is unique; therefore, generalizations about the performance of POs from alternative structures cannot be made. A CMO/REMIC model is required to analyze these alternative structures.

Combined Cash Flow Model

The monthly before- and after-tax cash flows of servicing and the PO are added together to calculate the net cash flows for the combined investment. The hedge performance must be calculated using a monthly cash flow analysis and not a dollar weighted average of the servicing's expected return and the PO's expected return. All calculated rates of return must be monthly cash flow rates of return. The rate of return of the servicing and the PO must be adjusted for settlement date and appropriate payment delay days.

Hedging Strategies

Strategy Structure

This section provides a brief guide to the steps of hedging your servicing portfolio with POs.
1. Identify your overall market expectation.
   - Bullish
   - Neutral
   - Bearish
2. Evaluate your servicing portfolio.
   - Identify which portions are prepayment rate sensitive. (Portions of the servicing portfolio that are not especially prepayment rate sensitive may have POs available which can completely eliminate.)
   - Determine the characteristics of those prepayment rate sensitive mortgages.
     - Note rate

- Average loan size
- CONV/FHA/VA
- Age
- Geographic location

3. Evaluate available POs as hedge instruments.

■ Which POs are available that have similar characteristics to the servicing to be hedged?

■ Does the expected return of the POs perform in an offsetting manner to the servicing to be hedged?

■ Could a combination of the POs perform better than a single PO?

4. Construct a hedge ratio with the POs consistent with your overall strategic view prepayment risk of that portion of the portfolio.

The following illustrative examples show the type of calculations necessary for regulatory and fiduciary purposes.

Matched Coupon and Collateral Level Yield Hedge

The PO used to hedge this servicing should have characteristics as similar as possible to those of the servicing. In this example, a portion of a large servicing portfolio is isolated such that it has similar characteristics and prepayment sensitivity as the PO. In this particular example, the WACs and WAMs and all other aspects of the servicing and PO are matched to minimize any deviation in the hedge's performance.

In this example, the par amount PO purchased is $2,930,000. The PO currently is trading at a PSA of 198 percent and a yield of 9.95 percent, resulting in a price of 57.875 percent. The portfolio was priced to return, or yield, 15 percent before tax. This translates into a price of 1.435 percent of the principal balance or $1,434,750.00. The prepayment speeds in different interest rate environments are estimated using a prepayment model. Table 8.5 shows the yield of the PO in various interest rate environments. The interest rate/prepayment rates changes in this and following examples are assumed to be instantaneous. (Other analyses assume a 100-basis-point interest rate change per quarter or per month).

If interest rates rise 100 basis points from current rates, the PSA falls to 159 percent from 198 percent and the before-tax yield rises from 15 percent to 16.81 percent. If interest rates fall 100 basis points, the PSA

Table 8.5   Level Yield Results

Interest Rate Environment	Combined Yield (%)	Combined Duration	Combined WAL
+300	12.46	4.34	9.58
+200	12.46	4.32	8.87
+100	12.47	4.32	8.32
Current	12.47	4.06	7.06
−100	12.48	3.34	4.96
−200	12.48	2.77	3.67

rises to 295 percent from 198 percent and the before-tax yield falls from 15 percent to 10.37 percent.

Example 1: Conventional Servicing: Conventional PO Level Hedge Sensitivity Analysis After Level Yield Hedge

Recognizing that all prepayment models have constraints and are only models, a sensitivity analysis is performed to determine the approximate bounds of an investment in mortgage servicing combined with POs. The servicing's PSA prepayment speed is assumed to behave in a nonparallel manner to that of the POs PSA prepayment speed. A 20 percent error in prepayment estimation is assumed in the +200 basis points, current and −200 basis interest rate environments. The PSA prepayment speed of the mortgage servicing is assumed to be 20 percent (lower/higher) and is combined with the FNMA PO whose PSA prepayment speed is 20 percent (higher/lower). The result is a conservative total PSA prepayment error estimate of 40 percent. The (lower/higher) PSA prepayment speed of servicing is combined with the (higher/lower) PSA prepayment speed of PO to produce (upper/lower) bounds on the rate of return of combined investments. The upper bound resulting from favorable PSA prepayment mis-estimation a 20-percent slowing of prepayment of the servicing and a 20-percent increase in the prepayments of the PO.

The lower bound resulting from unfavorable PSA prepayment mis-estimation of 20-percent increase in prepayment of the servicing and a 20-percent decrease in the prepayments of the PO.

Table 8.6   Level Hedge Cost

Servicing Basis	$1,434,750
Par Amount PO Purchased	$2,400,873
Purchase Cost PO @ Price	$1,389,505
Total Dollar Investment	$2,824,255
PO to Dollar Hedge Ratio	49%

In a +200 basis points interest rate environment, assuming the servicing does not prepay at the projected 145 percent PSA but prepays 20 percent (lower/higher) or (116 percent/174 percent) PSA the yield is (18.76/16.11 percent) duration (4.16/3.67 years) WAL, (10.18/7.75 years). The PO also projected to prepay at 145 percent PSA, prepays at a prepayment rate 20 percent (higher/lower) or (174/116 percent) PSA the yield is (8.87/6.45 percent), duration (4.48/5.46 years), WAL (7.82/10.25 years), this mismatch of PSA prepayment speeds results in (upper/lower) bounds on the combined yield (19.13/10.77 percent), duration (4.36/4.32 years), WAL (10.16/7.74 years).

The PSA prepayment speed of 40 percent is very extreme because the servicing portfolio and PO have identical aggregate characteristics, FNMA MBS 10.58 WAC, 335 WAM. The results of the sensitivity analysis indicates that the absolute range of returns should not deviate significantly from 9.44 percent minimum lower bound calculated to 14.55 percent the maximum upper bound calculated.

Example 2: Conventional Servicing: Conventional PO Bull-Hedge

The sample mortgage servicing portfolio has been combined with 1,000,000 par amount ($819,410.41 of principal amount) additional PO from the level hedge amount. The total par amount PO purchased is $3,930,000 ($3,220,282.91 of principal amount). The additional dollars of PO introduces the bull-biasness to this hedge. The dollar hedge ratio is increased from 49 percent to 57 percent as interest rates fall the combined return rises. An investor who believes that rates are more likely to fall than rise would consider this strategy, as the PO's bullish (the return rises as interest rates fall) characteristics are permitted to dominate.

A superior bullish structure has been created with only slight variations in duration and weighted average life. The investor has a maximum yield give-up versus the level-yield strategy of 82 basis points while having a maximum yield pick-up versus the level-yield strategy of 222 basis points. Because the investor is purchasing more PO, it is a more expensive strategy.

Example 3: Conventional Servicing: Conventional PO Bear Hedge

The sample mortgage servicing portfolio has been combined with $1,000,000 par amount ($819,410.41 of principal amount) less PO from the level hedge amount. The total par amount PO purchased is $1,930,000 ($1,581,462.09 of principal amount). The reduction in dollar amount of PO purchased introduces the bear-business to this hedge, as the mortgage servicing portfolio's bearish (the return rises as interest rates rises) characteristics are permitted to dominate. The dollar hedge ratio is decreased from 49 percent to 39 percent. As interest rates rise, the combined return rises. An investor who believes that rates are more likely to rise than fall would consider this strategy.

A superior bearish structure has been created with only slight variations in duration and weighted average life. The investor picks up 52 basis points in the current interest rate environment, and this pick-up in return rises to 117 basis points above the level hedge performance in the +300 basis points interest rate environment.

Because the investor is purchasing less PO, it is a less expensive strategy.

Executing this strategy generates a cost savings of $474,233.77 (due to $1,000,000 of par amount PO not purchased). This return is level-interest-rate insensitive return. The prepayment risk is completely eliminated in this case because of the obvious strong correlation in prepayments of two identical portfolios. The Bear Hedge has an absolute lower bound of 7.94 percent and an absolute upper bound of 15.13 percent.

Example 4: Differing Collateral and Coupon Level Yield Hedge

Sometimes it is desirable to structure a hedge ratio with differing underlying collateral and coupon because of the desired return structure. In this example, a higher coupon GNMA is used as a hedging tool for FNMA servicing because of the more bullish bias of the GNMA PO.

Table 8.7 Bull Hedge Results

Interest Rate Environment	Combined Yield (%)	Combined Duration	Combined WAL
+300	11.64	4.41	9.58
+200	11.74	4.39	8.88
+100	11.84	4.39	8.32
Current	12.10	4.12	7.03
−300	12.79	3.38	4.93
−200	13.57	2.79	3.64
−100	14.68	2.22	2.64

Table 8.8 Level Hedge Results

Interest Rate Environment	Combined Yield (%)	Combined Duration	Combined WAL
+300	12.46	4.34	9.58
+200	12.46	4.32	8.87
+100	12.47	4.32	8.32
Current	12.47	4.06	7.06
−100	12.48	3.34	4.96
−200	12.48	2.77	3.67
−300	12.46	2.21	2.63

Table 8.9 Differential Bull Hedge Results Less Than Level Hedge Results

Interest Rate Environment	Combined Yield (%)	Combined Duration	Combined WAL
+300	−.82	0.07	0.00
+200	−.72	0.07	0.001
+100	−.63	0.07	0.00
Current	−.37	0.06	0.00
−100	+.31	0.04	0.00
−200	1.09	0.02	0.01
−300	2.22	0.01	0.01

Table 8.10 Bull Hedge Cost/Level Hedge Cost

Bull Hedge Cost	
Servicing Basis	$1,434,750
Par Amount PO Purchased	$3,220,283
Purchase Cost PO @ Price	$1,863,739
Total Dollar Investment	$3,298,489
PO to Dollar Hedge Ratio	57%
Level Hedge Cost	
Servicing Basis	1,434,750
Par Amount PO Purchased	$2,400,873
Purchase Cost PO @ Price	$1,389,505
Total Dollar Investment	$2,824,255
PO to Dollar Hedge Ratio	49%

Table 8.16 lists the GNMA PO's characteristics. Table 8.17 shows the PO performance in different interest rate environments. Table 8.18 shows how the hedge performs.

Other Types of Hedges

There are as many different hedges as there are servicing portfolios and POs. An investor can structure a hedge ratio to accomplish any number of objectives.

Zero Return Hedge

Using a hedge ratio with fewer POs enables the servicing portfolio characteristics to dominate the combined portfolio's return. Therefore, the investor is taking a risk that rates may fall and prepayments rise. A major variation of this hedge is to purchase just enough POs to protect the return in a falling interest rate environment of the combined portfolio from becoming negative.

Table 8.11   Bear Hedge Results

Interest Rate Environment	Combined Yield (%)	Combined Duration	Combined WAL
+300	13.63	4.24	9.57
+200	13.48	4.22	8.86
+100	13.36	4.23	8.31
Current	12.99	3.98	7.02
−100	12.04	3.30	4.92
−200	10.94	2.74	3.63
−300	9.38	2.19	2.62

Table 8.12   Level Hedge Results

Interest Rate Environment	Combined Yield (%)	Combined Duration	Combined WAL
+300	12.46	4.34	9.58
+200	12.46	4.32	8.87
+100	12.47	4.32	8.32
Current	12.47	4.06	7.03
−100	12.48	3.34	4.93
−200	12.48	2.77	3.63
−300	12.46	2.21	2.63

Table 8.13   Differential Bear Hedge Results Less Level Hedge Results

Interest Rate Environment	Combined Yield (%)	Combined Duration	Combined WAL
+300	1.17	−0.10	−0.01
+200	1.02	−0.10	−0.01
+100	0.89	−0.09	−0.01
Current	0.52	−0.08	−0.01
−100	−0.44	−0.04	−0.01
−200	−1.54	−0.03	−0.00
−300	−3.08	−0.02	−0.01

Table 8.14   Bear Hedge/Level Hedge

Bear Hedge
Servicing Basis	$1,434,750
Par Amount PO Purchased	$1,581,462
Purchase Cost PO @ Price	$915,271
Total Dollar Investment	$2,350,021
PO to Dollar Hedge Ratio	39%

Level Hedge
Servicing Basis	1,434,750
Par Amount PO Purchased	$2,400,873
Purchase Cost PO @ Price	$1,389,505
Total Dollar Investment	$2,824,255
PO to Dollar Hedge Ratio	49%

Floating Rate Hedges

Floating rate hedges are hedges where the amount of PO purchased/sold is changed as interest rates change to maintain a fixed basis-point spread of a specific index. The alternative hedges described previously are fancy customized hedges that require considerably more maintenance than the level yield hedges that, once in place, need be as closely monitored.

Rewards, Benefits, and Relative Risk of Hedging Servicing Portfolio with POs

Rewards and Benefits

The major reward of this strategy is that a level yield can be achieved. Typically, a yield spread of at least 300 basis points over a similar duration treasury can be locked in. The correlation of a prepayments servicing portfolio and PO is extraordinarily high. Sometimes the mortgages that serve as collateral of the PO are exactly the same as the mortgages that comprise the servicing portfolio. One would expect an FNMA 10.58-percent servicing portfolio to prepay at essentially, if not exactly, the same

Table 8.15   PO Level Hedge Cost

Government POs

Estimated Servicing Basis	$1,434,750
Par Amount PO Purchased	$2,559,250
Purchase Cost PO @ Price	$1,497,161
Total Dollar Investment	$2,931,912
PO to Dollar Hedge Ratio	51%

Conventional POs

Estimated Servicing Basis	1,434,750
Par Amount PO Purchased	$2,400,873
Purchase Cost PO @ Price	$1,389,505
Total Dollar Investment	$2,824,255

Table 8.16   Principal-Only SMBS Characteristics

Par Amount PO	$3,350,000
Collateral WAC	11.500%
Collateral Servicing Fee	0.440%
Agency Guarantor Fee	0.60%
Collateral Pass-Through	11.000%
Weighted Average Maturity	322
Original Maturity	360
Trading Factor	0.72500000
Price of PO	58.500%

Table 8.17   Government PO SMBS Dynamics

Interest Rate Environment	PO SMBS PSA (%)	PO SMBS Yield (%)	PO SMBS Duration	PO SMBS WAL
+300	111	6.19	5.25	10.35
+200	121	6.57	5.28	9.85
+100	139	7.28	5.16	9.03
Current	205	10.15	4.34	6.79
−100	313	15.46	3.37	4.63
−200	379	19.01	2.99	3.81
−300	470	24.27	2.54	3.02

Table 8.18   Level Yield Results (Government PO)

Interest Rate Environment	Combined Yield (%)	Combined Duration	Combined WAL
+300	11.67	4.42	9.58
+200	11.52	4.43	8.88
+100	11.68	4.41	8.32
Current	12.52	3.99	7.01
−100	12.90	3.24	4.91
−200	12.23	2.80	3.62
−300	11.66	2.35	2.63

rate as an FNMA PO whose collateral (underlying) WAC is 10.58 percent. Hedging with Treasury options has not been effective in the past. Hedging with POs has several benefits:

- High prepayment rate/interest rate correlation.
- Similar Basis.
- Most POs are AAA investments—no default to date.
- The asset is usually blend of AAA PO and unsecuritized servicing; therefore, the required discount rate is lower.

Premium Servicing Bidding Strategy

Premium servicing can be aggressively bid for. A lower required yield can justify purchasing premium servicing if a hedging strategy is in place at the time of a bid. A bid for a premium servicing portfolio can easily be won with a yield in 20-percent range when combined with a PO for a yield of 15 percent.

Relative Risks

The reason the strategy works so well is that the risks the investor takes are the same for the combined asset as for most of each asset separately. These risks are drastically reduced:

- *Prepayment risk* can be completely eliminated or at least minimized by choosing an appropriate PO as a hedge tool and hedge ratio.

- *Basis risk*, the risk that the hedge tool return is based on different base, is minimized. Both assets are mortgage assets.

- *Correlation risk* relates to the fact that the hedge tool performs in an off-setting manner to the instrument being hedged. There is high correlation risk because both are mortgage-related assets.

- *Interest rate risk* is not specifically addressed by this hedging strategy. However, most of the interest rate risk is related prepayment risk, and that correlation as previously discussed is high.

In this chapter, the most successful strategy for hedging the prepayment risk of a mortgage servicing is discussed in detail. Hedging with POs can effectively eliminate prepayment risk. In fact, all major risks are minimized.

Note 1

Calculation of Price

$$P = \frac{1}{1} = 1 \frac{CF_i}{(1+Y)^i}$$

P = Price

CF_i = Cash flow in period i.

Y = Required return (expressed as percent).

t = Term of investment, for a mortgage-related asset, the remaining term.

Note 2

Calculation of Rate of Return or Yield

$$0 = t/i = 1 \frac{CF_i}{(1+Y)^i} - P$$

Y is solved for above by trial and error. A simple algorithm for solving the above is this:

$$Y_{i+2} = \frac{Y_{i+1} + P - P(Y_{i+1})}{P_{(Y_{i+1})} - P(Y_i)}$$

P = Price to be solved for.

i = Iteration number of trial.

This yield must take into account the payment delays which are defined as follows:

- Mortgage Servicing—31 days
- GNMA—45 days
- FNMA—55 days
- FHLMC—75 days

Note 3

Calculation of Macauly Duration

$$D_m = t/i = \frac{1\,(i-1+2)CF_i}{(1+Y)^{i-1+2}}$$

$$t/i = 1\,\frac{CF_i}{(1+Y)^{i-1+2}}$$

CF_i = Cash flow in period i.

Y = Required return discount rate (expressed as a percent).

a = Fraction of a period remaining until the next cash flow anniversary date (a = 1 on a Cash flow anniversary date).

t = Term of investment, for a mortgage-related asset, the remaining term.

Note 4

Calculation of Weighted Average Life in Years

$$WAL = \frac{t\ i.P_i \quad i=1}{12\,.\,Principal}$$

P_i = Principal received in period i.

t = Term of investment, for a mortgage-related asset, the remaining term.

Practical Application: The Plain Vanilla Deal

The plain vanilla deal can be defined as the deal that most buyers find acceptable at a given point in time. The characteristics of a plain vanilla deal change over time due to market conditions that are constantly changing. At the time of this writing, the following characteristics have been considered plain vanilla or generic:

$100MM	U.P.B.
GNMA	Investor
Fixed Rate	Rate Type
65,000	A Loan Size
10% Rate	Current Market Note Rate
.44%	W. Average Service Fee
360	W.A.O.T.
3336	W.A.R.T.
1%	W. A. Esc. Bal.
4%	Total Delinquencies

Regional	Location
25%	VA Properties
75%	FHA Properties
90%	Single Family
95%	Owner Occupied
85%	Retail Originated

Assuming that these characteristics were plain vanilla, we can use them as benchmarks with which to compare other deals. This section takes you through a specific example of a real deal that traded in the marketplace as a result of a competitive auction. This plain vanilla example demonstrates the actual process, from the seller's initial need to sell to the actual transfer of the servicing.

Aug. 3

The seller, a southeast financial institution, calls Cohane Rafferty to ask for assistance in selling $109mm of GNMA mortgage servicing rights. The seller already has identified approximately $109mm of GNMA product that it intends to sell to supplement earnings. The seller requests that Cohane Rafferty put together a proposal that includes an evaluation of the portfolio, the likely market range, number of expected bids, and marketing plan for the portfolio. The seller requests similar feedback from other servicing brokerage firms. It plans to review the information provided by all brokerage firms and pick one by August 10.

Aug. 3–6

Cohane Rafferty prepares a proposal that includes an evaluation showing conservative and aggressive bid ranges, the likely market high bid, and an overview of how they would market the portfolio.

Aug. 9

Cohane Rafferty visits the client to review its proposal. The economic valuation suggests a conservative bid of 1.94 percent and an aggressive bid of 2.59 percent. Based on other recent trades, we explain that the likely winning bid will fall between 2.20 and 2.40 for this particular portfolio. The seller suggests that in order to sell the portfolio it must receive the higher end of this range. We discuss the attractiveness of the portfolio in the market particularly its regional nature with more than 9 percent of the loans being located in three desirable contiguous states—North Carolina, South Carolina, and Virginia. The 12e loans located in New York cause a little concern because quite often southeast regional buyers will not bid on a package if it contains a state outside their local region, such as New York, that they do not currently service. Extracting these pooled New York loans from the portfolio in order to entice these potential bidders would cause the unpaid principal to fall substantially, making it unlikely that the seller's cash needs would be met.

We expressed confidence that we could generate 10 to 15 bids on this portfolio and get the higher end of the likely market range (2.20 to 2.40 percent). We also discussed the timing of the sale, which would be set up for the end of August. The purchase and sale would be negotiated and signed during September to allow a third-quarter profit, and transfer would be scheduled tentatively for October.

Aug. 10

The seller announces selection of Cohane Rafferty to assist in this sale.

Aug. 10–13

Cohane Rafferty and ABC Co. set the following immediate goals from Aug. 10–13:

1. Work together to obtain any additional information deemed necessary by Cohane Rafferty to include in the servicing being sold.

2. Make sure that the information in the offering is accurate.

3. Start preparing for additional questions such as county breakdowns, weighted average escrow information, etc. that will be needed by bidders but would not be ready by the distribution (mail-out) date.

4. Complete a professionally designed mortgage servicing portfolio offering in the Cohane Rafferty format (Exhibit 9.1) for distribution on August 16.

5. Get ready to mail the offering to more than 800 potential bidders (including a final review of the offering by both Cohane Rafferty and ABC Co. to detect any inaccuracies).

6. Schedule mailing date and the bid date. The distribution date was set for August 16 with an auction date of August 30. This provided 10 working days for all potential bidders to receive, review, ask appropriate questions. Just as important, the 10 working days allow Cohane Rafferty adequate time to follow up with phone calls to more than 90 percent of the institutions to which the portfolio was mailed.

Aug. 16

The portfolio is mailed to more than 800 financial institutions, which include thrifts, mortgage banks, some insurance companies with mortgage subsidiaries, and other financial institutions.

Aug. 16–29

Cohane Rafferty sales teams make phone calls to create interest in the portfolio and ensure that each institution actually reviews the portfolio's characteristics with the salesperson over the phone. This is the single most important step in the marketing process. Sending a mortgage servicing and not calling each individual to review the characteristics would most likely lead to a dismal auction with few or no bids being received on the auction date. The job of the sales team is to get this portfolio to the top of the in-basket and to discuss with potential buyers the opportunities and benefits that the offering provides.

Many additional questions come from potential interested bidders. Some of these additional questions are as follows:

- Weighted average escrow balance
- County breakdowns of loans in New York, North Carolina, and Virginia
- Any subsidy loans such as section 235 loans
- Number of correspondent lenders are represented in portfolio
- Delinquency of correspondent loans
- Number of FNMA polls
- Percentage of loans with optional insurance
- Identity of optional insurance carriers
- VA no-bid experience of the seller
- Foreclosure history of seller
- Refinance loans
- All loans escrowed
- Timing of certification for uncertified loans
- Location of condo loans
- Bankruptcy or foreclosure loans in the over-90 category
- Location of bankruptcy or foreclosure loans
- Transamerica Tax Service loans "life of loans contacts"
- Negative amortization on GPM loans
- Seller acceptance of VA indemnification

- Type of buydowns in portfolio
- Year in which buydowns and GPM originated
- Delinquencies by 15- and 30-year loans separately

Aug. 16–29

It would have been highly desirable to have all this information in the portfolio offering when it was mailed out. However, the seller and the broker must work together to balance the needs of the buyer/seller and the broker. There is no substitute for accurate data. If a seller finds itself in the undesirable position that it must sell quickly and does not have the time to put every detail of the portfolio's characteristics in the marketing package, it is better that the portfolio go out without the information. Normally a two-week span exists between the mail date and the auction date during which time the seller can retrieve accurate additional information and provide it to interested bidders. Bidders get very discouraged when they see data that is represented incorrectly. It damages the credibility of both the seller and the broker and the offering for sale. Receiving a lot of questions on an offering is generally a good sign; it shows that the package is creating interest in the market. The seller must be prepared to answer questions in an efficient manner. If a seller cannot or will not provide the necessary resources to get accurate answers in a reasonable time period, a lower price undoubtedly will result. This problem is most often a result of a computer system that is not user-friendly when it comes to extracting servicing data particularly to the portfolio being sold. A seller of servicing should address this with management if it intends to be an ongoing seller.

In the case of this sale, the seller is easily accessible and working extremely hard to provide answers. However, it is a first-time seller, and the computer system it uses (an outside service bureau) is not flexible when it comes to extracting servicing data. They work diligently to respond to questions, and in many circumstances they must manually obtain information that might otherwise have been easily obtained with a more user-friendly computerized servicing system. Obtaining information by manual means allows for greater potential error.

Aug. 30

The bid is scheduled for 3 p.m. Eastern time. Every morning at 8 a.m., Cohane Rafferty has a 15- to 30-minute meeting to discuss the day's priorities. Today, all salespeople and the principals of the company are focused on today's auction. During the meeting, we review what we call our short list. The short list is so called because it is generally an extremely short list of interested bidders relative to the number of people to whom the initial deal was sent. In the case of this sale, the initial deal went to more than 800, and on this day approximately twenty-five institutions were still interested and potential bidders at 3 p.m. Our first priority today will be to call all of these twenty-five companies to make sure they are still interested and that all their questions have been answered.

We call the seller in the morning to discuss today's auction process and to review still outstanding questions and additional questions we just received. We tell the seller that twenty-five companies are on the short list but that it is expected that ten to fifteen of these potential bidders will probably fall out by 3 p.m. We anticipate a strong auction will be somewhere between ten and fifteen bids. This is shaping up to be a good auction. In the trading room of Cohane Rafferty, the atmosphere gets intense with anticipation and excitement of the final outcome. In the trading room, each trader hopes to bring in the winning bid and thus be a major contributor in getting the deal done. At 3 p.m., all bids are received by Cohane Rafferty. Most of the bids have been faxed in between 2 and 3 p.m.

The bids received are as follows:

- 2.35
- 2.30
- 2.27
- 2.25
- 2.20
- 2.15

- 2.08
- 2.06
- 2.05
- 2.05
- 2.03
- 1.993
- 1.86
- 1.84
- 1.64
- 1.59
- 2.004 average bid

2.04–average bid

2.15–average bid (excluding four of the lowest bids falling below economic valuation of 1.94 to 2.59 percent)

2.20–2.40–expected winning bid

2.35–high auction bid

At approximately 3:15 p.m., Cohane Rafferty calls the seller to inform the seller of the results of the auction. The seller expresses that although it had hoped to get someone to pay in excess of 2.40 percent, it is obvious that the portfolio was well represented by the number of bids received. The top four bid letters will be faxed and mailed to the seller for review and discussion by the seller and Cohane Rafferty tomorrow. Cohane Rafferty calls all clients who bid to tell them the results. The top four bidders are informed that they should be available for questions tomorrow because their bid letters are being reviewed. No two bid letters are the same. It is possible for different bid letter caveats to cause wide price differences. Therefore, it is possible that even though the 2.35 percent is the high numerical bid, it may well not be the winning bid. Also, other issues come into play that are important:

- When can the bidder do a due diligence?
- When can the bidder sign a P&S?
- When can the bidder transfer?

Aug. 31

Bid letters are reviewed. Cohane Rafferty intermediates the negotiations between the seller and the top numerical bidder. Typically, the main issues in negotiating a bid letter tend to revolve around accounting/bookability issues. In the case of this transaction, the seller requires a 15 percent deposit upon written acceptance of the buyer's bid letter in order to be able to bank the sale. The buyer had stated a 5 percent deposit in its bid letter. The buyer agrees to make this change to a 15 percent deposit. In calculating the purchase price, the buyer had a requirement that "a lump sum of $3,500 would be deducted from the purchase price for each delinquent loan." Delinquent loans were defined as all loans that are three or more payments past due, in bankruptcy, litigation, or foreclosure. This represented eight loans in the portfolio. A compromise was met in which the buyer dropped the $3,500 in price per delinquent loan, but a new clause was incorporated that required the buyer to remove these loans from the portfolio. The third and final issue resolved when both parties agreed to share in the costs putting 630 loans (35 percent total number of loans) on a tax service.

September 1

The bid letter is executed by the seller.

September 7

The buyer visits the seller's operation to conduct due diligence. The due diligence goes well with the exception of one issue. The seller instructs

Cohane Rafferty and the seller that it will be reducing its bid one basis point because the weighted average escrow balance represented by the seller was not accurate.

Exhibit 9.1

Exclusive Servicing Offering

NO. 307

BID DATE: August 30, 1988/3 p.m. New York Time

Winning Bid:
2.35
2.27
2.25
2.25
2.25
2.20
2.15
2.08
2.06
2.05
2.05
2.03
1.86
1.84
1.59

Cohane Rafferty Securities, Inc. is acting as an exclusive agent in the sale of $109,261,616.50 of GNMA I servicing by a sourtheast financial institution.

The information in this report has been obtained from sources which Cohane Rafferty Securities, Inc. believes to be reliable. However, we do not guarantee its accuracy, as such information may be incomplete or condensed.

Bids must be received by Cohane Rafferty by 3 p.m. New York Time, August 30, 1988.

To facilitate your analysis of the offering, this portfolio contains the following information:

	Page
GNMA I Total/Fixed Rate	
Essential Details	1
Note Rate Distribution	2
Loan Characteristics	3
Geographical Distribution	4
GNMA I 30-Year/Fixed Rate	
Essential Details	5
Note Rate Distribution	6
GNMA I 15-Year/Fixed Rate	
Essential Details	7
Note Rate Distribution	8
Additional Information	9

Essential Details

GNMA I Total

Date of Information	July 21
Product Type	Fixed Rate
Principal Balance	$109,261,616.50
Number of Loans	1,793
Average Loan Size	$60,937.88
Note Rate Range	8.00–11.00%
Weighted Average Note Rate	9.47%
Weighted Average Net Service Fee	0.44%
Weighted Average Original Term (months)	343
Weighted Average Remaining Term (months)	322
Average Monthly Escrow Balance	$866,285.95
Monthly Tax and Insurance Constant	$133,274.76
Monthly Principal and Interest Constant	$948,471.54

Delinquencies

	Number of Loans	Percentage of Loans
30 days	12	0.67
60 days	2	0.11
90 days and over	8	0.45
Total delinquencies	22	1.23

Note Rate Distribution

GNMA I Total

Interest rate (%)	Number of loans	Principal balance	Weighted average servicing fee (%)
8.00	14	941,626.73	0.44
8.50	210	12,832,504.28	0.44
9.00	400	23,675,471.44	0.44
9.50	648	40,129,268.18	0.44
9.75	18	1,077,379.72	0.44
10.00	308	19,015,587.78	0.44
10.50	157	9,375,251.84	0.44
11.00	38	2,214,526.53	0.44
Total	1,793	$109,261,616.50	0.44

Loan Characteristics

GNMA I Total

Loan Types

	Number of loans	Dollar amount
FHA	1,362	79,279,657.84
VA	431	29,981,958.66
Total	1,793	$109,261,616.50

Property Types

	Number of loans	Percentage of total loans (%)
Single family	1,655	92.30
Condos/townhouse	138	7.70
Total	1,793	100.00

Occupancy

	Number of loans	Percentage of total loans (%)
Owner occupied	1,699	94.76
Non-owner occupied	94	5.24
Total	1,793	100.00

Loan Source

	Percentage of total loans (%)
Retail	85.00
Purchased/correspondent	15.00
Total	100.00

Geographical Distribution

GNMA I Total

State	Number of FHA loans	Number of VA loans	Total loans	Percentage of total loans (%)	Dollar amount
NC	1,143	209	1,352	76	80,100,733.74
VA	115	117	232	13	16,305,331.38
SC	86	74	160	9	10,062,274.31
NY	12	31	43	2	2,491,950.72
AL	6	0	6	0	301,326.35
Total	1,362	431	1,793	100	$109,261,616.50

Essential Details

GNMA I 30-Year

Date of Information	July 21
Product Type	Fixed Rate
Principal Balance	$100,469,245.91
Number of Loans	1,624
Average Loan Size	$61,865.30
Note Rate Range	8.00–11.00%
Weighted Average Note Rate	9.50%
Weighted Average Net Service Fee	0.44%
Weighted Average Original Term (months)	358
Weighted Average Remaining Term (months)	335
Average Monthly Escrow Balance	$779,294.56
Monthly Tax and Insurance Constant	$119,891.47
Monthly Principal and Interest Constant	$853,609.54

Note Rate Distribution

GNMA I 30-Year

Interest rate (%)	Number of loans	Principal balance	Weighted average servicing fee (%)
8.00	14	941,626.73	0.44
8.50	175	11,010,668.09	0.44
9.00	329	20,088,769.84	0.44
9.50	585	36,745,435.58	0.44
9.75	18	1,077,379.72	0.44
10.00	308	19,015,587.78	0.44
10.50	157	9,375,251.84	0.44
11.00	38	2,214,526.53	0.44
Total	1,624	$100,469,245.91	0.44

Essential Details

GNMA I 15-Year

Date of Information	July 21
Product Type	Fixed Rate
Principal Balance	$8,792,370.59
Number of Loans	169
Average Loan Size	$52,025.86
Note Rate Range	8.50–9.50%
Weighted Average Note Rate	9.09%
Weighted Average Net Service Fee	0.44%
Weighted Average Original Term (months)	180
Weighted Average Remaining Term (months)	162
Average Monthly Escrow Balance	$86,991.39
Monthly Tax and Insurance Constant	$13,383.29
Monthly Principal and Interest Constant	$94,662.00

Note Rate Distribution

GNMA I 15-Year

Interest rate (%)	Number of loans	Principal balance	Weighted average servicing fee (%)
8.50	35	1,181,836.19	0.44
9.00	71	3,586,701.80	0.44
9.50	63	3,383,832.60	0.44
Total	169	$8,792,370.59	0.44

Additional Information

Computer: EDS System (outside service bureau)
Files and Records: On hard copy and microjackets
Tape-to-tape transfer is available.
Loans have been solicited for insurance through Germantown, Minnesota, Mutual and Monumental
With the exception of 630 loans in the Forsyth and Guilford county areas, all loans are being serviced by Transamerica Tax Service.
Payments are due on the first with interest collected in arrears.
Loan package represents 8 percent of the seller's portfolio.
All loans are subject to a 4-percent late charge.
82% of the pools have final certification.

Buydown Loans

Number of loans	**Principal balance**
4	$253,399
Weighted average net servicing fee	0.44%
Weighted average note rate	9.50%

GPM Loans

Number of loans	**Principal balance**
38	$2,214,525
Weighted average net servicing fee	0.44%
Weighted average note rate	11.00%

Flow Deals

===============

A great deal of servicing is bought and sold as soon as it is originated. These transactions generally are considered flow deals. In their simplest form, the transaction is the typical correspondent/wholesaler transaction where the loan is originated by the correspondent, according to the wholesaler's pricing and underwriting guidelines. When the relationship is taken beyond this, the terms often are negotiated privately and a special arrangement is created that is somewhat exclusive between the two parties involved. These arrangements become necessary when the volume of loans being transferred becomes too great for each loan to be underwritten and approved by the buyer prior to funding the loan or the servicing. The arrangements generally are driven by a seller seeking to exceed the premiums paid by a wholesaler for the servicing and a buyer who desires to add product in volume on a predictable basis in addition to or instead of purchasing product through the usual correspondent/wholesaler relationship.

Definition and Formats

It may be helpful to define what flow servicing is and to explore the variations of flow transactions that typically exist. *Flow servicing* is the simultaneous sale of the rights to service mortgage loans with the sale or securitization of the underlying mortgage loans.

Most flow servicing transactions fall within one of two formats:

- Assignment of trade
- Co-issuance

The formats can be differentiated in two major areas:

- Who is the servicer of record/pool issuer?
- Does the transaction include the purchase of whole mortgage loans plus servicing, or servicing only?

Notice the difference in these areas as the steps to assignment of trade and co-issuance is outlined.

Assignment of Trade

1. Seller originates mortgage loans within the guidelines of an investor (FHLMC, FNMA, GNMA).
2. Seller negotiates the sale of the underlying mortgages into the secondary market. This may take the form of a forward sale (trade) of mortgage backed securities to a broker/dealer.
3. As the seller's pipeline of loans matures and specific allocations of closed loans can be forecast, the seller assigns the trade with the broker/dealer to the buyer. The buyer and the broker/dealer both must acknowledge acceptance of this assignment. At this point, the buyer becomes responsible to make delivery of the mortgage backed security to the broker/dealer. The terms of the trade that were negotiated by the seller and the broker/dealer do not change. The amount, date, and price are set by the seller, and the buyer steps into the seller's place with a matched transaction—a commitment to buy at a prearranged price, and a commitment to sell at a prearranged price. It generally is accepted, therefore, that the assigned trade transaction does not have marketing risk from the perspective of the buyer.
4. The seller must now deliver the closed loans to the buyer. The buyer in turn will use them to form securities for delivery to the broker/dealer. The price paid to the seller will be the price at which the forward trade was done plus the premium payable for the servicing. This involves the sale of whole mortgage loans plus servicing, and that the pools are formed and issued by the buyer.
5. The seller must deliver closed loans early enough to allow time for the buyer to form the pools. An important clause in a flow contract between buyer and seller is the deadline by which the seller must

deliver loans and the penalty for failure to do so. As mentioned previously, an assignment of trade generally does not carry marketing risk for the buyer. Therefore, the customary penalties for failure to meet loan delivery deadlines to the buyer will cover the costs incurred by the buyer for failing to deliver mortgage-backed securities to the broker/dealer. These costs may include lost interest and/or marketing losses incurred when trades must be bought back. There may be additional penalties to compensate the buyer for administrative expenses.

6. If the seller has met the required deadlines, it becomes the buyer's responsibility to form pools and make delivery against the security trades with the broker/dealer. The broker/dealer pays the buyer the same price the buyer paid for the loans less the servicing premium. Therefore, the seller's net outlay is only the servicing premiums.

Co-Issuance

1. Seller originates mortgage loans within the guidelines of an investor (FHLMC, FNMA, GNMA).

2. Seller negotiates the sale of the underlying mortgages into the secondary market. This may take form of a forward sale (trade) of mortgage backed securities to a broker/dealer.

3. Seller closes the loans and forms pools to be delivered against the forward sale. During the pooling process, the seller can designate a new servicer who will be responsible for making the first remittance to the investor.

4. Seller delivers loan files for servicing transfer to buyer prior to the first reporting/remitting cycle.

5. The buyer pays the seller the servicing premium. The seller has formed and issued the pools, and the sale involved only a servicing premium.

Flow Transactions Versus Bulk Transactions

Advantages to Seller

1. Flow sales provide a predictable stream of revenue on a monthly basis, making it easier to measure operating results on a continuing basis.
2. Contracts for flow servicing usually cover extended periods, thereby locking in prices. The seller is not subject to downswings in price caused by changes in interest rates or market imbalances.
3. The seller avoids the expense of setting up the loans on its own servicing system only to take them off a short time later as with a bulk sale. Transfer fees, conversion costs, and other expenses associated with bulk sales also are avoided.
4. Prices for flow sales generally are based on long-term goals and expectations. Historically, flow pricing has been inherently more stable than prices paid in the bulk market. A seller can price production with a high degree of certainty that would not be the case if it elects to accumulate and sell in bulk.
5. Diligent marketing may bring out multiple buyers. Flow sellers can take better advantage of multiple buyers who may have stronger prices for a particular product in the seller's mix (i.e. conventional, government, fixed, and ARM). Bulk sales may not always be split.
6. The seller has the flexibility to adjust the volume sold as production and profitability require.

Advantages to Buyer

1. The buyer is assured of filling acquisition requirements without relying on hit or miss results in bidding on bulk portfolios.
2. A buyer can add loans from a large number of flow sellers rather than a fewer bulk sellers, thereby reducing the amount of risk from any one lender. Flow transactions also give the buyer more control over from whom and how much it buys.
3. Transfer of servicing can be handled more smoothly with less disruption to the borrowers. It is possible to notify customers prior

to their making the first payment. Servicing departments are not deluged with phone calls and complaints which may occur with bulk transfers.

4. Buyers are acquiring new, current coupon loans that will have maximum value at the time of acquisition.

5. The prices paid for flow have generally been below those required to win bulk sales of high quality product when offered on a competitive basis.

6. Cash outlays are smoother and easier to budget when compared with large sums of capital required to fund bulk purchases.

7. Flow buyers can structure their deals to acquire servicing that meets very specific requirements with respect to geographic locations and loan type.

8. A buyer who develops a strategy to acquire flow will find less competition than in the bulk market.

Appendices

Normal Paper Trail in Servicing Sale

This documentation outlines the routine procedures for the sale of a servicing portfolio.

     I.   ***Agency Agreement***

     II.   ***Offering*** - This is marketed to prequalified buyers nationwide.

     III.   ***Bid Letter*** - Submitted by the buyer February 2, 1989 and accepted by the seller February 3, 1989.

     IV.   ***Purchase and Sale Agreement*** - Signed March 10, 1989

     V.   ***Payment of Fee*** - Received April 7, 1989

XXXXXXXXXXXXXXXX

XXXXXXXXXXXXXXXX
XXXXXXXXXXXXXXXX
XXXXXXXXXXXXXXXX
XXXXXXXXXXXXXXXX

Dear XXXXXXXXXXX:

Cohane Rafferty Securities, Inc. ("we", "our", or "us") understand that XXXXXXXXX ("you" or "your") propose to sell all or a portion of your right, title, and interest in the servicing of mortgage notes serviced by you under servicing contracts with the Government National Mortgage Association (GNMA), the Federal National Mortgage Association (FNMA), and the Federal Home Loan Mortgage Corporation (FHLMC) described in Schedule A, hereto. You have proposed that we act as your exclusive agent in obtaining commitments from one or more purchasers to purchase such servicing rights from the date hereof and until any extensions pursuant to the terms hereof. We hereby accept the appointment subject to the terms and conditions set forth herein.

(1) **Services to be Rendered by Us:** As your exclusive agent, we will assist and advise you in connection with the structure of the proposed sale and use our best efforts to locate potential purchasers and assist you in negotiating the amount and other terms of sale.

(2) **Compensation:** As compensation for our services hereunder, you agree to pay an amount equal to ____ basis points (___%) of the unpaid principal balance plus ____ percent (___%) of any sum received by you in excess of _____ basis points. This fee shall be deemed earned upon acceptance of a bid and paid as funded.

We will be compensated ____ basis points (___%) of the unpaid principal balance on any additional servicing, negotiated and sold to the same buyer within eighteen months of the transfer.

It is understood that, for the purpose hereof, any purchaser which is approved to service mortgage loans of the type you are selling and is financially ready, willing and able to perform under the applicable servicing contracts, will be an acceptable purchaser.

(3) <u>Obligations Limited:</u> You acknowledge that the descriptions of the Servicing Rights have been furnished by you are not representations by Cohane Rafferty Securities. We shall be under no obligation to make an independent investigation or inquiry as to the correctness of any information or data given to us, and shall have no liability in regard thereto.

(4) <u>Exclusive agency;</u> **Confidentiality:** You agree that we shall be your sole and exclusive agent during the term and any extensions hereof. You agree that (i) you will not communicate with or contact purchasers; (ii) any inquiries you receive directly from any proposed purchasers will be referred to us; and (iii) the entry into a commitment by any purchaser prior to the termination hereof, whether or not such purchaser is introduced by us, will entitle us to the compensation set forth in paragraph (2) hereof. Except for any required recording in connection with sales, you will keep confidential and will not, without written consent, divulge the identity of any prospective purchaser introduced by us to any other person, except to the extent necessary in working with legal counsel, auditors, taxing authorities or governmental agencies.

(5) <u>Termination; Subsequent Closings</u>. This agreement may not be terminated prior to sixty (60) days from the date hereof, but may be terminated thereafter on (2) days written notice from either party to the other. Notwithstanding such termination, if within one year of the date of such terminations you shall arrange for a commitment to sell any Servicing Rights to a purchaser introduced to you during the term hereof by us, we shall be deemed to have earned the compensation set forth in paragraph (2) hereof, which shall be payable on the transfer of such Servicing Rights.

(6) <u>Indemnification:</u> You agree to indemnify and hold harmless Cohane Rafferty Securities, Inc., including any affiliated companies, and their respective officers, directors, controlling persons and employees and any persons retained in connection with a transaction or proposed transaction (whether or not consummated), from and against all claims, damages, losses, liabilities and expenses as the same are incurred (including any legal or other expenses incurred in connection with investigating or defending against any such loss, claim, damage or liability or any action in respect thereof), related to or arising out of its activities hereunder.

Notwithstanding the foregoing, you shall not be liable under this agreement in respect of any loss, claim, damage, liability or expense if a court having jurisdiction shall have determined by a final judgement that such loss, claim, damage, liability or expense primarily resulted from our willful misconduct or gross negligence in performing the services described above. This provision shall survive any termination of our engagement.

(7) <u>**Miscellaneous:**</u> This agreement is made solely for the benefit of the parties hereto, and no other person shall acquire or have any right under or by virtue of this agreement. This agreement shall be governed by and construed and enforced in accordance with the laws of New York and may be executed in several counterparts, each of which shall be deemed to be an original, but all of which together shall constitute one and the same instruments. Nothing contained herein shall be deemed or construed to create a partnership or joint venture between the parties hereto, and our services shall be rendered as an independent contractor.

A late fee of one percent (1%) per month will be charged on any outstanding compensation due Cohane Rafferty ten (10) business days after funding. In addition, you agree to forward to us a signed copy of the Purchaser and Sale Agreement upon its execution.

If the foregoing correctly sets forth our understanding, please execute the enclosed copy of this letter and return it to Tim Cohane or Larry Rafferty whereupon it shall become a binding agreement.

Very truly yours,

H. J. Renz
Cohane Rafferty Securities, Inc.

Accepted and Agreed to:

XXXXXXXXXXXXXXXX

By:_____
    XXXXXXXXXXXXX

Dated:_____

EXCLUSIVE SERVICING OFFERING

NO. 362

BID DATE: January 23, 1989/2 P.M. New York Time

550 Mamaroneck Avenue
Harrison, New York 10528
(914) 381-6300
(914) 381-6307 (FAX)

Denver West Office Park
1746 Cole Blvd., Golden, CO 80401
(303) 279-4830
(303) 278-0092 (FAX)

ESSENTIAL DETAILS

FNMA LASER

Date of Information:	1/9/89
Product Type:	30 Year ARM
Principal Balance:	$15,222,057.60
Number of Loans:	182
Average Loan Size:	$83,637.68
Weighted Average Net Servicing Fee:	.5098%
Weighted Average Note Rate:	9.841%
Weighted Average Original Term:	360
Weighted Average Remaining Term:	315
Tax & Insurance Constant:	$50,682.56
Principal & Interest Constant:	$145,063.13

Delinquencies

(As of 12/31/88)

	No. of Loans	% of Total Loans
30 days	8	4.40%
60 days	1	.55
90 days and above	1	.55
Total Delinquencies	10	5.49

NOTE RATE DISTRIBUTION

FNMA LASER

(30 Year ARM)

Note Rate	No. of Loan	Principal Balance	Percent of Balance	Net Servicing Fee
7.500	1	$96,570.07	0.00%	.500%
8.500	2	180,109.89		.500
8.625	1	76,491.61		.500
8.750	2	163,932.30		.500
8.875	2	195,266.75		.500
9.000	6	604,683.80		.500
9.125	15	1,182,595.36		.500
9.200	1	93,762.45		.500
9.250	23	1,830,158.53		.516
9.375	5	370,166.27		.500
9.500	15	1,405,207.24		.509
9.625	4	328,421.50		.500
9.675	1	113,948.54		.500
9.750	7	602,189.16		.500
9.875	13	1,112,120.15		.500
10.000	11	955,193.11		.475
10.125	15	1,137,368.48		.479
10.250	5	450,664.71		.671
10.375	2	168,236.79		.500
10.500	3	321,436.05		.500
10.625	42	3,373,809.13		.500
10.750	2	135,897.22		.500
10.875	1	66,550.98		1.625
11.000	1	70,080.95		.500
11.375	1	110,940.92		.500
11.625	1	78,845.64		.500
Total	182	$15,224,647.60		.5096

GEOGRAPHICAL DISTRIBUTION

FNMA LASER

(30 Year ARM)

State	No. of Loans	Principal Balance	% of Balance
NJ	27	$2,219,470.49	14.58%
NY	155	13,002,587.11	85.42
Total	182	$15,222,057.60	100.00%

ESSENTIAL DETAILS

FNMA LASER

Date of Information:	1/9/89
Product Type:	Total Fixed
Principal Balance:	$38,347,616.10
Number of Loans:	408
Average Loan Size:	$93,989.26
Weighted Average Net Servicing Fee:	.4360%
Weighted Average Note Rate:	10.25%
Weighted Average Original Term:	322.36
Weighted Average Remaining Term:	298.63
Tax & Insurance Constant:	$120,791.25
Principal & Interest Constant:	$367,448.39

ESSENTIAL DETAILS

FNMA LASER

Date of Information:	1/9/89
Product Type:	30 Year
Principal Balance:	$30,697,073.97
Number of Loans:	321
Average Loan Size:	$95,629.51
Weighted Average Net Servicing Fee:	.4259%
Weighted Average Note Rate:	10.33%
Weighted Average Original Term:	357.96
Weighted Average Remaining Term:	334.01
Tax & Insurance Constant:	$92,226.96
Principal & Interest Constant:	$281,124.71

ESSENTIAL DETAILS

FNMA LASER

Date of Information:	1/9/89
Product Type:	15 Year
Principal Balance:	$7,650,542.13
Number of Loans:	87
Average Loan Size:	$87,937.27
Weighted Average Net Servicing Fee:	.4764%
Weighted Average Note Rate:	9.95%
Weighted Average Original Term:	179.54
Weighted Average Remaining Term:	156.68
Tax & Insurance Constant:	$28,564.69
Principal & Interest Constant:	$86,323.68

NOTE RATE DISTRIBUTION

FNMA LASER
(Total)

Note Rate	No. of Loan	Principal Balance	Percent of Balance	Net Servicing Fee
8.685 - 8.975	10	$802,239.69		.4807%
9.125 - 9.425	17	1,612,422.47		.3935
9.525 - 9.995	93	9,019,503.60		.4156
10.000 - 10.475	142	13,033,097.33		.4282
10.500 - 10.925	120	11,379,946.61		.4148
11.000 - 11.250	22	2,238,060.99		.6354
11.625 - 11.875	3	136,451.67		.2869
12.125	1	125,893.74		1.550
Total	408	$38,347,616.10		.4362 *

* Differences are due to rounding.

* Servicing fees are calculated as of 1/10/89.

GEOGRAPHICAL DISTRIBUTION

FNMA LASER
(Total)

State	No. of Loans	Principal Balance	% of Balance
NJ	79	$7,491,622.73	19.54%
NY	329	30,855,993.37	80.46
Total	408	$38,347,616.10	100.00%

February 2, 1989

XXXXXXXXXXXXXXXXXX
XXXXXXXXXXXXXXXXXX
XXXXXXXXXXXXXXXXXX
XXXXXXXXXXXXXXXXXX

Dear XXXXXXXXXXXXX:

We have reviewed the information you provided us concerning the above captioned servicing offering, and we have relied on the attached information in making this offer. We represent that were are an approved FNMA/FHLMC/GNMA Servicer in good standing with requisite financial criteria and adequate resources necessary to complete the transaction.

This letter will serve to notify you of (Purchaser) offer and intent to purchase from (Seller) the servicing rights to the loans, aggregating approximately $53 million as described in the attached schedules supplied by Cohane Rafferty (hereafter the "loans or the servicing") on the terms and conditions expressed in this Letter of Intent.

1.   Purchaser Price: The Purchaser Price shall be the result of multiplying the bid percentage of 1.95% by the unpaid principal balance on the transfer date of all loans which are not sixty days or more past due or in foreclosure as of the transfer date. The payment of the purchase price will be as follows:

   A.   5% of the estimated final purchase price will be paid within 5 days of acceptance of this commitment.

   B.   An additional 75% of the purchase price shall be paid to the Seller in cash within 5 days of the sale date.

C.   The remaining 20% of the purchase price will be paid by Buyer within 5 days of the transfer date.

2.   The Sale Date will be the date of execution of the Loan Servicing Purchase and Sale Agreement (the "Agreement") and the Interim Loan Servicing Agreement. At the time of execution of the Agreements, all rights to the servicing will be transferred to the Purchaser.

The Sale Date - as soon as possible, but in no event any later than February 28, 1989.

3.   The Transfer Date - will be the date the Purchaser assumes the servicing of the loan portfolio, this is anticipated to be March 30, 1989 for all FNMA servicing rights.

4.   Prior to the Transfer Date, Seller will continue to service the loans and pools in accordance with all applicable laws, rules, regulations and procedures, and with any contractual obligations with FNMA, GNMA and FHLMC, the owners of the loans and the borrowers under the loans, and shall have the rights, including, but not limited to, the right to earn and receive servicing fees and other income incidental to servicing.

5.   Seller will continue to service all loans which, as of the Sale Date, are in the process of foreclosure, bankruptcy, or litigation. Any and all losses resulting from foreclosure action on loans 60 days or more delinquent on the transfer date shall be the responsibility of Seller.

6.   Purchase of the servicing rights is subject to the following conditions:

A.   Determination by Purchaser that the books, records and accounts of Seller with respect to the loans ar in order and acceptable to Purchaser, and verification by Purchaser that the information provided as part of the offering package is substantially correct.

B.   Delivery by Seller to Purchaser of written approval of transfer of Seller/Servicer rights and responsibilities from the owner or holder of each of the loans, and any other consents or approvals; if necessary to transfer the servicing from Seller to Purchaser.

C.   Execution by Purchaser and Seller of a Loan Servicing Purchase and Sale Agreement mutually acceptable to both parties and which will contain, among other provisions, the Seller's agreement to hold Purchaser harmless, by loan repurchase or otherwise, for any and all expenses resulting form servicing, prior to the transfer date of loan under any applicable laws, rules, regulations or guidelines or requirements, including but not limited to contractual obligations with FNMA/GNMA/FHLMC, private mortgage insurers, the owners of the loans and the borrowers under the loans.

D.   Approval and acceptance by Purchaser and Seller of any and all documentation (including a Loan Servicing Agreement) which may be required to effectuate the sale and assignment of the servicing rights to Purchaser.

E.   Buyer is responsible for the transfer of all tax service contracts to Transamerica from Ticor or any other tax service and any costs associated with such transfer. Seller must provide complete histories and a copy of each ARM change letter, where applicable.

F.   Seller shall transfer to Purchaser on the transfer date, in immediately available funds, all loan escrow monies and unearned fees.

7   Seller represents that it has the sole right and authority to sell the servicing rights and is not contractually obligated to sell the rights to any other party.

8.   This bid is predicated on the attached information supplied by Seller. To the extent these figures change we maintain the right to amend our bid.

9.   Seller shall pay the costs of securing any approvals of the owners or holders of any loan or of any other persons and transfer fees due them, and shall bear the costs of preparing and recording assignments of mortgages as required. Blanket assignments may be used where permitted. Seller agrees to pay any brokerage fees due Cohane Rafferty. Other than as provided herein, each party represents that it is not obligated to pay any brokers or other fees on this transaction.

This Letter of Intent is subject to Buyer approving Seller's financial statements, delinquency ratios of its servicing portfolio, and a satisfactory reference and due diligence of its servicing, investor reporting and underwriting procedures.

Unless accepted sooner, this offer will be valid until 5:00 p.m., February 6, 1989. Upon return of a copy of this letter duly executed by any authorized officer of Seller, this letter will constitute a binding agreement between the parties for the purchase and sale of servicing.

Sincerely,

By:_____ Date:_____

By:_____ Date:_____

February 2, 1989

XXXXXXXXXXXXXXXXXX
XXXXXXXXXXXXXXXXXX
XXXXXXXXXXXXXXXXXX
XXXXXXXXXXXXXXXXXX

RE: *Purchase and Transfer of FNMA Servicing Rights*

Enclosed you will find an original commitment letter for your signature. After signing it please return.

After receiving the signed copy, I will send you our proposed Purchase and Interim Servicing Agreement for your review. In the mean time if you have any questions please use myself as the main contact.

March 10, 1989

XXXXXXXXXXXXXXXXX
XXXXXXXXXXXXXXXXX
XXXXXXXXXXXXXXXXX
XXXXXXXXXXXXXXXXX

RE: *Transfer of Servicing Rights*

Dear XXXXXXXXXXXXX:

Enclosed please find initialed copies of the pages you amended in the Purchase and Servicing Agreement. I appreciate your sending the Board minutes.

Please advise me as to when the goodbye and welcome letters are being mailed so I may put our Customer Service area on notice to expect these calls. I will contact you closer to the transfer dat about the timing of the shipment of the loan files.

I would like to thank you and your staff for the cooperation that has been extended in regards to this transfer. If you have any questions please contact me.

Mortgage Servicing Purchase and Sale Agreement

This is a Mortgage Servicing Purchase and Sale Agreement (referred to herein as "Agreement") made and entered into as of February 8, 1989.

WHEREAS, Purchaser and Seller have entered into a Letter of Intent dated February 2, 1989 ("Letter") pursuant to which Seller agreed to sell to Purchaser the right to service approximately $53,000,000 of loans secured by first mortgages on residential real estate ("Loans") all on the terms and conditions described herein and in the Letter; and

WHEREAS, the Loans are owned _____ or by investors in their respective securities representing interest in the Loans; and

WHEREAS, Buyer and Seller wish to state more fully the terms and conditions of the sale and transfer of the Servicing.

NOW, THEREFORE, in consideration of premises and the mutual covenants contained herein and in the same Letter, Purchaser and Seller agree as follows:

ARTICLE I

DEFINITIONS

As used herein, the following terms shall mean:

1.1   "Business Day": Any day other than (a) a Saturday or Sunday, or (b) a day on which banking institutions in the State of Illinois are authorized or obligated by law or by executive order to be closed.

1.2   "Delinquent Mortgage": A Mortgage which is sixty (60) days or more past due.

1.3   "FHLMC": Federal Home Loan Mortgage Corporation.

1.4   "FNMA": Federal National Mortgage Association.

1.16   "Servicer": The Seller is sometimes referred to herein as the Servicer.

1.17   "Servicing": All of Seller's rights, title, and interest and to the servicing of Mortgages and the Loans which are sold pursuant to this Agreement.

1.18   "Servicing Agreements": The mortgage loan servicing agreements pursuant to which Seller is currently servicing the Mortgages.

1.19   "Total Servicing Fee": For each loan, the excess of any amounts with respect to interest received on a Loan by the Seller over any amounts with respect to interest or guaranty fees the Seller remits to FHLMC, FNMA or other investors or security holders.

1.20   "Transfer Date": The day servicing responsibilities on a particular Loan are actually transferred to Purchaser. This will be a day or days mutually agreed to in writing by Seller and Purchaser, not later than March 3, 1989 for Loans owned by Federal National Mortgage Association.

ARTICLE 2

SALE AND TRANSFER OF SERVICING

2.1   Sale of Rights to Servicing. Subject to, and upon, the terms and conditions of this Agreement, Seller as of the Sale Date does hereby sell, transfer, assign and deliver to Purchaser all right, title and interest in and to (a) the Servicing, including, without limitation, the right to receive servicing fees on the Loans and (b) Related Escrow Accounts.

2.2   Transfer Date. On the Transfer Date:

    (a)   Purchase shall assume all servicing responsibilities related to, and Seller shall cease all servicing responsibilities related to, the Loans; and

    (b)   Seller shall transfer to Purchaser the rights to all accrued receivables relating to servicing the Loans including but not limited to accrued late charge balances.

2.3   Examination of Mortgage Documents. Purchaser shall have the right to conduct, prior to the Transfer Date, a review of the Loan documents and of Seller's books, records and accounts with respect to the Loans to verify the accuracy of the information provided by Seller. If Purchaser's examination reveals that any information provided by Seller or any of the representations contained herein concerning a Loan is not true and accurate, Seller shall have five (5) Business Days following notice, not later than February 24, 1989 from Purchaser to cure all defects in the Loan or purchase such Loan as provided in Paragraph 9.3 hereof. Seller shall provide Purchaser, within three (3) Business Days after request, with all information reasonably requested of Seller with respect to the Loans and the Servicing in order to permit Purchaser to fully underwrite its investment in the Servicing.

2.4   Obligations of Seller. Seller covenants and agrees, from the Sale Date until the Transfer Date, the Seller shall pay, perform and discharge all of the liabilities and obligations relating to ownership of the Servicing and all the rights, obligations and duties with respect to the Related Escrow Accounts until the transfer of such items on the Transfer Date.

2.5   Undertaking by Purchaser. Purchaser covenants and agrees, upon acceptance of the assignment of the Servicing and Related Escrow Accounts, to service the same in accordance with the terms and conditions of the Servicing Agreements. Purchaser shall not be responsible for the acts or omission of Seller or Prior Services, nor for any other obligations or liabilities of Seller or Prior Servicers whatsoever, except those obligations or liabilities specifically set forth in the Servicing Agreements accruing on or after the Transfer Date.

2.6   Approval to Transfer Servicing.

(a)   Seller shall obtain all FHLMC and FNMA approvals and any other approvals necessary to transfer the Servicing from Seller to Purchaser. Seller shall prepare the requests for approval in a manner to secure from FHLMC and FNMA a prompt written determination of the acceptability of the transfer of Servicing. Seller must obtain any necessary approvals on or before the Transfer Date.

(b)   On or before the Transfer Date, Seller shall prepare and execute all forms, documents, and other information requested by FHLMC,

FNMA or others in connections with the transfer of the Servicing
Blanket assignments may be used where permitted.

2.7   Cooperation. To the extent possible, the parties hereto shall cooperated
with and assist each other, as requested, to assure the orderly transfer of
the Servicing from Seller to Purchaser under this Agreement and in
connection therewith shall execute and deliver all such documents and
instruments as shall be necessary and appropriate in the furtherance
thereof. Each party shall designate an employee to coordinate and be
responsible for orderly transfer of the Servicing.

ARTICLE 3

PURCHASE PRICE

3.1   Purchase Price. In full consideration for the sale of the Servicing as
specified in Article 1 hereof, and upon the terms and conditions of this
Agreement Purchaser shall pay to Seller the purchase price (the
"Purchase Price") computed as follows:

   (a)   1,95% (the "Purchase Price Percentage") of the aggregate unpaid
principal balance of all Loans as of the respective Transfer Dates,
excluding the unpaid principal balances of Delinquent Mortgage
and Foreclosure Mortgages; and

   (b)   It is understood and agreed that if the principal balance of any
of the Loans used in computing the amount of the Purchase Price
shall be found, within ninety (90) days after payment of such
amount, to be incorrectly computed, the Purchase Price shall be
promptly and appropriately adjusted on the basis of the Purchase
Price Percentage, and payment shall be promptly made by the
appropriate party.

3.2   Payment. The Purchase Price shall be paid as follows:

   (a)   5% of the estimated final Purchase Price ($51,675.00) was paid
upon execution of the Letter, and Seller acknowledge receipt of
that amount.

(b)   Within five (5) days after Sale Date, Purchaser shall pay
        Seller an amount equal to 75% of the estimated final Purchase
        Price ($775,125.00).

(c)   Within five (5) days after each Transfer Date, Purchaser shall
        pay Seller the remainder of the Purchase Price for the Loans
        transferred on that Transfer Date.

(d)   The requirement of this paragraph concerning payment shall not
        apply if the transfer of servicing is not completed on the Transfer
        Dates. In the event Seller has not complied with all provisions
        hereof on or before the Transfer Dates with respect to a Loan,
        Purchaser's obligation to pay the Purchase Price for such Loan
        shall be postponed until all required performance and all reasonably
        requested information is provided by Seller and the transfer of
        Servicing on that Loan is completed.

3.3.   Other Costs.

(a)   Seller shall bear the entire cost of securing any approvals for the
        transfer of Servicing from Seller to Purchaser, including all transfer
        fees due to FHLMC or FNMA.

(b)   Seller shall comply, at its sole cost and expense, with Purchaser's
        reasonable requirements pertaining to the processing and shipping
        of loan files, insurance files, tax records and collection records
        which are reasonably necessary to service the Loans.

(c)   On or prior to the Transfer Date, Seller shall assign to Purchaser,
        by appropriate endorsements and assignments, all of Seller's rights,
        title and interest in and to the Servicing Agreements, and the
        promissory notes and Loans as required by FHLMC or FNMA or as
        reasonably requested by Purchaser. Seller shall execute or cause
        to be executed assignments of promissory notes and assignments
        for each Mortgage as Purchaser may reasonably request. Seller
        shall prepare and record the assignments at its sole cost and
        expense. Seller shall also prepare assignments of Loans from
        Purchaser to FHLMC or FNMA, if required by FHLMC or FNMA.

3.4   Refund of Purchase Price. In the event all required approvals are not obtained don or before the Transfer Date, or if Seller has not complied with the requirements of the Agreement on or before the Transfer Date, at Purchaser's option and upon Purchaser's request, Seller shall refund to Purchaser any amounts paid pursuant to Paragraph 3.2 hereof with interest on the amount refunded hereunder at a rate equal to five percent (5%) plus the average Fed Funds rate for the period between the Sale Date and the date of the refund and Purchaser shall reassign to Seller all right, title and interest in and to the Servicing and related Escrow Accounts. Section 3.4 refers to the non-compliance or non-performance solely on behalf of the company.

ARTICLE 4

GENERAL REPRESENTATIONS AND WARRANTIES OF SELLER

As an inducement to Purchaser to enter into this Agreement, Seller represent and warrants as follows, it being acknowledged that each such representation and warranty relates to material matters upon which Purchaser relied, and it being understood that each such representation and warranty is made to the Purchaser as of the Sale Date and shall be deemed remade as of the Transfer Date:

4.1   Due Incorporation and Good Standing. Seller and all Prior Servicer were Corporations duly organized, validly existing and in good standing under the laws of their states of incorporation during the time of their activities with respect to the Mortgages and the Servicing. Seller and all Prior Servicers were properly licensed and qualified to transact business in all appropriate jurisdictions to conduct all activities performed with respect to origination and servicing of the Loans.

4.2   Authority and Capacity. Seller has all requisite Corporate power, authority and capacity to enter into this Agreement and to perform the obligations required of it hereunder. The execution and delivery of this Agreement and the consummation of the transactions contemplated hereby, have each been duly and validly authorized by all necessary corporate action. This Agreement constitutes the valid and legally binding agreement of Seller enforceable in accordance with its terms, and no offset, counterclaim or defense exists to the full performance of this Agreement.

4.3   Effective Agreement. The execution, delivery and performance of this Agreement by Seller, its compliance with the terms hereof and the consummation of the transactions contemplated (assuming receipt of the various consents required pursuant to this Agreement) will not violate, conflict with, result in a breach of, constitute a default under, be prohibited by or require any additional approval under its certificate of incorporation, bylaws, or any instrument or agreement to which it is a party or by which it is bound or which affects the Servicing, or any state or federal law, rule or regulation or any judicial or administrative decree, order, ruling or regulation applicable to it or to the Servicing.

4.4   Compliance with Contracts and Regulations. Seller and Prior Servicers have complied with all material obligations under all contracts to which they were parties, and with all applicable federal, state and local laws and regulations, with respect to and which might affect any of the Servicing and assets being purchased by Purchaser hereunder. The laws and regulations which Seller has complied with include but are not limited to all applicable FHLMC and FNMA requirements. Seller has done and shall do no act or thing which may adversely affect the Servicing. Prior Servicers have complied with all applicable FHLMC and FNMA requirements and have done no act or thing which may adversely affect the Servicing.

4.5   Filing of Reports. For each Loan, Seller or Prior Servicers have file dor Seller shall file through the Transfer Date, all required reports including but not limited to investor reports to FHLMC and FNMA, reports to all governmental agencies having jurisidiction over the Servicing and all appropriate private mortgage insurance companies.

4.6   Title to the Servicing and Related Escrow Account. Seller is the lawful owner of the Servicing, is custodian of the Related Escrow Accounts and has the sole right and authority to transfer the Servicing and the Related Escrow Accounts as contemplated hereby. The transfer, assignment and delivery of the Servicing and of the Related Escrow Accounts in accordance with the terms and conditions of this Agreement shall vest in Purchaser all rights as servicer free and clear of any and all claims, charges, defenses, offsets and encumbrances of any kind or nature whatsoever, including but not limited to those of Seller or Prior Servicers.

4.7   Related Escrow Accounts. All Related Escrow Accounts are being maintained in accordance with applicable law and in accordance with Servicing Agreements and the terms of the Mortgages related thereto.

Except as to payments which are past due under the Loans, all escrow balances required by the Loans and paid to Seller for the account of the Mortgagors are on deposit in the appropriate escrow/impound accounts.

4.8   Schedule of Prior Servicers. All Prior Servicers are enumerated in Exhibit B attached hereto.

4.9   Litigation; Compliance with Laws. There is no litigation, proceeding or governmental investigation pending, or and order, injunction or decree outstanding which might materially affect any of the Mortgages, Loans or the Servicing, except for Foreclosure Mortgages. Additionally, there is no litigation, proceeding or governmental investigation existing or pending or to the knowledge of Seller threatened, or any order, injunction or decree outstanding against or relating to Seller, a Prior Servicer or the Servicing, which could have a material adverse effect upon the Servicing or the other assets being purchased by Purchaser hereunder, no does Seller know of any basis for any such litigation, proceeding, or governmental investigation. Seller or Prior Servicer has not violated any applicable law, regulation, ordinance, order, injunction or decree, or any other requirement of any governmental body or court, which may materially affect any of the Mortgages, the Loans or the Servicing.

4.10   Statements Made. No representation, warranty or written Statement made by Seller in this Agreement, the Letter or in any schedule, written statement or certificate furnished to Purchaser in connection with the transactions contemplated hereby contains or will contain any untrue statement of a material fact or omits or will omit to stat a material fact necessary to make the statements contained herein or therein not misleading.

4.11   No Accrued Liabilities. There are no accrued liabilities of Seller with respect to the Mortgages, the Loans or the Servicing or circumstances under which such accrued liabilities will arise against Purchaser as successor to the Servicing, with respect to occurrences prior to the Transfer Date.

4.12   FHLMC and FNMA Requirements. Seller and Prior Servicers have performed all obligations to be performed under FHLMC and FNMA requirements, and no event has occurred and is continuing which, but for the passage of time or the giving of notice or both, would constitute an event of default thereunder. Seller and Prior Servicers have serviced the

Loan and have kept and maintained complete and accurate books and records in connection therewith, all in accordance with FHLMC and FNMA requirements.

4.13   Compliance with insurance Contracts. Seller and Prior Servicers have complied with all obligations under all applicable insurance contracts, including private mortgage insurance, with respect to, and which might affect, any of the Servicing. Seller and Prior Servicers have not taken any action or failed to take any action which might cause the cancellation of or otherwise adversely affect any of the insurance policies on a Loan.

4.14   Private Mortgage Insurance ("PMI")

(a)   Each Mortgage which is represented by Seller to have private mortgage insurance is insured in the amounts represented, the Seller shall provide a list to the Purchaser that specifies all loans that have PMI.

(b)   At Purchaser's option, any Loan that is not properly insured as specified in Paragraph 4.14 (a) shall be repurchased by Seller within ten (10) Business Days after written demand for repurchase by Purchaser. Such Loans which Purchaser requests to be repurchased by Seller at the price computed under Section 9.3. In addition to such purchase price, Seller shall also pay any advances made by Purchaser.

(c)   As to each private mortgage insurance certificate, Seller further warrants that it has complied with applicable provisions of federal statutes and regulations and applicable PMI requirements, the insurance is in full force and effect with respect to each Mortgage, and no event or condition exists which can result in a revocation of any such insurance of which Seller is aware or of which Seller should be aware.

(d)   Any other provision of this Agreement to the contrary notwith-standing, if a Loan transferred and/or assigned to Purchaser pursuant to this Agreement fails to have, or subsequently loses, its PMI reason of any act or omission occurring prior to the Transfer Date then, upon receipt of written notice from Purchaser Seller shall have thirty (30) Business Days to remedy the problem causing loss of insurance. If Seller is unable within thirty (30) Business Days after receipt of notice to remedy the problem, then Seller shall repurchase such Mortgage within ten (10) Business Days after receipt of such written notice at the price computed according to Section 9.3.

4.15 Title Insurance. A title policy currently in effect running to the benefit of the owner of the Loan has been issued for each Loan insuring that the Mortgage relating thereto is valid first lien on the property therein described, which has not been modified, and that the mortgaged property is free and clear of all encumbrances and liens having priority over the first lien of the mortgage or deed of trust, except for liens for real estate taxes and specials assessments not yet due and payable and except for easements and restrictions of record identified in title policy.

4.16 Non Recourse Servicing. All Loans are serviced without recourse to the Servicer.

ARTICLE 5

REPRESENTATIONS AND WARRANTS AS TO LOANS

As further inducement to Purchaser to enter this Sale Agreement, Seller represent and warrants, to the best of its knowledge, to Purchaser as of the Sale Date and the Transfer Date, with respect to each Loan that:

5.1 Mortgage Documents. The Mortgage documents are genuine, duly executed by a borrower of legal capacity, and all insertions in any loan document are correct.

5.2 Unpaid Balance. All of the information for each loan reflection on Exhibit A is correct as of the date of Exhibit A and there are no defenses, setoffs or counterclaims against the Loan.

5.3 Security Interest. The security interest granted by the borrower in the property described in the Mortgage is a valid first lien on the property described therein.

5.4   Validity of Note. There is nothing which would impair the validity or value of the promissory note, the Mortgage/Dead of trust, any other loan document or the collateral.

5.5   Compliance with Law. The Mortgage and Loan Transaction and the origination and servicing thereof, complies in all material respects with each of the federal or state laws or regulations which pertain to the origination, closing and servicing of the Mortgage.

5.6   Payment of Taxes, Insurance Premiums, Etc. All applicable taxes, special assessments, ground rents, flood insurance premiums and mortgage insurance premiums have been paid when due by Mortgagor, Seller or Prior Servicer.

5.7   Effective Insurance. All required insurance policies, including hazard, flood, and PMI, remain in full force and effect, and such policies are with companies approved by FHLMC and FNMA.

5.8   Tax Identifications. All tax identifications and property descriptions and legally sufficient. Tax segregation, where required, has been completed.

5.9   Payoff Statements. All payoff and assumption statements with respect to each Loan provided by Seller to Mortgagors or their agents were complete and accurate.

5.10   Interest on Escrows. Seller has paid to the mortgagor all interest required to be paid on any escrow/impound account through the Transfer Date. Evidence of such payment shall be provided to Purchaser upon request.

ARTICLE 6

COVENANTS

6.1   Notice to Mortgagors. Seller shall, at Seller's expense, mail to the Mortgagor of each Loan a letter advising the Mortgagor of the transfer of Servicing to Purchaser no later than fifteen (15) days prior to the Transfer Date; provided, however, the content and format of the letter shall have the prior written approval of Purchaser, which consent shall not be unreasonably withheld.

6.2   Notice of Mortgage Insurers. Seller shall, at Seller's expense, notify all relevant private mortgage insurance companies no later than five (5) Business days prior to the Transfer Date by certified mail, return receipt requested, that all insurance premium billings for the Loans must thereafter be sent to Purchaser. Seller shall provide Purchaser with a copy of the certificate receipt. Additionally, Seller shall, prior to the Transfer Date, obtain the written consent of any private mortgage insurance companies which have the contractual right to approve transfer of the Servicing.

6.3   Notice to Taxing Authorities and Insurance Companies. On or before the Transfer Date, unless otherwise agreed by the parties, Seller shall, at Seller's expense, notify applicable taxing authorities and insurance companies and/or agent, by certified mail of the assignment of the Servicing and instructions to deliver all notices, tax bills and insurance statements, as the case may be, to Purchaser from and after the Transfer Date.

6.4   Delivery of Loan Documents. Seller shall provide Purchaser on or prior to the Transfer Date the loan documentation described in Exhibit D.

6.5   Delivery of Servicing Records. Seller shall forward to Purchaser on or prior to the Transfer Date all servicing records in Seller's possession relating to each Mortgage including the information enumerated in Exhibit C.

6.6   Escrow/Impound Balances. Seller shall provide Purchaser on the Transfer Date with immediately available funds in the amount of the net escrow and suspense balances and all loss draft balances associated with the Loans, in a manner reasonably acceptable to Purchaser. Seller shall provide Purchaser with an accounting statement of escrow and suspense balances and loss draft balances sufficient to enable Purchaser to reconcile the amount of such payment with the accounts of the Loans.

6.7   Payoffs and Assumptions. Seller shall provide to Purchaser on the Transfer Date copies of all assumption and payoff statements generated by Seller on the Mortgages within the preceding sixty (60) days. Seller shall notify Purchaser prior to the Transfer Date of all payoffs and assumptions in process.

6.8   Mortgage Payments Received Prior to Transfer Date. Prior to the Transfer Date, all payments received by Seller on each Mortgage shall be properly applied by Seller to the account of the particular Mortgagor.

6.9   Mortgage Payments Received After Transfer Date. The amount of any Mortgage payments received by Seller after the Transfer Date shall be paid to Purchaser within two (2) Business Days after receipt by Seller, properly endorsed by Seller to Purchaser. Seller shall notify Purchaser of the particulars of the payment, which notification shall be satisfied if Seller forwards with its payment sufficient information to permit appropriate processing of the payment by Purchaser. Seller shall assume full responsibility for the necessary and appropriate legal application of Mortgage payments received by it after the transfer Date with respect to Loans then in foreclosure or bankruptcy; provided, for purposes of this Agreement, necessary and appropriate legal application of such Mortgage payments shall include endorsement of a Mortgage payment shall include endorsement of a Mortgage payment to Purchaser with the particulars of the payment such as the account number, dollar amount, date received any special mortgagor application instructions.

6.10   Misapplied Payments. Misapplied payments shall be processed as follows:

     (a)   Both parties shall cooperate in correcting misapplication errors.

     (b)   The party receiving notice of a misapplied payment occurring prior to the Transfer Date and discovered after the Transfer Date shall immediately notify the other party.

     (c)   If a misapplied payment, that occurred prior to the Transfer Date cannot be identified by either party and said misapplied payment has resulted in a shortage in a Mortgage account, Seller shall be liable for the amount of such shortage. Seller shall reimburse Purchaser for the amount of such shortage within thirty (30) days after receipt of written demand therefor from Purchaser.

     (d)   If a misapplied payment has created an improper Purchase Price as the result of an inaccurate outstanding principal balance, a check shall be issued to the party shorted by the improper payment application within ten (10) Business Days after notice thereof by the other party.

(e) Any check issued under the provisions of this Paragraph 6.10 shall be accompanied by a statement indicating the purpose of the check,

  the Mortgagor and property address involved, and the corresponding Seller/Purchaser account number.

6.11 Accomplishment of Transfer. Seller and Purchaser shall each use their best efforts to accomplish transfer of the Servicing from Seller to Purchaser as contemplated hereunder in accordance with standards for servicing transfers approved by the Mortgage Bankers Association of America.

6.12 Payment of Taxes and Insurance. Before the Transfer Date, Seller will pay all insurance premiums payable from escrow accounts, including hazard and PMI policy premiums, which are due prior to or within thirty (30) days after the Transfer Date. Before the Transfer Date, Seller will pay all taxes payable from the escrow accounts on all loans which taxes are due prior to or within ten (10) days after the Transfer Date.

6.13 Missing Payments. Seller agrees to indemnify and remit to Purchaser any missing escrow funds or unremitted principal and interest which preceded the transfer of Servicing.

6.14 Tax Contracts. Seller agrees to assign the Purchaser "lifetime" tax contracts with a reputable tax service company on each Loan and to notify said tax service company of the transfer of the Servicing. In the event no "lifetime" tax contracts are presently in force which are assignable to Purchaser, buyer agrees to purchase a tax contract for each Loan in this category. The Purchaser is solely responsible for the cost of the tax contracts.

6.15 Annual Report to Mortgagors. Seller agrees o provide each Mortgagor whose Loan Servicing is transferred under this agreement with an annual year-end sttement in accordance with FHLMC and FNMA regulations or as reasonably requested by Purchaser. Such statement shall reflect the status of the Loan up to the Transfer Date. Purchaser shall have no responsibility for providing this information for the period of time the Loan was serviced by the Seller. Seller agrees to mail this information to the mortgagor on or after January 1, 1990 along with a 1099 (Interest on Escrow), if applicable.

6.16 Servicing Delinquent Mortgages and Foreclosure Mortgages. Seller shall continue to Service any Foreclosure Mortgage on the Sale Date and the Servicing on those Loans shall not be transferred to Purchaser. Seller shall reimburse Purchaser for Purchaser's costs incurred in foreclosing Loans which are transferred to Purchaser and are Foreclosure Mortgages on the Transfer Date. Costs to be reimburse include, but are not limited to, Purchaser's expense for the following:

(a) Principal and interest not paid by PMI.

(b) Costs of foreclosure including attorneys' fees and court costs.

(c) Recovery of advances for principal and interest, escrow or foreclosure costs and PMI funds advanced while the property is designated REO.

(d) Any amounts resulting from sale of property if a Loan becomes Real Estate Owned ("REO") including all costs of sale and closing.

(e) Any amounts Seller is required to pay to FHLMC, FNMA or investors to repurchase the Loan from any mortgage pool.

Seller shall reimburse Purchaser for these costs within ten (10) days after receipt of the Purchaser's request for reimbursement.

ARTICLE 7

INTERIM SERVICING AGREEMENT

7.1 Servicing of Mortgages. In the event the Transfer Date with respect to the Servicing or any portion thereof occurs later than the Sale Date, Seller shall service the Loans relating thereto on behalf of Purchaser during that time period (the "Interim Period") as provided herein. In the event the Transfer Date with respect to the Servicing occurs simultaneously with the Sale Date, the provision of this Article 7 shall be null and void as to those Loans already transferred.

7.2   Assumption of Duties; Standard of Care. Seller agrees that, throughout the Interim Period, it shall observe and perform all warranties, representations, covenants and agreements with respect to the Loans and the Servicing required to be observed and performed by Seller as servicer under the Servicing Agreements. Seller shall at all times service the Loans in accordance with all applicable statutes, regulations, contractual provisions, and in accordance with prudent mortgage banking practices. It is understood and agreed that the Seller shall exercise the same standard care it exercises in the servicing of mortgages for its own account. Among the services to be provided by Seller during the Interim Period are:

     (a)   Receive and process Mortgagor's payments;

     (b)   Make all escrow disbursements in its own name;

     (c)   Handle all collection efforts with Mortgagor in its own name;

     (d)   Provide and handle insurer delinquency notices in its own name;

     (e)   Prepare and forward all remittances due for the months during the Interim Period;

     (f)   Prepare and submit all cut-off reports for the months of the Interim Period.

7.3   Servicing Fee. As consideration for servicing the Mortgages during the Interim Period, Seller shall receive for each Loan for each month the Loan is serviced by Seller a servicing fee equal to (1) $5.00 plus (ii) 20% times the difference, if any, between (a) the total Servicing Fee for such month and (b) $5.00. This servicing fee is payable monthly out of the interest actually received on the related Loan. Seller shall promptly remit to Purchaser on the day remittances are due to the FHLMC, FNMA or the investors for each month during the Interim Period, the Total Servicing Fee for each Loan less the servicing fee retained by Seller under this Section 7.3. Servicing fees for partial months shall be ported based on the actual number of days in the month. Section 7.3 will be enforceable only if the projected Transfer Date is not met or the Seller fails to comply or fails to perform its duties as servicer as defined by FNMA guidelines. Seller shall receive all service fees and late charges prior to March 3, 1989.

7.4   Reporting by Seller. Servicer shall provide to Purchaser by the tenth (10th) day of each month a report which shall set forth the prior month for each Mortgage, subtotaled by pool (as applicable): (a) collections of principal and interest; (b) the remaining principal balance; (c) the mortgage interest rate; (d) the servicing fee retained by Servicer; and (e) such other information as may be reasonably requested in writing by Purchaser with reasonable notice.

7.5   Notifications. If required by FHLMC or FNMA, Servicer shall upon execution of this Agreement notify FHLMC and FNMA in writing that Servicer shall service the Loans during the Interim Period. Purchaser hereby authorizes FHLMC and FNMA to communicate with, issue instructions to, accept directives from and otherwise deal with Seller in the manner and to the extent permitted pursuant to applicable rules and regulations.

7.6   Fees and Advances. During the Interim Period, Servicer shall be responsible for payment of all guarantee fees to FHLMC and FNMA and for all advances required by FHLMC and FNMA in the form of payments to security holders. Servicer shall also be responsible for any advances required for the various Mortgage escrow/impound accounts, and shall be responsible for prompt payment of all mortgage insurance premiums, hazard insurance premiums and real estate taxes during the Interim Period. If adequate funds are not held in escrow to pay, when due, real estate taxes or insurance premiums on nay property securing a Loan, Servicer shall advance sufficient funds to cover any such deficiency in a manner to ensure timely payment of such taxes or insurance premiums.

7.7   Escrows. During the Interim Period, Servicer shall maintain all escrow/impound accounts.

7.8   After Transfer Date. Following the Transfer Date, Servicer shall endorse and forward to Purchaser all funds received by Servicer related to the Loans as provided in Section 6.9.

7.9   FHLMC or FNMA Suspension. Should Seller at any time during the Interim Period have its right to service for FHLMC or FNMA temporarily or permanently suspended by FHLMC or FNMA, then Purchaser shall have the following options:

       (a)   Purchaser may immediately terminate this Agreement, at which time Seller shall be required to refund to Purchaser all portions of the Purchase Price which have been previously paid by Purchaser plus interest as provided for in Section 3.4; or

(b) Immediately accelerate performance of the provisions of this Agreement to required immediate transfer of the Servicing and payment of the Purchase Price, provided all necessary approvals can be obtained.

7.10 Termination Upon Transfer. The provisions of this Article 7 shall terminate with respect to the Servicing or portion thereof transferred on the Transfer Date.

7.11 Maintenance of Books and Records. Seller shall keep full and complete records pertaining to (i) each Mortgage and the collections made thereon, and (ii) each check paid as distribution of principal interest collected, to appropriate parties (investors, security holders, etc.) which records are and shall be the property of Purchaser. During the Interim Period, Purchaser or its representative, upon three (3) Business Days' written notice to Seller may examine any and all at such time or times as it may elect during the Seller's regular business hours.

7.12 Transfer of Books and Records. All books, records, documents, files, and other information and data in Seller's possession pertaining to the Loans (Collectively "Date") are and shall at all times remain the property of Purchaser. Upon termination of the Interim Period, Servicer shall be obligated, immediately, at its own expense, to transfer in an orderly manner and in accordance with Purchaser's transfer instructions, to Purchaser or a designee of Purchaser the Data held by it. Seller shall also, upon termination of the Interim Period, account for and turn over to Purchaser all funds collected and held by it with respect to each loan.

7.13 Insurance. In addition to insurance required to be maintained by Seller under the Servicing Agreements, Seller shall also at its own expense maintain at all times during the Interim Period policies of fidelity, theft, forgery and errors and omissions insurance. Such policies shall be responsible amounts with acceptable standard coverages in accordance with industry standards.

7.14 Relationship of Parties. Nothing herein contained shall be deemed or construed to create a partnership or joint venture between the parties.

The duties and responsibilities of the Seller shall be rendered by the Seller as an independent contractor and not as an agent of Purchaser. The Seller shall have full control of all of its acts, doings, proceedings, relating to or requisite in connection with the discharge of its duties and responsibilities under this Agreement.

ARTICLE 8

CONDITIONS PRECEDENT T OBLIGATIONS OF PURCHASER

This obligations of Purchaser under this Agreement are subject to the satisfaction of the following conditions:

8.1   Schedule of Servicing. On or prior to the Sale Date, Purchaser shall have received from Seller the Mortgage Loan Schedule with respect to each Loan and Related Escrow Account. By signing this Agreement, Seller warrants that such information is true and correct.

8.2   Documentation to be Delivered. On or prior to the Transfer Date, Purchaser shall have received the documentation described in Exhibit B and the information described in Exhibit A. The books, records and accounts of Seller with respect to the Loans being transferred shall be in order according to all applicable regulations.

8.3   Correctness of Representations and Warranties. The representations and warranties made by Seller in this Agreement are true and correct, to the best of its knowledge, and shall continue to be true and correct on the Sale Date and Transfer Date.

8.4   Compliance with Conditions. All of the terms, covenants and conditions of this Agreement required to be complied with and performed by Seller at or prior to the Transfer Date shall have been duly complied with and performed.

8.5   Corporate Certificate. On or prior to the Sale Date, Purchaser shall have received from Seller a certified copy of its corporate resolution approving the execution and delivery of this Agreement and the consummation of the transactions contemplated hereby and thereby, together with such other certificates of incumbency and other evidences of corporate authority as Purchaser or its counsel any reasonably request.

ARTICLE 9

MISCELLANEOUS

9.1 Costs and Expenses. Costs and expenses incurred in connection with the transactions contemplated hereby shall be paid as follows except as otherwise provided in this Agreement.

    (a) Seller shall pay all the costs associated with the transfer of the Servicing to Purchaser, including without limitation, any recording or filing fees, FHLMC and FNMA transfer fees, any fees related to obtaining any required approvals, custodian charges, and all other costs associated with the preparation and filing of Mortgage assignments or any other transfer documents; and

    (b) Except as provided in (a) above, Purchaser shall pay the expenses incurred by it or its affiliates in connection with the transactions contemplated hereby whether or not the transactions hereby contemplated shall be consummated.

9.2 Indemnification by Seller. Seller shall indemnify and hold Purchaser harmless from and shall reimburse Purchaser for any losses, damages, deficiencies or expenses of any nature (including attorneys' fees) incurred by Purchaser before or after the Transfer Date which:

    (a) Result from any knowing or intentional misrepresentation made by Seller in this Agreement, or any inaccurate information or omission in any schedule, statement or certificate furnished by Seller pursuant to this Agreement;

    (b) Result form any breach of a representation or warranty by Seller, or the non-fulfillment of any covenant or condition of Seller contained in this Agreement, or in any schedule, statement or certificate furnished by Seller pursuant to this Agreement;

(c)   Result form any defect in any Loans existing as of the Transfer Date (including those defects subsequently discovered), or as a result of any act or mission of Seller prior thereto;

(d)   Result from errors in originating or servicing any of the Loans (e.g., misquoted payoffs, misapplied payments, failure to file timely notice of default or failure to pay taxes or other charges including penalties and interest) prior to the Transfer Date or as a result of Seller's act or omission prior thereto. Such errors may include improper action or failure to act when required to do so; or

(e)   Result from Seller's failure to permit Purchaser to examine records, failure to comply with the provisions hereof or Purchaser's reasonable instructions regarding the transfer of Servicing or failure to provide accurate information requested by Purchaser regarding the Mortgages or the Servicing.

9.3   Repurchase of Servicing. In the event that any of the representations and warranties contained in Articles IV and V hereof were not accurate as of the date they were made or deemed to be made by Seller, or if Seller fails to comply with this Agreement, and as otherwise provided in this Agreement, Purchaser may demand that Seller remedy the inaccuracy or breach within thirty (30) days or such shorter period of time as may otherwise be provided in this Agreement. If Seller fails to remedy the inaccuracy or breach within this period, Purchaser may demand that Seller repurchase from Purchaser the right to service those Loans which are affected by the inaccurate representation and warranty or breach of covenant. Seller shall pay Purchaser a repurchase price equal to the Purchase Price Percentage paid for that Loan multiplied by the then outstanding principal balance for that Loan within fifteen (15) Business Days following receipt from Purchaser or written demand for repurchase pursuant hereto. In addition, Seller shall reimburse Purchaser for any advances or other costs and expenses made or incurred by Purchaser with respect to such Loan. Upon receipt by Purchaser of such repurchase price an reimbursement, Purchaser shall, within five (5) Business Days, forward to Seller all servicing records and all documents relating to such repurchased Loans, and reassign the Servicing on the repurchased Loans to Seller.

If FHLMC or FNMA requests Purchaser to purchase any Loans out of any pools because of some action or failure to act by the Seller or because of a breach of representation or warranty made to FHLMC or FNMA regarding the Loans, Seller shall promptly purchase such Loans out to the appropriate pools or repurchase such Loans from Purchaser and shall reimburse Purchaser fr any costs Purchaser incurred in handling the Loan. The seller will receive a copy of such notice within three (3) days of receipt by the Purchaser and shall have the right to respond and/or dispute the repurchase request of FNMA.

9.4   Supplementary Information.   From time to time prior to and after the Transfer Date, Seller shall furnish to Purchaser upon Purchaser's request such incidental information, which is reasonably available to Seller, supplementary to the information contained in the documents and schedules delivered pursuant hereto as Purchaser may request.

9.5   Access to Information.   Seller shall give to Purchaser and its counsel, accountants and other representatives, upon receipt of written notice not less than three (3) Business Days in advance, reasonable access during normal business hours throughout the period to the Transfer Date, to all of Seller's files, books and records relating to the Servicing and Related Escrow Accounts.

9.6   No Broker's Fees.   Each party hereto represents and warrants to the other that it has made no agreement to pay any agent, finder, or broker or any other representative, any fee or commission in the nature of a finder's or originator's fee arising out or in connection with the subject matter of this Agreement.   The Seller is responsible for all related broker fees to Cohane Rafferty.

9.7   Survival of Representations and Warranties.   Each party hereto covenants and agrees that the representations and warranties in this Agreement, and in any document delivered or to be delivered pursuant hereto, shall survive the Transfer Date.

9.8   Notices.   All notices, request, demands and other communications which are required or permitted to be given under this Sale Agreement shall be in writing and shall be deemed to have been duly given upon the delivery or mailing thereof, as the case may be sent by registered or certified mail, return receipt requested, postable prepaid to such address as Purchaser or Seller shall have specified in writing to the other.

9.9   Waivers.   Either Purchaser or Seller may, by written notice to the other:

(a)   Extend the time for the performance of any of the obligations or other transactions of the other:

(b)   Waive compliance with any of the terms, conditions or covenants required to be complied with by the other hereunder; and

(c)   Waive or modify performance of any of the obligations of the other hereunder.

The waiver by any party hereto of a breach of any provision of this Agreement shall not operate or be construed as a waiver of any other subsequent breach.

9.10   Entire Agreement; Amendment. This Agreement and the Letter constitute the entire agreement between the parties with respect to the sale of the Servicing and supersede all prior agreements with respect thereto. This Agreement may be amended and any provision hereof waived, but only in writing signed by the party against whom such amendment or waiver is sought to be enforced.

9.11   Binding Effect. This Agreement shall inure to the benefit of and be binding upon the parties hereto and their successors and assigns. Nothing in this Agreement, express or implied, is intended to confer on any person other than the parties hereto and their successors and assigns, any rights, obligations, remedies or liabilities.

9.12   Headings. Headings on the Articles and Paragraphs in this Agreement are for reference purposes only and shall not deemed to have any substantive effect.

9.13   Applicable Law. This Agreement shall be construed in accordance with the laws of the State of Illinois.

9.14   Incorporation of Exhibits. Exhibits A and B attached hereto shall be incorporated herein and shall be understood to be a part hereof as though included in the body of this Agreement.

IN WITNESS WHEREOF, each of the undersigned parties to this Agreement has caused this Agreement to be duly executed in its corporate name by one of its duly authorized officers, all as of the date first above written.

EXHIBIT A

SCHEDULE OF SERVICING INFORMATION

The following information with respect to each Mortgage in a format sufficient to enable its tape-to-tape transmission to Purchaser:

1.	Property Address	10.	Type of Loan
2.	Borrower's Name	11.	Term of Loan
3.	Mailing Address	12.	Maturity Date of Loan
4.	Loan Number	13.	Delinquency Pattern
5.	Interest Rate	14.	Date and Type of Last Activity
6.	Principal Balance	15.	Principal and Interest Constant
7.	Original Loan Amount	16.	Social Security Number of Mortgagor
8.	Interest Due	17.	Calendar year-to-year history, if required by Purchaser
9.	Next Due Date		

EXHIBIT B

ADDITIONAL INFORMATION/DOCUMENTATION TO BE DELIVERED

A.   The following information and documents with respect to each Mortgage:

1.   Twelve (12) month transaction history file, if available.

2.   For each Mortgage on which Seller escrows real estate taxes, tax payments receipt for past twelve(12) months which Seller has received, if available.

3.   Collection records and property address listing.

4.   All flood, hazard insurance and mortgage insurance policies.

5.   All available tax records including prior year receipts.

6.   All title policies and title opinions.

7.   Microfilm of case files to the extent available.

8.   Copy of letter to appropriate insurance companies/agents requesting endorsements to reflect transfer to Purchaser and new address.

9.   Other documents or information that Purchaser may reasonably request which are reasonably available.

10   Original Note and recorded Mortgage or certified copy of Mortgage.

11.   Copy of letter to the Seller's real estate tax service notifying them of the transfer of Servicing to Purchaser.

12.   Copy of credit package.

13.   Available information governing all pending items, including but not limited to partial releases, mortgage life or mortgage disability claims and litigation.

14.   FHLMC and FNMA reports for the past six months.

15.   A schedule listing each Loan which requires special handling with a
       statement of the reasons therefor and all relevant documentation attached.
       Loans which require special handling are Loans on which there are
       pending assumptions or payoffs, partial releases, building code violations,
       escrow repairs, hazard losses, pending lawsuits, property tax problems,
       title company problems and similar circumstances which could require
       special servicing.

April 3, 1989

Mr._____
_____
_____
_____
_____

Re: <u>The Sale of $53,572,263 FNMA Servicing Offering</u>

Agency Fee Due $25,509.59
(100% of total fee due Cohane Rafferty)

Please wire to:

_____
_____
_____
_____
_____
_____

Due Diligence and Transfer Procedures

Due Diligence Review Process

There are basically five ways in which a portfolio can be reviewed by a buyer during a due diligence.

1. **Verification of the Essential Details:** The buyer may request the detailed reports which represent your offering. That information would be verified to your monthly system reports. They will be reviewing you trial balance, pool reports and delinquency reports. They may ask to see recent FHLMC, FNMA, and GNMA HUD audits. If you have any open items I suggest you work on those to clear them up.

2. **Servicing Capability:** The buyer may request to speak to your managers or supervisors within the servicing area. During the interview they can establish the degree of knowledge and controls your management team has within the servicing departments. If they can establish a comfort level they can usually feel confident that the portfolio has been serviced correctly. They may ask to see departmental manuals.

3. **System Integrity:** The buyer may have you pull loan files at random and verify that the essential information about the loan has been entered into your system correctly. Note rate, original term, original balance etc. Usually this is a one percent (1%) selection of the loans being sold.

4. **File Documentations:** From a random loan selection the buyer will determine if all the essential information is included in the loan files and the conditions of the file for organization. They will check to determine if all information required by the investors underwriting guidelines are in the file. They will verify that all insurance and tax payments are current. They will also verify documentation of collection calls.

5. **Cash:** The buyer may ask to review T&I and P&I bank statements to tie back to the trial balance per investor group and to test minimum can requirements.

Transfer Fees

GNMA

GNMA charges a transfer fee of $250.00 per pool

FHLMC

Transfer fee s the larger of $500.00 or one basis point (0.01%) of the total dollar amount of FHLMC's participation in the unpaid principal balance of the mortgages being transferred.

FHLMC considers waiving fees for transfers of servicing that meet the following criteria's; 1) where one receiving the servicing is the originator of the mortgages; 2) where the transfer of servicing is between affiliates (e.g., a parent to a subsidiary); and 3) where the transfer is a result of a merger and acquisition or a regulatory takeover.

FNMA

FNMA has removed all transfer fees on sales of FNMA servicing between approved sellers. FNMA will not absorb the excess yield or yield differential in servicing transfers.

The FNMA servicing transfer fee had ranged from 5 to 10 basis points assessed on the amount of servicing being sold.

Transfer

Transfer Fees Per Agency

Flow Servicing: Unlike transfer of block servicing the buyer in flow is frequently designated as the initial servicer of record on newly originated loans.

Eliminate borrower confusion as to who will be servicing the loan.

Monthly arrangement must be made for loan delivery and setup, and typically will be handled manually instead of 1 tape-to-tape transfer.

FHLMC: Concurrent transfer of servicing Form 960 (revised 5/86) is used to notify FHLMC at the time of loan purchase that the seller of the loans will not be the servicer. It is from this 960 form that FHLMC sets up their accounting records to reflect the servicer of these loans.

FNMA: Assignment of servicing at point of sale.
FNMA MBS - Form 2011 - Notifies FNMA
FNMA Laser + SRS Form 1068 - Fixed Rate
Form 1069 - ARM
Forms 1068, 1069 - Block #6 - Seller ID #
Block #7 - Seller ID #

It is recommended that a seller first notify either agency of spending monthly servicing flowsale prior to loan and form submission.

FHLMC Transfer Procedures

Procedures for the transfer of FHLMC servicing are found in the Seller/Servicer's Guidelines in Chapter 63, Section II.

The seller initiates the transfer process by submitting a written request to FHLMC of the servicing transfer which contains the names of both parties, their FHLMC Seller/Servicer numbers, along with the total number of loans, unpaid principal balance and the effective date of transfer. All FHLMC servicing transfers occur on the 16th of each month. The seller will also complete Form 981 which will list all accounting groups in the transfer.

FHLMC charges a flat transfer fee of $500.00 for bulk servicing transfers. There is no transfer cost for concurrent transfers of FHLMC servicing.

After FHLMC receives the completed Form 981 and written request, FHLMC will send their approval letter, checklist, and three page triparty agreement. Once the triparty agreement is executed, the transfer can take place on the following 16th of the next month.

FHLMC

1. FHLMC PC program requires all loan payoff (prepayments) to be remitted within five (5) business days (or seven calendar days) of receipt.

2. Scheduled principal, if collected, and scheduled interest, whether collected or not, are remitted on the first Tuesday of the month following the month of collection.

3. FHLMC reporting cycle is scheduled on the 15th of every month.

4. Servicer holds the homeowner's payments for approximately 33 days on scheduled payments.

FNMA MBS

1. Principal and interest payments due on the first of the month.

2. Payment due the 18th of each month.

3. Remittance to investor on the 25th of each month.

4. Payment has one month interest in arrears:

    A. 55 day interest delay:
        1. 30 day interest in arrears and
        2. 25 day interest free period

5. FNMA collects its guaranty fee in a separate payment due at the time the account]report is submitted on the 7th day of the month.

Pre-Transfer Questionnaire

Loan Summary

Provide printouts showing servicing by the following categories. If printouts by category are not available or do not show number of loans, indicate loan count in the spaces provided below.

A. Mortgage Types
   1. First Mortgages _____   3. Third, etc. _____
   2. Second Mortgages _____

B. Loan Types
   1. FHA _____   8. Conv. Insured _____
   2. FHA 235 _____   9. Conv. Uninsured_____
   3. FHA 265 _____   10. Commercial _____
   4. FHA 246 _____   11. Multi-Family _____
   5. FHA 245 _____   12. Farm _____
   6. FHA 255 _____   13. Misc. _____
   7. VA _____

C. Program Type
   1. ARMS _____   9. Participants _____
   2. ARMS/RRMS _____   10. PUD _____
   3. GPMS _____   11. Housing Agency _____
   4. GEMS _____   12. Texas VLB _____
   5. Balloons _____   13. Employee Loans _____
   6. Call Options _____   14. Buydowns _____
   7. ARM Buydowns _____   15. Wraparounds _____
   8. _____

D. Property Types
   1. Single Family _____   6. Condo Unit _____
   2. Duplex _____   7. Income Product _____
   3. Triplex _____   8. Land Only _____
   4. Fourplex _____   9. Mobile Homes _____
   5. Multi-Family _____   10. _____

Data (Global)

A. Computer Information
1. Name of Service Bureau _____
2. What type of hardware is being used? _____
   Is the data ASCII or EBCDIC? _____
3. Can you use a tape-to-tape method? NO _____ YES _____
   Number of Tracks: 7 _____ 9 _____
4. What is format of loan number? _____
   Is check digit used? NO _____ YES _____ Type _____
   Is loan number ever changed? NO _____ YES _____
   WHEN? _____
5. Are subsystems used? NO _____ YES _____
   List all subsystems _____
6. Where is history file? _____
7. Are check numbers and payees shown on history? NO _____ YES _____

B. Computer Data
1. Are the following items on the computer and how valid is the data?

   a. Full Mortgagor Name(s) _____
   b. Property Address _____
   c. Property Zip Codes _____
   d. Mailing Address _____
   e. Contract Purchasers _____
   f. Legal Description _____
   g. Social Security Numbers _____
   h. Phone Numbers _____
      How do you cross-reference co-mortgagors with different last names?
      _____
      How do you cross-reference different loans on the same property?
      _____
      How do you identify the property type (single family, condo, duplex, etc.)
      on a loan? _____

Records

A. Files
1. How are mortgage files maintained?
   - ( ) a.   Microfilm   ( ) d. Hard Copy Side Tab
   - ( ) b.   Microfiche   ( ) e. _____
   - ( ) c.   Hard Copy Top Tab
2. Where are mortgage files maintained? _____
3. What type of filing system is used? _____
   - ( ) a.   Numeric by Loan Number ( ) c. Alphabetical
   - ( ) b.   Terminal Digit   ( ) d. _____
4. Are original documents in the loan file? NO _____ YES _____
   If no, where? _____
5. Do you maintain abstracts in the file? NO _____ YES _____
   If no, where? _____
6. Is general correspondence in the loan file? NO _____ YES _____
   If no, where? _____
   For what period of time is it maintained? _____
7. Are commercial loan files segregated from residential files?
   NO _____ YES _____

B. Type of Loan Records (Specify location of each.)
1. Current History _____
2. Prior Years Histories _____
3. Last Escrow Analysis _____
4. Hazard Insurance Policies _____
5. Optional Insurance Certificates/Policies _____
6. Tax Receipts _____
7. Collection Records _____
8. Collection Correspondence _____

GNMA Pools

A. What is your GNMA Issuer Number? _____
   GNMA I Pools in Transfer:
   1. Total Number of pools _____
   2. Number of loans _____
   3. Total Unpaid Principal Balances $_____
   4. Total number of security holders _____
   5. Number of IR's _____
   6. Number of CD's _____
   7. Number of GP's _____

   GNMA II Pools in Transfer:
   1. Total Number of pools _____
   2. Number of loans _____
   3. Total Unpaid Principal Balances $_____
   4. Total number of security holders _____
   5. Number of IR's _____
   6. Number of CD's _____
   7. Number of GP's _____

B. Are all the GNMA pools final certified? NO _____ YES _____
   If no, please provide a list of the pools that are not final certified.

C. What is the date of cutoff for GNMA pools? _____

D. Have the pools been audited by GNMA? NO _____ YES _____
   When? _____ Please attach copy.

E. Name and Address of Custodian(s) _____
   _____

F. Is there a tax ID number on each pool? NO _____ YES _____
   How is tax ID number formatted? _____

G. Are 1099's or 1041/K-1's used for interest income reporting to security
   holders? _____

H. Are Security Holders' names and addresses current? NO _____ YES _____

I. What is the format for Security Holders' name and address ?
   _____ Is it free form input? NO _____ YES _____

J. Are Security Holder transfer transactions entered manually or by bank tape method? _____

K. Do you have a Security Register in pool number order? NO ____ YES ___

L. Do you flag Security Holders to differentiate a social security number
    (individual) from a tax identification number (corporation)? NO __ YES __
M. How may manual checks are produced monthly? _____

N. Have mortgage been reconciled to security balances?
    NO ____ YES ____ When? _____
    Reconciled Monthly? NO ____ YES ____

O. Has minimum P&I been reconciled? NO ____ YES ____ How many? ____
    Amount to be recaptured? $_____

P. Do you have any differences between rial balance and 1710A Section I?
    NO ____ YES ____

Q. Do you have any pools where you are waiting on liquidations to recapture
    funds overremitted to the Security Holder? NO _____ YES ____ How
    many? _____ Amount to be recaptured? $_____

R. At what stage of the foreclosure do you remove the principal balance from
    the GNMA Pool and pass the funds to the Security Holders? _____
    _____

S. P&I advances as of the 15th of previous month $_____

FNMA Pools

A. What is your FNMA seller servicer number? _____

B. 1. Total number of pools in transfer _____
        MBS _____ MRS _____
    2. Number of loans _____
    3. Total unpaid Principal Balance $_____
    4. Total number of ARM loans _____
    5. Total escrows impounded $_____
    6. Total escrows non-impounded $_____

C. Have mortgages been reconciled to security balances? NO ____ YES ____
    When? _____
    Reconciled monthly? NO _____ YES _____

D. Has minimum P&I been reconciled? NO _____ YES _____
   When? _____ Reconciled monthly? NO _____ YES _____

E. Do you have any differences between trial balance and 2010 Section I?
   NO _____ YES _____ Please provide details.

F. Do you have any pools where you are waiting on liquidations to recapture
   funds overremitted to the Security Holder? NO ___ YES ___ How many? ___

G. Have pools been audited by FNMA? NO _____ YES _____
   When? _____ Please attach copy of audit.

H. What is the date of cutoff for FNMA pools? _____

I. P&I advances are of the 18th of previous month? _____

J. Name and address of Custodian(s) _____
   _____
   _____

K. Have all FNMA investor number been entered into your records? _____

L. Are there any buydown funds in FNMA? NO _____ YES _____ If so, who
   holds the funds? _____

M. Do you plan to transfer your FNMA stock? NO _____ YES _____

N. Number of loans with Special Servicing Option _____
   Number of loans with Regular Servicing Option _____

FHLMC Loans

A. What is your FHLMC servicer number? _____

B. FHLMC Portfolio being transferred:
   1. Total Unpaid Principal Balances $ _____
   2. Number of Loans _____
   3. Number of Participation Loans _____
   4. Number of Participation Investors _____
   5. Percent Owned by FHLMC _____ %
   6. Number of Control Groups _____
   7. Number of ARM Loans _____

C. Are all FHLMC loan numbers entered correctly on your system?

NO _____ YES _____

D. Provide detail of line 5 adjustments to Form 330 for prior three (3) months.

E. Are any groups out of balance between the 308 and the trial balance?
   NO ·____ YES ____ If yes, how many? _____ Amounts $_____

F. Do you use the P40X? (CPI Clients) NO _____ YES _____

Cash Processing/Payment Information

A. Billing Method
   1. Coupons? NO _____ YES _____ Vendor _____
   2. Monthly Billing? NO ____ YES ____ Computer _____ Manual ____
   3. Drafts? NO ____ YES ____ Checking _____ Savings _____
      Number of loans _____ Are only local banks drafted? NO ____
      YES ____ How are draft loans identified? _____
      _____
   4. Are there any military allotments, and how are they handled? _____
      _____
   5. Are there any pay-by-phone arrangements, and how are they handled?
      _____
   6. Other _____

B. Payment Application
   1. Do your loan records show interest paid through date or next due date?
      _____
   2. Are payments processed by a lockbox? NO ____ YES ____
      Please provide name and address of lockbox bank and contact person.
      _____
      _____
   3. If a lockbox is used, how are "exception" payments processed?
      _____
      How many per month? _____
   4. Are late charges applicable to all loans? NO ____ YES ____
   5. How are curtailments applied? _____
      a. Pools? _____
   6. What is your policy on rejecting payments?_____
      _____
   7. How are HUD funds and mortgagors funds applied on 235, 265 and 246
      loans? _____
      Do you maintain separate due dates?_____
   8. How are subsidy funds and mortgagors funds applied on buydown
      loans? _____

9. How are buydown funds handled? _____

10. How do you handle returned checks? _____

Where are the returned checks filed after reversals?_____

11. Are payments accepted in related bank branches? NO ____ YES ____
Origination branch offices? NO _____ YES _____

Payoffs

A. Number of Payoffs last 12 months _____

B. Is a separate payoff file created, or is payoff information added to an existing servicing file? _____

C. How do you identify on your system loans on which payoff statements have been issued? _____

D. Do your payoff statements include a void/expiration date? NO ___ YES ___
When? _____

E. Do you net the escrow balance from the total required for payoff? NO ____
YES ____ Do you net remaining buydown funds? NO ____ YES ____

F. Do you consider a request for a payoff statement to be "Notice of Prepayment"? NO ____ YES ____

G. Do you require certified funds for payoff? NO ____ YES ____

H. Do you stop payment of escrowed items due to a pending payoff?
NO ____ YES ____ How? _____

I. Do you have a special procedure for quoting payoffs on loans pending force placement of hazard insurance? NO ____ YES _____

J. Do you charge any type of payoff fees? NO _____ YES ____
What? _____

K. Are any special or unusual payoff reports required? NO _____ YES ____

L. Are old payoff files maintained? NO _____ YES _____ Where? _____
_____ For who long? _____

M. Do you use a paid in full tracking subsystem? NO _____ YES _____
On-line? _____ PC based? _____

N. Did you originate all loans to be transferred? NO _____ YES _____
Who is the present noteholder? (For assignment, merger, etc. information)
_____

FHA 235, 265 and 246 Loans

A. Number of 235's _____ Number of 265's _____
Number of 246's _____ (includes terminated & susp.)

B. Date of last HUD Billing _____

C. How are billing records maintained? _____

D. How are recertification records maintained? _____

E. Have recertifications been performed annually? _____

F. Are Recertifications performed on the anniversary date or an arbitrary
certification date? _____
If an arbitrary date, when? _____

G. How many suspended loans do you have? _____
How are they identified? _____

H. How many terminated loans do you have? _____
How are they identified? _____

I. What is the normal timing for escrow analysis on 235 loans? _____
_____

J. How are escrow overages handled? _____
_____

K. How are escrow shortage handled? _____
_____

L. When was the last HUD 235 review? _____
Can we obtain a release statement? NO _____ YES _____

M. Are 235/265 loan files held in the department? NO _____ YES _____

N. Are loans reviewed for overpaid assistance? _____
_____

O. How is overpaid assistance on HUD Subsidy 235 loans handled? _____
_____

P. How is overpaid assistance reflected on the loan records? _____
_____

Q. Are any mortgagors on repayment plans for overpaid assistance? NO _____
YES _____ Method _____

R. How is progress on the recertification process tracked? _____
_____

S. Are there any 235 Assumptions in progress? _____

T. How are accounts suspended for termination, after three years, tracked?
_____

U. How will the assistance for the month of the transfer be handled? _____
_____

V. If you have 246 loans, how is the assistance billing handled? _____
_____
Is it included with the 235 billing, or is it done separately? _____
_____

GEM / GPM's

A. How are GPM's identified? _____

B. Is the entire payment schedule on the computer? NO _____ YES _____

C. How are payment changes handled? _____

D. What is the normal timing for escrow analysis on GPM's _____
_____

E. How did Borrowers get notice of P&I change? _____
_____

F. Does P&I schedule show on the ledger/Master Record dump? _____

G. Attach sample Master Record dumps and ledgers showing GEM/GPM identification and application.

H. Attach sample copies of GEM/GPM Notes showing P&I schedules.

I. Attach a list of the GEMs / GPMs.

Buydowns

A. How are buydowns identified? _____
_____

B. Is the entire buydown schedule on the computer? NO _____ YES _____

C. Where are buydown funds held? _____

D. How do Borrowers get notice of buydown changes? _____
_____

E. How are buydown funds reconciled? _____

F. Attach a sample loan history marked to demonstrate receipt of buydown funds.

G. Attach a listing of buydown loans.

H. Attach sample copies of buydown agreements, closing statements and disbursements.

ARMS

A. How are ARM's identified? _____

B. How many different ARM plans do you have? _____

C. How are payment changes handled? _____

D. Are interest rate change parameters on your system? NO _____ YES _____

E. What is the normal timing for escrow analysis on ARM's? _____
_____

F. What kind of ARM's are included? _____
   Standard FHA, FNMA programs? _____
   In-house products? _____

G. What indexes are used? _____

H. How often are changes made to the Interest Rate? _____
   _____ To P&I? _____

I. How were Borrowers notified of changes in Interest Rate and/or P&I?
   _____
   Attach copies of notices.

J. When are ARM notices sent? _____
   Are they geared to the Interest Rate change date or the payment effective
   date? _____

K. How are all previous ARM changes stored on-line? _____
   _____

L. How do you identify the various types of ARM's? _____
   _____ Are they grouped by product type? _____
   Loan type? _____ How are caps identified within the
   groups? _____

M. Attach sample copies of Master Record dumps showing ARM data and
   Account and Loan Histories.

N. Attache detail listing of ARM Loans being transferred, listing to include the
   following:

   1. ARM Program Parameters (Basic Code)
   2. Original Rate
   3. Current Rate
   4. Next Interest Rate Change Date
   5. Next P&I Change Date

O. Attach ARM Parameter listing, which describes each type of ARM Loan,
   margins, caps, etc.

Escrow on Portfolio

A. Escrow Loans
   1. Number of Escrowed Loans _____

    2. Do you have any non-escrowed VA loans? NO _____ YES _____
       How Many? _____
    3. Do you have any non-escrowed FHA loans? NO _____ YES _____
       How Many? _____

B. Interest on Escrow
    1. Do you pay any interest on escrow? NO _____ YES _____
    2. When do you normally credit interest? _____
       _____
    3. How do you calculate amount of interest due? _____
       _____
    4. Attach complete listing indicating various states you pay interest on
       Escrow, the Interest Rate, the number of loans receiving interest on
       Escrow, and the criteria for paying interest on Escrow.

C. Analysis
    1. Do you escrow for any special assessments? NO _____ YES _____
       Ground Rents? NO _____ YES _____ Condo Association Fees?
       NO _____ YES _____
    2. Is any sort of cushion collected or maintained? NO _____ YES _____
       What? _____
    3. Is analysis based on amount of last disbursement? NO ____ YES ____
    4. Are individual analyses run between annuals? _____
    5. Are previous analyses stored on the computer system? _____
       _____
    6. How are overages handled? _____
    7. How are shortages handled? _____
    8. Is pending payment information on your system? NO ____ YES ____
    9. Do you analyze all delinquent loans? NO _____ YES _____
       If no, which are excluded? _____
    10. Attach a sample Escrow Analysis with explanation.
    11. Attach an Escrow Analysis schedule indicating when states are analyzed
       and when are they effective.

D. Disbursements
    1. How do you track outstanding checks? _____
    2. How are overdrafts handled? _____
    3. Are advances shown on history? NO _____ YES _____
    4. Are all disbursements made from a clearing account? NO ___ YES ___

E. Escrow Advances
    1. What are procedures for handling escrow advances? _____
       _____
    2. How much and how many loans have escrow advances? _____
       _____

3. Attach sample loan history showing advance and its repayment.

Hazard Insurance

A. What type evidence of insurance do you require?
( ) 1. Original Policies
( ) 2. Certificate
( ) 3. Memorandum & Certificate
( ) 4. Declaration
( ) 5. _____

B. Do you presently have a policy on file for each account? NO ___ YES ___
Where are they filed? _____

C. Do you maintain all policies or just current policy? _____
_____

D. Are Best ratings used? NO ____ YES ____ Minimum rating _____

E. Is information included on computer records? NO ____ YES ____
Are Special characters such as hyphens, slasher, etc., included in the policy number? NO _____ YES _____

F. How do you identify loans which do not require insurance? _____
_____

G. How do you identify loans with multiple policies? _____
_____

H. How do you identify expired policies? _____
_____

I. How do you identify continuous coverage policies? _____
_____
Is previous year's premium amount paid automatically? NO ___ YES ___

J. How do you identify loans on which flood insurance is required? _____
_____

K. Do you maintain and/or track flood policies which are not required? NO ____
YES ____ How are they identified? _____

L. How do you identify binder coverages? _____

M. How do you identify cancelled policies? _____

N. How do you identify Fair plan or pool polices? _____

O. Payments
1. When are premiums usually paid? _____
   How far in advance? _____
2. When are the heaviest billing periods? _____
3. Do you pay any premiums tape-to-tape? NO _____ YES _____
   Who? _____
4. How are premiums usually remitted? With voucher? _____
   With payment stub? _____

P. Condominiums
1. Are master policies available on condominiums? NO _____ YES _____
   How are these filed? _____
2. How many different condo associations? _____
3. Do you maintain or pay personal property or liability policies on condos?
   NO _____ YES _____
4. How do you identify loans with blanket condo policies? _____
   _____

Q. Force Placement
1. Who is your default carrier? _____
2. What method do you use to force place? _____
   a. Hazard _____
   b. Flood _____
3. For how long do you force place? _____
4. What correspondence do homeowners receive? _____
5. What procedures are required for claims? _____
   _____

R. Do you currently have uninsured properties? NO _____ YES _____
   Why? _____
   Where? _____
   How are these loans identified? _____

S. What are your open items categories? _____
   How many? _____

Loss Drafts

A. Are there any loss drafts in progress? NO _____ YES _____
   How many? _____

B. Where are loss draft funds held? _____

C. How are loss drafts usually handled? _____

D. Have you had any uninsured losses? NO _____ YES _____ Will these be resolved prior to transfer? NO _____ YES _____

Optional Insurance

A. What types of insurance do you offer and through what companies?
   1. Life _____
   2. A&H _____
   3. AD&D _____
   4. Other _____

B. Is the following information on computer system:

Type Coverage	YES _____	NO _____
Premiums	YES _____	NO _____
Last Month Paid	YES _____	NO _____
Name of Insured	YES _____	NO _____
Amount of Coverage	YES _____	NO _____
Birthdate	YES _____	NO _____
Name/Code for Carrier	YES _____	NO _____
Policy Number	YES _____	NO _____

C. Are premiums co-mingled in the escrow account? NO _____ YES _____ If yes, funds must be disbursed prior to transfer date.

D. Are optional insurance payments identified on history? NO _____ YES _____ How? _____

E. Attach a list of loans with optional insurance, indicating insurance premium amounts, sorted by insurance type and state.

Mortgage Insurance

A. Are FHA/VA/PMI numbers on computer? NO _____ YES _____ How valid is data? _____

B. What is your HUD ID number? _____

C. What method do you use to pay FHA premiums? 1/2 monthly _____
   Amount collected $_____

D. Is cumulative figure available for amount paid FHA since last anniversary for
   each loan? NO _____ YES _____ Where? _____

E. How do you handle MIP on which you did not receive a bill? _____
   _____

F. How do you identify loans with MIP paid up front? _____
   _____

G. Do you have any FHA loans on which the FHA insurance has been
   cancelled? NO _____ YES _____ How many? _____

H. Are due dates for MIP and PMI included on computer? NO ____ YES ____
   Is due date for FHA updated monthly or annually? _____

I. Are any premiums paid tape-to-tape? NO _____ YES _____
   Who? _____

J. Are MIP premiums paid on current basis or in arrears? _____
   _____

K. Attach listing of all loans of which MIP premiums are being paid.

L. Attach listing of PMI Companies which insure loans in this transfer and
   indicate the number of loans insured by each company.

Taxes

A. Is a tax contract vendor used? NO ___ YES ___ Who? _____
   Escrowed loans? NO ___ YES ___ Non-escrowed loans? NO ___
   YES ___ (Attach listing indicating states under tax service.)

B. Where are tax contracts kept? _____

C. Are all loans under contract? NO _____ YES _____ What loans are
   excluded? _____

D. Is tax information maintained on system? NO _____ YES _____ What? ___
   _____

E. Are parcel numbers on system? NO _____ YES _____

    1. How do you identify loans with multiple parcels?_____

    2. How do you tract parcel payments? _____

F. What type of payee code system do you use? _____

G. When are the majority of taxes due? _____

H. How many times per year are taxes being paid? _____

I. What is your policy concerning special assessments? _____

_____

J. How do you handle ground rents? _____

K. What kinds of major tax problems presently exist? _____

_____

    1. Number of Delinquent Tax Items _____

    2. Pending Reimbursements of Penalties from Vendor _____

    3. Pending Refunds form Taxing Authorities _____

    4. Do you owe vendor any money? NO _____ YES _____

       How much? $_____

    5. Other major problems? _____

L. Have you had any regulatory agency inquiries regarding taxes?

   NO _____ YES _____ From whom? _____

M. Have you paid tax penalties from any escrow account? NO ___ YES ___

N. Attach listing of open items (both Escrow and Non-Escrow.)

O. Attach listing of loans sorted by Payee with states, also attach listing
identifying various payees.

Assumptions

A. Number of Assumptions last 12 months:

   FHA/VA _____ CONV. _____ Qualifying FHA _____

B. Number of FHA Releases of Liability processed last 12 months _____

_____

C. What is your normal fee on conventional assumptions? $_____

D. How do you handle conventional assumption underwriting? _____

E. Do you have any unusual investor inquirements? NO _____ YES _____
   What? _____

F. Are old assumption files maintained? NO _____ YES _____
   Where? _____
   For how long? _____

G. How many pending loan assumptions are currently in process, for the loans
   being transferred? _____

H. Attach copies of sample Assumption documentation.

I. Attach Fee Schedule for FHA, VA and Conventional Assumptions and FHA
   Releases of Liability.

Partial Releases

A. How many Partial Releases have been processed during the past 12
   months? _____

B. Are there any Partial Releases currently being processed? NO __ YES __
   If yes, how many? _____

C. Briefly outline your procedures for processing a Partial Release. _____
   _____
   _____
   _____
   _____

Customer Service

A. Where is customer service function handled? Central location _____
   In the field _____

B. How is customer service handled? Are phone coverage, correspondence,
   and research considered separate functions? _____
   _____

C. At year end, are borrowers provided with tax and interest summaries or
   complete histories? _____

D. Have SSN/TIN numbers been solicited on all accounts? NO ___ YES ___
   Are numbers certified? NO _____ YES _____

E. Are mortgagors accustomed to receiving mass solicitations, i.e., life insurance, TIN's etc? _____

F. Attach sample copy of loan history with explanations for reading the history.

G. Attach sample copy of microfiche and/or the Customer Service File.

H. Attach sample copy of Goodbye Letter.

I. Attach stop and flag listings with definitions.

J. Attach sample Master file printouts with explanations/definitions of the various fields and their usage.

K. Attach fee listing for various customer service functions, i.e., Amortization Schedules, document requests. etc.

L. Attach sample coupon book, with an escrow analysis.

Collections

A. What is your delinquency ratio excluding foreclosures? _____
   1 30 days - number of loans _____ Ratio _____
   2. 60 days - number of loans _____ Ratio _____
   3. 90 days - number of loans _____ Ratio _____
   4. 120+ days- umber of loans _____ Ratio _____
   5. Total Number of loans _____ Ratio _____

B. How is information on collection activities recorded and filed? _____
   _____

C. Is more than one phone number available? NO _____ YES _____
   Where? _____

D. Where is second lien information recorded? _____ Are these
   records complete? NO _____ YES _____

E. Are field call reports on file? NO _____ YES _____ Where? _____
   _____ Where? _____
   Have they been made timely? NO _____ YES _____ Do you use an in-
   house representative or contract? _____

F. Have notices of default been filed timely and HUD requirements generally met? NO _____ YES _____

G. Are any loans on repayment plans? NO ___ YES ___ How many? _____
    How are these loans identified? _____
    Are the plans current and properly administered? NO ____ YES ____

H. What is your policy on refusing payments? _____
    _____

I. Do any investors have special inspection requirements? NO ___ YES ___
    What? _____

J. Do you have any loans more than 90 days delinquent and not in foreclosure?
    NO ____ YES ____ How many? _____

K. Do you have any loans pending HUD assignment? NO ____ YES ____
    Loans identified? _____

L. What is your frequency and method of contact with homeowners? _____
    _____
    30 day delinquent: Telephone _____   Letters _____
    60 day delinquent: Telephone _____   Letters _____

Bankruptcies

A. How many loans in bankruptcy? _____

B. How are loans in bankruptcy identified? _____
    _____

C. Where do you record the trustee's name and address? _____
    _____

D. Where is the information regarding the bankruptcy? _____
    _____

E. Are Escrow Analyses performed on loans in bankruptcy? NO ___ YES ___
    If yes, what is your criteria? _____
    _____

Foreclosures

A. How many loans in foreclosure? _____

B. How many loans are within 60 days of sale date? _____

C. How many loans have already been to sale and are pending claims? _____

D. How many loans not yet purchased from pools/portfolio on which claims are pending? _____

E. Do you use in-house trustee or attorney? _____

F. Have proper precautions been taken to protect vacant property? NO ___ YES ___

G. Are there any current board-ups? NO ___ YES ___ How many? _____ Where? _____

H. Do you have restrictions on securing or boarding vacant properties? NO ___ YES ___ What? _____

I. Are majority of foreclosures judicial or non-jurdicial? _____

J. Are redemption periods usually applicable? NO ____ YES ____ Average number of days _____

K. Are foreclosure advances shown on history? NO _____ YES _____

L. Average Loss on Pool Foreclosures $_____ Total Pool Losses Last Year $_____

M. Do you have a foreclosure tracking system? NO _____ YES _____

N. At what point do you remove the principal balance on a foreclosure? _____

Miscellaneous

A. Is there any pending litigation of any kind? NO _____ YES _____ What? _____

Transfer of Servicing

When making transfers of servicing, sellers and buyers have a responsibility to each other and to the mortgagors whose loans are transferred. In such transactions, mortgage companies should have a contract that details their several responsibilities and provides a timetable for completing agreed-upon tasks. In undertaking large transfers, sellers and buyers should make certain that sufficient manpower and facilities are dedicated to the transfer to ensure that their obligations to one another and to mortgagors are met. The following is a list of the principal responsibilities of sellers and buyers:

Sellers' Responsibilities. It is recommended that sellers should:

1. Send a notice of transfer of servicing to mortgagors, which includes:

    -   The effective date of transfer to the buyer;

    -   The new servicer's name, address, and telephone number (toll-free number, if available);

    -   The name of a referral person or department in the buyer's company;

    -   Instructions concerning interim payments (until notice of the transfer of servicing is sent from the buyer);

    -   Reassurance that the transfer of servicing does not affect the terms and conditions of the mortgage;

    -   Information about mortgage life insurance, mortgage disability insurance, or any other form of optional mortgage insurance, if applicable.

2. Provide the hazard insurance agent or carrier with a notice of transfer in the form of a corrected mortgagee clause.

3. Notify the tax-bill service or taxing authority of the transfer, if applicable.

4. Notify the FHA, VA (in the case of loans in foreclosure), or mortgage insurance company of the transfer.

5.   Bring escrow (impound) accounts current by paying outstanding bills.

6.   Transfer escrow (impound) balances and buydown subsidy funds to the buyer, together with any interest owing to the mortgagor.

7.   Provide the following documents and information to the buyer, when appropriate:

   - Complete loan files or photocopies and/or microfiches of loan files;

   - Insurance policies or certificates and related Correspondence, including any pending loss claims;

   - Contracts with a tax-bill service or a listing of tax-service contract numbers, if applicable;

   - Servicing history, such as the last twelve months' payments and disbursements and the last escrow analysis;

   - Collection history on all loans;

   - Foreclosure information on loans transferred during the foreclosure process;

   - Bankruptcy information and documents;

   - Pending payoff and/or assumption statements;

   - Other information concerning pending items, including, for example, partial releases, mortgage life or mortgage disability claims, and any matters in litigation;

     Photocopies of letters and notices concerning the transfer of servicing addressed to mortgagors, hazard insurance agents and carriers, tax-bill services, the FHA, the VA, mortgage insurance companies, etc.

8.   When the physical transfer of servicing is completed:

   - Answer mortgagor's questions about the transfer;

   - Forward mortgage payments daily to the buyer (for a period of at least thirty (30) days);

- Forward correspondence, bills, receipts, and documents relating to the transferred loans promptly.

Buyers' Responsibilities. It is recommended that buyers should:

1. Send a notice of the transfer of servicing to mortgagors, recapitulating and elaborating on the information contained in the seller's notice. The buyer's notice should be sent concurrently with the seller's, or shortly thereafter.

2. Prepare for the transfer of servicing by ensuring that adequate facilities and staff are available to set up loan information from transferred file quickly.

3. Conduct a legal review of state requirements before buying servicing, in order to ensure compliance with state laws, statutes, and regulations and with industry standards for servicing.

4. When the transfer of servicing is completed:

    - Respond to mortgagor's questions and requests concerning payoff, assumptions, year-end statements, servicing practices (e.g., procedures for making payments, acceptance of toll-free or collect telephone calls), etc. (A buyer should make every effort to avoid referring mortgagors back to the previous servicer. If a mortgagor's request cannot be honored without recourse to the seller, it is the buyer, not the mortgagor, who should communicate with the seller);

    - Handle questions from insurance agents or carriers, taxing authorities, government agencies, etc

    - Practice forbearance with mortgagors when sorting out transfer-related problems (delinquencies, the assessment of late charges).

Tape-to-Tape Transfers

The following information with respect to each Mortgage in a format sufficient to enable its tape-to-tape transmission to Purchaser:

1. Loan Number
2. Investor/Category Number
3. Investor Loan Number
4. Loan Type
5. State Code
6. Current Principal Balance
7. Escrow Balance
8. Escrow Advance Balance
9. Escrow Suspense Balance
10. Deficit Balance
11. Late Charge Balance
12. Replacement Reserve Balance
13. Mortgagor Name
14. Co-Mortgagor Name
15. Mortgagor Social Security Number
16. Co-Mortgagor Social Security Number
17. Interest Rate
18. Principal & Interest Amount
19. Payment Frequency
20. Payment Due Date
21. Next Payment Number
22. Total Payment Amount
23. Annual Service Fee
24. Level of Service Fee
25. Original Principal Balance
26. First Payment Date
27. Loan Maturity Date
28. FHA Section & Number
29. Loan Term
30. Mortgagor's Phone Number (Home & Business if possible)
31. Late Charge Factor
32. Late Charge Code
33. Grace Days
34. Assumptions Date
35. Last Escrow Analysis Date
36. Pending Payment Change Information
37. SMSA Code
38. Census Tract
39. Occupancy Code

Hazard Insurance Items (Including Flood)

40. Coverage Amount
41. Property Value
42. Premium Amount

Schedule of Servicing Information

43. Last Premium Paid Date
44. Payee Code Listing of Agents & Companies
45. Condo Flag (if applicable)
46. Premium Due Date/Expiration Date
47. Term
48. Policy Number
49. Any Other Pertinent Information

MIP/PMI Insurance Items

50. Premium Amount
51. Indication of Prepaid or Monthly Premium
52. Amount of Premium Paid YTD (FHA only)
53. PMI Rate
54. Payee
55. Anniversary Date

Real Estate Taxes (County, City, School & Special Assessments

56. Amount Last Paid
57. Date Last Paid
58. Date Next Due
59. Payee
60. Payee Code Listing of Counties, Cities, Schools & Special Assessments
61. Parcel Number/Tax ID Number/Tax Service Contract Number (if available)
62. Legal Description (lot, block, section)

GPM, ARM, Buydown or 235 Loans

63. All Pertinent Information on nay of these loan types.

Additional Information/Documentation to be Delivered

A. The following information and documents with respect to each Mortgage:

1   Twelve (12) month transaction history file
2. For each Mortgage on which Seller escrows real estate taxes, tax payments receipt for past twelve (12) months which Seller has received.
3. Collection records and property address listing.
4. All flood, hazard insurance and mortgage insurance policies.
5. All available tax records including prior years receipts.
6. All title policies and title opinions.
7. Microfilm of case files to the extent available.
8. Copy of letter to appropriate insurance companies/agents requesting endorsements to reflect transfer to Purchaser and new address.
9. Other documents or information that Purchaser may reasonably request which are reasonably available to Seller.
10 Copy of Note and recorded Mortgage or certified copy of Mortgage.
11. Copy of letter to the appropriate taxing authorities notifying them of the transfer of Servicing to Purchaser.
12. Copy of credit package.
13. Available information concerning all pending items, including but not limited to partial releases, mortgage life or mortgage disability claims and litigation.

B. On an aggregate basis, a schedule enumerating each Mortgage which requires special handling with a statement of the reasons therefor and all relevant documentation attached.

Servicing Transfer Checklist

A. Pre-Closing Requirements.

1. Fully executed Purchase Agreement to include Seller's representations and warranties as prescribed.
2. Review of Mortgage Portfolios for (also function of new custodian-recertification of pool):
    a. Note and proper endorsements
    b. Original mortgages
    c. Assignment
    d. FHA or VA insurance or guaranty certificate
    e. Title insurance policy and proper endorsements
    f. Hazard insurance policy
    g. Flood insurance policy, if required
    h. Letter agreement guaranties and other documents relating to securities
    i. Other documents, as required (e.g., RESPA form, Truth-in-Lending Disclosures, etc.)
3. Written request for agency approval
4. Receipt of agency approval/payment of agency pool fee
5. Post-approval, pre-transfer submission to agency:
    a. Corporate Resolution of Seller approving request for transfer
    b. Custodial Agreement executed by Buyer and Custodian for each pool
    c. Servicing Agreement executed by Buyer for each pool
    d. (P&I) (T&I) Agreements executed by Buyer and new Custodian for each pool
    e. Executed Assignment Agreement in form prescribed by Agency with agency approval of consolidated forms b-d
6. Execution of Assignment Agreement for transfer of servicing
7. Notice to borrowers of transfer
8. Requests for endorsement of hazard and casualty insurance
9. Listing of taxing authorities for new servicer
10. Endorsement of Mortgage Notes from seller to buyer
11. Following signing of Assignment Agreement, submit to agency of:
    a. Copy of release of documents from prior custodian
    b. Documentation for each pool certified by new custodian
12. Endorsement of Mortgage Notes from buyer in blank
13. Preparation of individual mortgage assignments from buyer to agency.

B. On Or Before Closing Requirements.

1. Certified trial balance of each mortgage identified by pool number and loan number
   a. Current Balance
   b. Balance required for P&I custodial account
   c. Current Balance for T&I custodial account
   d. Due date of next P&I payment
   e. Due date and amount of each delinquent payment
   f. Amount of sellers P&I and T&I advances
2. FHA notification
3. Most recent tax receipts
4. Copy (mircofiche) of seller's most recent T&I custodial account analysis
5. Individual YTD loan ledgers and definition of transaction codes
6. Previous year's loan ledgers
7. IRS forms

C. Documents To Be Delivered at Closing

1. Original notes properly endorsed
2. Original recorded mortgages (Deeds of Trust, etc.)
3. Original Title policy, together with endorsements, if applicable
4. Delivery of mortgage insurance certificate, guaranty certificate
5. All recorded assignments as applicable
6. Recordable replacement assignments from buyer to seller
7. Seller's certified Corporate Resolution and Incumbency Certificate
8. Buyer's certified Corporation Resolution and Incumbency Certificate
9. Opinion of attorney for seller
10. Opinion of attorney for buyer
    a. Check of states of qualification of buyer
11. President's certificate as to representations and warranties
12. Reconciliation of pool principal to security price
13. Certification by mortgage pool as to warranty that reconciliations are true and correct.
14. Certification and schedule of unreimbursed advances
15. Schedule of documents which are not in custodial bank's possession
16. Escrow Agreement with custodian bank
17. Letter Agreement with custodian bank
18. Buyer's receipt for documents

19. Delivery of:
    a. Balance required for P&I custodial accounts as of cut-off
    b. Actual balance of T&I accounts as of cut-off
20. Evidence of agency approval of custodian bank
21. The custodian bank release of documents
22. Delivery of loan payments to buyer after transfer date
23. Payment of purchase price to seller

D. Post-Closing Requirements

1. Substitution of recordable assignments from seller to buyer; to agency for all pooled mortgages
2. Acknowledgement by custodian of receipt of new assignment and release of old assignment
3. Recording of assignment from seller to buyer
4. Delivery of loan payments after transfer date received by seller after cut-off
5. Notice to agency certificate holders of assignment
6. Statement of interest paid (YTD) to borrowers
7. Buyer to reimburse seller for seller's P&I advances
8. Buyer to reimburse seller for T&I advances
9. Buyer to pay seller for delinquent mortgages (3 months or more) which are brought current, if applicable
10. Seller to pay buyer for costs of completed foreclosures, if applicable
11. Follow-up on hazard insurance endorsement
12. Seller, upon deposit of buyer, will make first payment to security holders following closing
13. Follow-up on recording and delivery of possession of assignments from seller to buyer
14. Follow-up on documents defects
15. Follow-up on notes and mortgage guaranties and insurance of loans in foreclosure
16. Completion of all final certifications

Acquisition of Servicing
Requirements and Checklist

I. General

    A.   Determine Contacts
        1.
        2. Data Center
        3. Seller
        4. Seller Data Center
        5. Seller Lockbox Site

    B.   Determine File Dates
        1. Test Tape Delivery Date
        2. Final Tape Delivery Date
        3. Update (Conversion Date)
        4. Seller File Cutoff Date

    C.   Obtain File Description
        1. Definition (and Keys)
        2. Field Layout and File Segmentation
        3. Tape Characteristics
           a. Record size
           b. blocking factor
           c. format
           d. density
           e. number of bites per record
           f. labelled
        4. Multiple File Issues
        5. Balancing Methodologies
           a. Seller File to Itself (Here vs. There)

    D.   Determination of Conversion
        1 Automated Process

Appendix 2

II.   REQUIREMENTS

A.   General reports, records and/or listings required

    1.   Complete loan files

    2.   Two copies of name and address listing alpha order, hard copy.

    3.   Two copies of name and address listing number order, hard copy

    4.   Transaction codes cross reference

    5.   Payee codes cross reference

    6.   State code cross reference

    7.   Two copies of reconciled trial balance dated _____ hard copy

    8.   Identify and VA Vendee loans

B.   Reports and/or records required for each loan with following information:

    1.   Original Loan Amount

    2.   Term of Loan

    3.   Maturity Date

    4.   First Payment Due Date

    5.   P & I Payment

    6.   Name and Property Address

    7.   Mailing Address

    8.   Escrow Amount

    9.   Total Payment

    10.   Unpaid Principal Balance

    11.   Escrow Balance

    12.   Next Payment Due

    13.   SS Number

    14.   Most recent escrow analysis

15. Year end statement

16. History records.

(Missing Page)

2. Manual Process

3. Balancing Process

    1. File to Seller File

4. Testing Methodologies

E. Test Conversion Process

    1. Balance Files

       a. Seller file to Itself (Here vs. There)

    2. Run Conversion Stream

    3. Balance Files

       a. File to Seller File

    4. Test Report Production and Q C Review

    5. Recommend Changes for Final

F. Final Conversion Process

    1. Balance Files

       a. Seller file to Itself (Here vs. There)

    2. Run Conversion Stream

    3. Balance Files

       a. File to Seller File

    4. Conversion Report Production and Q C. Review

    5. Notify Related Departments of Conversion Status

G. Post Conversion Process

    1. Report Production

    2. Testing and Balancing

    3. Q C Review

4.   Begin Lockbox Interim Processes

5.   Receive Folders

6.   Recommendations for Changes to Enhance Conversion
      Process

<u>NOTIFICATION OF TRANSFER</u>

A.   Preparation in and mailing of letter to Borrower Advising of Transfer

     1.   Letter should be mailed by Seller

     2.   Use of   Seller Letter preferred

     3.   Copies to be placed in file

B.   Preparation in and mailing of Welcome Letter to Borrower

     1.   Letter to be mailed by

     2.   Use of   Welcome Letter

CUSTOMER SERVICE

A. Reports and Records

1. Listing of state(s) requiring payment of interest on escrows and method of application for each.

2. Listing of all accounts requiring payment of interest on escrow.

3. Evidence that all accrued interest due on escrows has been posted to accounts through cut-off date.

4. If interest has not been deposited to escrow account, _____ agrees to provide   with a check, representing interest due, and a detailed breakdown of accounts to be credited and amount due to each.

5. _____ agrees to credit interest on escrow to all accounts as of the cutoff date.

6. _____ agrees to prepare all 1099 forms required reflecting interest on escrow paid to borrowers for the period of January through ____. Copies to be supplied to _____.

7. _____ agrees to prepare tax and interest statements for the period of January through ____ and provide these statements along with a copy hard copies or fiche) to _____.

B.   Interview - Contact

     1.   History Records

         a.   Minimum of Two Years

         b.   Format

             -    Fiche

             -    hard copy

         c.   Definitions - Tran Codes

     2.   Last Escrow Analysis

         a.   Date

         b.   Distribution

         c.   Obtain Sample

     3.   Correspondence

         a.   In Process

         b.   Files

     4.   Year End Statements

     5.   Interest on Escrow Requirements

         a.   Method and frequency of crediting

         b.   Existing Servicer <u>Must</u> Credit Escrows on the Cutoff Date

     6.   Drafting

         a.   Existing Servicer <u>Must</u> delete customer from drafting (not an ACH originator)

     7.   Current Billing Method

         a.   Monthly Statement

         b.   Coupons

         c.   Passbook/Payment Book

     8.   Interest Method

         a.   Advance

       a.   **Advance**

       b.   Arrears

       c.   Capitalized

       d.   Rule of 78's

9.   Due Dates Other than the First

10. Late Charge Calculations/Rates

11. Lock Box for Mortgage Payments

12. Stop Value Definitions

REAL ESTATE TAXES

A. Reports and Records

    1. _____ should be provided with the following
       (if available)

    a. All tax control records
    b. Payee listing indicating the following for each
       payee:

       1. Name
       2. Address
       3. Due Dates
       4. Discount Dates, if applicable
       5. Penalty Dates

    c. Multipayee listing
    d. Multiparcel listing
    e. Listing of all overdue taxes and/or assessments
       as of transfer date
    f. Listing of all individual taxing authorities with
       tax processing fee, if applicable
    g. Complete listing of tax payment schedule
       applicable to all loans included in transfer. (at
       least 30 days prior to transfer date).
    h. Most recent paid bills and/or receipts for loans
       included in transfer.

    2. On condominiums and townhouses, seller will supply
       _____ with copies of the associations by-
       laws, also copies of the master policies, if in
       possession of the seller.

B. Verifications and Confirmations

    1. At the time of transfer _____ agrees to provide
       _____ with the following.

       a. Verification that all taxes and assessments due on
          or before _____ have been paid, except as
          provided for in Section D (1) and (2) below.

C. Past Due Taxes

    1. At time of transfer _____ will provide _____ with
       all unpaid tax bills in their possession except those
       provided for in Section D (1) and (2).

    2. _____ should be provided with a listing of all
       taxing authorities for which tax statements have not
       been paid _____ agrees to obtain any such statements
       and promptly forward them to _____.

3.

D. Taxes and Assessments

    1. _____has agreed to assume responsibility for payment of taxes and assessments due and payable for the month of _____.

    2. _____ will provide_____ with a listing of all taxing authorities having a due and payable date of _____.

    3. _____ agrees to assume responsibility for payment of any and all penalty and/or interest assessed as a result of delinquent payment of tax items due and payable prior to and including _____.

E. Interview - Contact

    1. Geographical Distribution of Loans

    2. Taxes Due During Conversion

        1. Define Disbursement Responsibilities (see Section D)

        2. Tax Bill Forwarding Instructions

    3. Format of Disbursement Data

        1. Tax Cards

            a. Obtain Sample

        2. Computer Generated Reports

            a. Obtain Sample

    4. Escrowed/Non Escrowed Loan Distribution

        1. ID

        2. Pledge Accounts

        3. Basis for allowing Non Escrow

    5. Tax Contracts

        1. Service Provided by ?

        2. Transferable ? Existing Contracts ? Full Fee Contracts ?

            a. Source of Contract Numbers and Date

6. New Contracts Required

    1. Negotiate Fee

    2. Determine Method

7. Tax Receipts

    1. Availability

    2. Storage Method

8. Unknown Expense Agreement

    1. Tax Penalties

    2. Erroneous Disbursements

9. Open Items Report (as of conversion)

HAZARD INSURANCE

A.   Reports and Records

    1.   Should be provided with the following:

        a.   Name and address listing of all hazard insurance payees

        b.   Errors and Omissions Report (open-end items)

        c.   Listing of loans having an insurance expiration date in _____.

        d.   Payee Insurance Master List in numeric and alph order.

        e.   Listing of all loans on direct or mass billing

        f.   Listing of all accounts with no insurance

        g.   All Hazard/Flood insurance control records

        h.   A separate listing showing those loans for which flood insurance is required-including the expiration date.

        i.   Listing of user defined codes for policy types if applicable.

B.   Insurance Files

    1.   _____ will supply _____ with the original hazard insurance files for each loan which should contain the following:

        a.   Current Homeowner's or Fire and EC policy
        b.   Current Flood Insurance Policy, if applicable
        c.   Current Catastrophe Policies, if applicable
        d.   Current Boiler Insurance Policy, if applicable

    2.   Coverage on loans secured by condominiums and townhomes may be evidenced by individual certificates of insurance, however, must be provided with a copy of the Master Policy of Insurance for each condominium, townhome project, as available. Copies of any master policies should be provided in a separate file labeled as such.

C.   Binders

    1.   Provide a listing of all loans with Forced Place Coverage along with the name of the company and expiration date.

D.   Change Endorsements

1. _____ will prepare an original and one (1) copy of the request for Change of Mortgagee (Loss Payable Clause) for each loan included in the transfer, including assumption.

2. The new mortgage clause should read as follows:

E. Interview - Contact

   1. Notice to Carriers

   2. Source of Policy Data

   3. Insurance Files

      a. Segregated

      b. Format

         - fiche
         - hard copy

   4. Escrowed/Non Escrowed Loan Distribution

      a. Identification
      b. Pledge Accounts
      c. Basis for allowing non escrow
      d. Identify co-ops

   5. Existing Forced Coverage (Section C)

   6. Existence of Impairment Policy

      a. Notice to company
      b. Hold harmless agreement from carrier

   7. Pay all premiums in house

FHA INSURANCE

A.   Notice of Change of Servicer to HUD

1.   _____ shall prepare an original and one (1) copy of HUD form 92080 for each FHA loan included in the transfer or bulk form 92080.

2.   If a bulk form 92080 is utilized, it must contain the following information:

    a.   _____ loan number
    b.   FHA case number
    c.   Mortgagor's name
    d.   Maturity date of loan
    e.   Original loan amount
    f.   Amount of MIP
    g.   Date MIP was last paid
    h.   For HUD co-insurance loans, if applicable, complete HUD Form 8084.

Please group the above in loan number order according to Section of the Act.

3.   The original and copy of the 92080 should be forwarded to _____ who will in turn forward the original to HUD.

B.   Payment of Premiums

1.   _____ will pay all premiums due for _____.

2.   For each FHA loan included in the transfer, please provide the following:

    a.   Method of MIP payment
    b.   Next payment due date
    c.   MIP year to date amount paid for each loan

3.   Lump sum payment at closing

    a.   Due Date of Insurance Certificate
    b.   Disbursement amount

4.   Monthly payment

    a.   Anniversary Date
    b.   Annual Premium
    c.   Mortgage Insurance Certificate endorsement date
    d.   Pending MIP Anniversary

FHA INSURANCE

A. Notice of Change of Servicer to HUD

    1. _____ shall prepare an original and one (1) copy of HUD form 92080 for each FHA loan included in the transfer or bulk form 92080.

    2. If a bulk form 92080 is utilized, it must contain the following information:

        a. _____ loan number
        b. FHA case number
        c. Mortgagor's name
        d. Maturity date of loan
        e. Original loan amount
        f. Amount of MIP
        g. Date MIP was last paid
        h. For HUD co-insurance loans, if applicable, complete HUD Form 8084.

    Please group the above in loan number order according to Section of the Act.

    3. The original and copy of the 92080 should be forwarded to _____ who will in turn forward the original to HUD.

B. Payment of Premiums

    1. _____ will pay all premiums due for _____.

    2. For each FHA loan included in the transfer, please provide the following:

        a. Method of MIP payment
        b. Next payment due date
        c. MIP year to date amount paid for each loan

    3. Lump sum payment at closing

        a. Due Date of Insurance Certificate
        b. Disbursement amount

    4. Monthly payment

        a. Anniversary Date
        b. Annual Premium
        c. Mortgage Insurance Certificate endorsement date
        d. Pending MIP Anniversary

MORTGAGE INSURANCE

A. Reports and Records

    1. _____ should be provided with the following:

        a. Name and address listing of all company payees
        b. Open items report
        c. All mortgage insurance control records
        d. Certificate number
        e. Date of next premium due date

B. Payment of Premiums

    1. _____ agrees to pay premiums due for _____.

OPTIONAL INSURANCE

A.   Reports and Records

     1.   _____ shall provide _____ with a listing for each carrier of the following that will transfer to

         a.   Loan number
         b.   Mortgagor's name
         c.   Policy/Certificate number
         d.   Type of insurance
         e.   Effective date
         f.   Amount of premium
         g.   Due date of premium
         h.   A list of mortgagors receiving benefits under a policy claim, including the name, loan number, insurance benefit amount, and insurance company. A copy of the claim file should also be sent.
         i.   Copy of certificate/policy

A. Copy of master policy and/or any agreements signed between yourselves and the insurance company.

B. Certificates of insurance or policy and copy of signed application for each insured.

C. Loan Listing showing the following information:

   1. Loan Number

   2. Customer Name

   3. Customer Address

   4. Company/Carrier Name

   5. Policy Number

   6. Type of Coverage

   7. Monthly Premium

   8. Premium Currently Collected

   9. Outstanding Premium Due

D. List of all carriers - including address, phone number and contact person.

E. Number of insured accounts by coverage program including annual premium volume.

F. Brief description of each program,/coverage provided.

G. Copies of sample policies and any applications, brochures used for solicitation.

H. Schedule of how rates are calculated.

I. Any information regarding commissions received.

   1. How are premiums paid--monthly, quarterly, semi-annually or annually?

   2. How are they collected--separate field, included in escrow deposit?

   3. When were they last paid?

J. Premium Remittance:
    (Reconciliation)

   1. How much is due to each carrier?

    2.   What has been collected?

    3.   When funds are transferred, how will they be identified?

K.   Please advise of all outstanding claims, carrier name, location of claim office, length of time claim has been pending and any other relevant information.

L.   Disability Claims:

    1.   Name of customer on disability and disability carrier and address.

    2.   Length of time on disability.

    3.   Last disability payment received.

M.   On life and/or disability claims, are the claim forms originated by you or are they sent directly from the insurance company?

N.   How are the various plans identified?

O.   On those loans where a master policy and certificate of insurance or policy is not available, please provide a listing with these loans separate and identified as missing information showing:

    1.   Loan number, mortgagor name, address, carrier, type of insurance and premium amount.

INSURANCE CLAIMS IN PROCESS

A. Packaging Instructions

B. Forwarding Instructions

C. Loss Drafts

    1.   Information Required

        a.   Date of loss

        b.   Cause of loss

        c.   Amount of loss

        d.   Amount of insurance proceeds received to date

        e.   Information received from contractors or record of conversation with contractors

        f.   Correspondence from and/or record of conversation with borrowers and insurance companies

        g.   Status reports on repairs

        h.   Inspection reports, if any

        i.   Report on receipt of future proceeds (date expected, amount)

        j.   A check payable to _____ representing monies in a restricted field for loss drafts with a detailed listing, by loan number, showing how the funds are to be applied.

COLLECTIONS

A. Records and Reports

    1.   _____ shall provide to _____ the following:

        a.   Collection code cross reference listing

        b.   Current suspense trial balance

        c.   Listing of accumulated late charges

        d.   Listing of all loans presently on either automatic draft or allotment

        e.   Two copies of current trial balance on all delinquent loans

        f.   Listing of all accounts currently on a repayment plan

        g.   Listing of delinquent accounts sorted by state

        h.   Listing of delinquent subsidy loans

        i.   Report on delinquent ratios sorted by loan type

        j.   Copies of most recent collection reports (monthly)

        k.   All collection cards and related records

B. Files Required

    1.   All permanent collection files separated by status (30, 60, 90, Fore, Bank)

    2.   Files on accounts 30 or more days past due must include all collection documents

    3.   Collection files related to default reporting. Those files should contain copies of all required Default Notices on the FHA, VA and/or private investor forms unless these copies have been placed in the individual permanent collection files.

FORECLOSURES AND BANKRUPTCIES

A. Information Required-Loans in Foreclosure

    1. Listing of all loans in foreclosure status as of transfer date

    2. Current status report on loans showing current stages of foreclosure

    3. Name and address listings of foreclosure attorneys

    4. Foreclosure code cross reference listing

B. Loans in a Foreclosure Status which will transfer

    1. Loans subject to judicial foreclosure will transfer only if no judgment has been entered

    2. Loans subject to power of sale will transfer only if loan has not been posted for foreclosure. If referred to attorney file must be recalled.

C. Funds received on claims, on Loans Retained for Servicing

    1. Upon receipt of the 90% check, _____will remit to _____ enough funds to remove the loan from our control.

    2. Upon receipt of the 10% check _____ will forward funds to _____ to be applied towards the deficiency. Buyer will bill _____ for any remaining deficiency. If funds received are greater than the deficiency, _____ will reimburse the difference. If no deficiency exists, then the check will be endorsed over to _____.

D. Loans to be retained for servicing by _____.

    1. Loans where a judgment has been entered

    2. Loans posted for foreclosure

    3. Pending claim

    4. Loans conveyed - waiting for funds

    5. Loans foreclosed - waiting for expiration of redemption period

E. Expenses Related to Foreclosures

    1. _____ shall reimburse _____ for any and all losses incurred on foreclosures on all loans that as of the transfer date were:

a.   foreclosed
b.   in process of foreclosure

Expenses shall include, but are not limited to those
expenses that are not reimbursed by FHA, VA, PMI and
FNMA which is not reimbursed. Also, any escrow
advances made. _____ agrees to pay any and all
invoices, legal fees that remain unpaid as of the
transfer date.

BANKRUPTCIES

A.   Information Required-Loans in Bankruptcy

    1.   Complete listing of all loans in bankruptcy as of transfer date. Listing should include:

        a.   Type of chapter filed

        b.   Complete list of trustees and attorneys

        c.   Status report for each loan reflecting if current/ delinq. inside or outside of plan

    2.   Current report on the status of proceeding appearing on listing, including the name and address of attorney

    3.   Copies of notices forwarded to attorneys and trustees advising them of the transfer to _____.

    4.   Payment status on all loans, inside and outside plan.

    5.   _____ agrees to pay any and all invoices that remain unpaid as of transfer date.

        Seller will provide buyer with a list of personnel to contact after the sale (i.e., payoff, collections, foreclosure, etc.)

        Seller shall provide buyer with an updated status report for all loans retained for servicing as of the transfer date and a similar report every 30 days until all loans are liquidated.

COLLECTIONS/FORECLOSURE/BANKRUPTCY INTERVIEW - CONTACT

A.   Define Loss Responsibilities

B.   Source of Required Data

      1.   Collection Cards, Etc.

C.   Identify and Notify Attorney Handling File

D.   Packaging of Files

E.   Required Stops

F.   Pending Litigation

G.   Source of Late Charge Due Balance

H.   Obtain Delinquency/FC Report

CREATIVE FINANCING PLANS

A.   Records and Reports - Buydowns

    1.   Listing in loan number order, of all buydown loans included in transfer, listing/printout should include:

        a.   Original Loan Amount
        b.   First Payment Due Date
        c.   Last Paid Installment
        d.   Total P & I Payment
        e.   Homeowners Current Payment Amount
        f.   Current Payment Amount Due From Buydown Escrow

    2.   Copy of buydown computation sheets for each loan as available.

    3.   Reconciled report showing remaining balance of escrowed buydown funds for each loan.

    4.   Listing of all loans pending a change in payment amount, if applicable.

    5.   A check payable to _____ representing remaining buydown funds as of the cutoff date with a detail listing, by loan number, showing how the funds are to be applied.

Records and Reports - GPM's

    1.   Listing in loan number order, of all GPM loans included in transfer, listing/printout should include:

        a.   GPM Plan number applicable to each loan
        b.   Schedule of payment changes
        c.   GPM spreads for each loan

    2.   Listing of all loans pending a change in the P&I Payment.

B.   Interview - Contact

    1.   ARMS

        a.   Types of plans

        b.   Indices used to calculate new interest rate

        c.   How they are identified on system

    2.   GPMS

        a.   Types of plans

        b.   Scheduled changes

c. How they are identified on system
3. Buydowns
   a. Who holds funds?
4. WRAPS
5. Miscellaneous Products

PAYMENT PROCESSING

A. Definition of processing items

    1.   Non-CPI Coupons

    2.   MICR

    3.   OCR

    4.   Lockbox

B. Drafting Issues

C. Mortgage Payments Received after Transfer

D. NSF Checks Transfer

E. Other Checks Received after Transfer

F. Procedures for payments held between cutoff and conversion

    1.   Time held

<u>INVESTOR SERVICES</u>

A.   Reports and Records

     1.   Nemac should be provided with the following:

         a.   Reporting/Reconciliation Requirements and Methods

         b.   Reconciliations of Loan Balance and Custodial Accounts

         c.   Preliminary and Final Trial Balances

         d.   Copies of any investor reports (summary, single debit, delinq., as requested)

     2.   Servicing Agreements

         a.   Approval by Investor

         b.   Copies of Agreements

B.   Transfer/Establish Custodial Accounts

C.   Required Assignments

D.   Reporting

     1.   _____ agrees to assume responsibility of the _____ .

E.   Interview - Contact

     1.   Reporting information for

     2.   Normal cutoff

<u>RECORDS/MICROFILM</u>

A. Arrangements should be made for delivery of the files and records being transferred. Delivery should be made on or before _____.

B. Files, records and reports should be forwarded to the following address:

C. Packaging Instructions for files

    1. Files being shipped should be packaged as follows:

        a. Original Loan Files

            - Should be boxed in loan number order and labeled "Original Files"

            - Each box should be numbered (i.e. box 1 of ____) and include to and from numbers

        b. Microfiche

            - Should be forwarded under separate cover in loan number sequence

            - Fiche must be good readable negative fiche

        c. Custodial Documents

            Custodial filed must be separate from the hard files

        d. Miscellaneous files (i.e., customer service, insurance)

            - Should be in separate folders

<u>INVESTOR REPORTING</u>

I. <u>GNMA POOLS</u>

    A.   All all the GNMA pools final certified? NO_____ YES_____
           If no, provide a list of the pools that are not.

           What is the date of cutoff for GNMA pools? _____

    B.   Name and Address of Custodian(s)

    C.   Is there a tax ID number on each pool? NO_____ YES_____

    D.   Are 1099's or 1041/K1's used for interest income reporting
           to security holders? NO_____ YES_____

    E.   Are Security Holders' names and addresses current? NO_____
           YES_____

    F.   How many manual checks do you produce monthly?

    G.   Do you have a Security Register in pool number order?

    H.   In what order is security register?

    I.   Do you have pools where you overremitted to security
           holders and are awaiting liquidations to recapture?
           YES_____ NO_____ How Many?_____ Dollar Amount _____

    J.   Are there differences between your trial balance and 1710A
           Section I? YES_____ NO_____

           Do the 171) Section III balances equal the security holder
           balances? YES_____ NO_____

II. <u>FHLMC LOANS</u>

    A.   Does the 308 and trial balance equal for all groups?
           YES_____ NO_____

           If no, what is dollar amount? _____ How many?_____

    B.   If there are adjustments to line 5 form 330, provide
           detail for last 6 months.

III. <u>FNMA POOLS</u>

    A.   Are there differences between your trial balance and 2010
           section I? YES_____ NO_____

If yes, attach details.

B.   Do you have pools where you overremitted to security holders and are awaiting liquidations to recapture?
YES _____ NO_____ How many _____ Dollar Amount _____

C.   Provide name, address of custodian.

IV.   <u>FHA 235, 265 and 246 Loans</u>

    A.   Number of:

        1. - 235's _____

        2. - 265's _____

        3. - 246's _____

    B.   Describe how billing records are maintained.

    C.   Describe recertification records are maintained.

    D.   Describe how each of the following is handled.

        1.   Escrow shortages

        2.   Escrow overages

        3.   Overpaid assistance on HUD subsidy 235 loans

        4.   How is overpaid assistance reflected?

        5.   After 3 years, how are accounts suspended for termination?

        6.   Assistance billing for 246 loans.

IV.   <u>GPM's BUYDOWNS, ARMS</u>

A.   How are the following identified?

    1.   GPM's

    2..   Buydowns

    3.   ARM's

B.   How is the borrower notified of payment change?

    1.   GPM's

    2.   Buydowns

3.   ARM's

C.   How are the interest rate parameters tracked for ARM's?

Manually _____ System _____

D.   What indexes are used for ARM's?

BANKING

Bank Account Reconciliation

A. Are all your P & I accounts reconciled monthly?
    Yes_____ No _____

B. If no, explain.

C. Are there any large undefined reconciling items?
    Yes_____ No _____

D. If yes, explain.

10. A. Are all T & I accounts reconciled monthly? Yes___
        No _____

    B. If no, explain.

    C. Are there any large undefined reconciling items?
        Yes _____ No_____

    D. If yes, explain.

11. Are private investor accounts commingled? Yes_____
    No _____

12. A. How many bank accounts are there? _____

    B. List bank accounts:

    Bank   Acct. #   Acct. Type   Bank Last Balance

CASHIERING/PAYMENTS

1. Do you use a lockbox? Yes _____ No _____

2. A.) How do you handle exceptions? (Please explain)

    B.) How many exceptions do you have per month?

3. How do you handle the following?:

    Buydowns

    Subsidy Fund

    HUD 235, 265, and 246 Loans

    Returned checks

4. What type of billing method is used?:

    ( ) A. Coupons

    ( ) B. Monthly billings

    ( ) C. Drafts

    ( ) D. Other

GENERAL ESCROW

1.   How many loans are escrowed?

2.   How many loans are non-escrowed?

      VA _____

      FHA _____

      Other _____

3.   A)   Do you pay interest on escrow? Yes _____ No _____

      B)   When is interest credited to account?

      C)   Provide a list of the following:

            1.   State requiring interest

            2.   Interest rate

            3.   # of escrowed loans in each state

TAXES

1. Are all loans on a tax service? Yes_____ No_____

2. Do all loans have contract #s? Yes_____ No_____

3. A. How many times a year are taxes paid?

    B. If different states, provide a list with the following information:

        1. # of loans

        2. State

        3. Frequency

        4. Method

    C. Are all taxes paid directly to county or are they paid separately? (example: school)

        in total _____ separately _____

4. Are all taxes current? Yes_____ No _____

5. A. Delinquent taxes - Provide a list of the following by investor.

    B. Are they FHLMC/FNMA/GNMA?

6. A. How many are escrowed for taxes?

    B. How many are not escrowed for taxes?

7. Total T & I advance amount outstanding

8. How do you identify multiple parcels?

INSURANCE

HAZARD

1. How many loans are not escrowed for hazard insurance?

2. What type of evidence of insurance do you require?

3. Is insurance information maintained or to computer?
   Yes _____ No _____

4. How do you identify the following?:

   A) Expired policies

   B) Multiple policies

   C) Binder Policies

   D) Payment dates

   E) Flood insurance or other special required insurance

5. A) Who is default carrier?

   B) Payment method

OPTIONAL INSURANCE

1. List the types of optional insurance offered and to companies

2. A) If life insurance offered, do you have administrative
      contracts? Yes _____ No _____

   B) What is average percent received on premiums?

3. Are funds co-mingled with tax and hazard insurance funds?
   Yes _____ No _____

4. Are funds reconciled monthly? _____ Quarterly _____
   Annually _____

MORTGAGE INSURANCE

1. How do you handle the following?:

   A) Identify MSP paid in advance

   B) MSP with no billing

   C) Method of payment of FHA premiums

2. Provide the following lists:

A) All PMO companies used

B) All loans with MSP premiums

ANALYSIS

1. How many times per year do you analyze?
2. When was the last time you analyzed <u>all</u> loans?
3. How are overages handled?
4. How are shortages handled?
5. Where are previous analysis stored?
6. Do you analyze delinquent loans?

COLLECTIONS, DELINQUENCY, FORECLOSURE

1. Delinquency Ratios

   30 days   _____
   60 days   _____
   90 days   _____
   Foreclosure _____
   Bankruptcy _____

2. How many loans are on payment plans? _____

3. Are phone numbers on customer records?
   Yes _____ No _____

4. How are you recording collection histories?

5. Do you use in-house trustee or attorney?

6. Law firms you have relationships with. (Foreclosure & Bankruptcy)

7. How many of the following loan types are involved?

   ARM   _____
   FHA 235   _____
   Multi-family _____
   Commercial _____

8. How many different lenders are involved? What are their requirements for reporting delinquency?

9. Monitoring system of <u>bankruptcy plan</u> payments.
   # of and itemization of Chapter 7, 13, & 11 bankruptcies.

10. Stance on the following for collection:
    (1) delinquent taxes
    (2) escrow shortages

11. Typical "late charge deferred" limit before starting collection.

12. What is your frequency and method of contacting the borrower?

13. Explain your foreclosure tracking system.

14. Are advances indicated in the system records? Yes_____No_____

<u>PAYOFFS</u>

1.   If private investors - do you keep or split?

     A)   P.P. penalty _____ retained

     B)   Late Fees % _____ retained

2.   P.O. Rate - past 6 months

     A)   # of loans   _____   _____   _____   _____   ___

     B)   UPB   _____   _____   _____   _____   ___

     C)   States   _____   _____   _____   _____   ___

3.   Disbursement method - checks _____ wires _____

4.   Do files have copies of notes? Yes _____ No _____

5.   Do you have a void or expiration date on your payoff
     statements? Yes _____ No _____

6.   Are your files with pay-off statements separated from regular
     files? Yes _____ No _____

BALLOONS

1. Do they have balloon loans? Yes _____ # of loans _____
    No _____

2. A) Usual call

    5 years   _____
    10 years   _____
    Other   _____

    B) Are balloon dates in your system? Yes _____ No _____

3. Do they allow extensions on terms when loan is due?
    Yes _____ No _____

Assumptions

1. How many assumptions have been processed over the last 6
    months?

    FHA/VA   _____
    Conventional_____

2. Provide a list of private investors indicating the following:

    1. Investor's name

    2. Investor's #

    3. Investor's approval needed

    4. Servicer can approve

    5. Remittance reporting requirements

        A. Due dates

        B. Actual/Actual ____ Schedule/Schedule _____ Other ____

    6. Comments

FILES

1.   Do you use micro fische?

2.   If yes to 1:

    A)   What do you have on fische?

    B.   What is retention time?

3.   Loan file contents - (Specify location of each if not in file)

    a.   Current History
    b.   Prior Years' Histories
    c.   Last Escrow Analysis
    d.   Hazard Insurance Policies
    e.   Optional Insurance Certificates/Policies
    f.   Tax Receipts
    g.   Collection Records
    h.   Collection Correspondence

4.   What type of filing system is used?

    ( ) 1. Numeric by loan #

    ( ) 2. Alphabetical

SERVICING AGREEMENT - PRIVATE INVESTORS

1. Do you have in possession executed servicing agreements &
    documentation to support any change?
    Yes _____ No _____ Other _____

2. If you deal with a security holder, do you have a current
    certificate register?
    Yes _____ No _____

3. Cancellation without cause - (verify in agreements)

4. Advances P & I - (verify in agreements)

    A) How long does the servicer have to advance on delinquent
        loans?

5. Is servicer required to advance n taxes and insurance?
    (verify in agreements)

6. Are there any sub-servicing agreements in place? Yes _____
    No _____

7. Are there any participation agreements in place? Yes _____
    No _____

SYSTEM REQUIREMENT

1. Type of System

    A.   Service Bureau - name _____

    B.   In-house systems

         1)   Software used   _____

         2)   Hardware used   _____

    C.   Manual System   Yes _____ No _____

2. Can it be a tape to tape transfer? Yes _____ No _____

3. Dump of loan files to determine what exactly is stored.

4. Loan file specs to match up with #5.

5. ARM files - Are the adjustment periods set up?

6. Escrow files and Vendor files - layouts.

7. All file codes

         Property type

         Loan type

         Message/Stop codes, etc.

8. Are the following items on the computer and how valid is the data?

    a.   Full Mortgagor Names (s) _____

    b.   Property Address _____

    c.   Property Zip Codes _____

    d.   Mailing Address _____

    e.   Legal description _____

    f.   Social Security Numbers _____

    g.   Phone numbers _____

         How do you cross reference co-mortgagors with different last names?

         How do you cross reference different loans on the same property?

How do you identify property types (single family, condo, duplex, etc.) on a loan?

Appendix III

Procedural Guidelines
for Transfers of Servicing

Comparison of Current Fannie Mae Reporting Systems

Reporting Feature	AES	SRS[1]	Pooling Cost MBS/MRS
Loan Groupings	AES is loan level reporting. There are no loan groupings	One open-ended grouping for each product type for each lender. For participations, one closed-ended grouping for each certificate that a lender services.[2]	One closed-ended grouping for each pool the lender services.[2]
Accounting Cycle	Monthly; end-of-month cut-off date. Accounting reports due seventh calendar day.	Monthly; end-of-month cut-off date. Accounting reports due seventh calendar day.	Monthly cut-off date may be any day from the 25th through the end of the month. Accounting report due seventh calendar day.
Remittance Date	Remittance made whenever $2,500 of principal and interest net of servicing fee collected, or at least monthly.	Single remittance on the 20th of the month following the month actual principal is collected and of the same month scheduled interest is due.	Single remittance on the 18th of each month the scheduled payment is due.
Interest Payment	Actual interest collected	One month's scheduled interest at weighted pass-through rate, whether collected or not.	One month's scheduled interest calculated at the pool's pass-through rate, whether collected or not.
Principal Payment	Actual principal collected	Actual principal collected.	Scheduled principal whether or not.
Delinquent Loan Advances	An advances made.	Advance scheduled interest until loan is 90 days delinquent. Recovery made when final foreclosure claim settlement is received.	Lender advances scheduled principal and interest payment until loan is removed from pool or final disposition of the REO.
Prepaid Installments	Prepaid installments are sent to Fannie Mae under normal remitting guidelines. Lender does not have option of holding payments and applying them as they come due.	Lender remits prepaid principal in the month following collection. Scheduled interest based on the unpaid principal balance is remitted as it comes due.	Lender holds prepaid installments and remits them as they come due.
Absorption of Losses	Fannie Mae absorbs all losses	Fannie Mae absorbs all losses unless the loans are participations, in which case, losses are proportionately shared with participant.	Regular Servicing: Lender absorbs all losses.[4] Special Servicing: Fannie Mae absorbs all losses.[3]

[1] For participation sales, Fannie Mae receives its proportionate share of principal and interest based on the weighted pass-through rate.

[2] Lenders may add or remove loans from open-ended loan pools. Lenders may not add loans to closed-ended pools, but loans may be removed.

[3] This also applies to loans using MRS non-recourse servicing.

[4] This also applies to loans using MRS recourse servicing.

Reference

○ Selling
● Servicing
● MBS
○ Multifamily

This announcement amends the guide(s) indicated. Please keep it for reference until we issue a formal change.

Subject   Procedural Guidelines for Transfers of Servicing

We are amending our procedural guidelines related to approved transfers of servicing to assure that mortgagors receive sufficient notice of a servicing transfer and to clearly delineate the responsibilities of the transferring servicer (transferor) and the receiving servicer (transferee). Although we expect that most servicers are already following these procedures (or similar ones that accomplish the same thing), we are making these changes effective with transfer arrangements entered into on and after March 1, 1989 to assure that we do not impose additional requirements for transfers of servicing that are presently under negotiation. The following requirements supplement the specific instructions we provide when we approve a transfer of servicing.

Notifying Mortgagors

The two servicers must work together closely to assure that mortgagors receive not only prompt and accurate notification of a pending transfer but also prompt and courteous responses to their inquiries about the transfer. The transferee servicer should provide the transferor servicer with essential information to include in its notification letter to the mortgagor—the transferee's name, address, and telephone number (either a toll-free number or authorization to include a statement that "collect calls are acceptable") and the name and telephone number of a contact person (or department) that can answer the mortgagor's questions. Both servicers are responsible for sending specific notices to the mortgagors whose mortgages are being transferred.

<u>Before the date of the actual transfer</u>, the transferor servicer must send each mortgagor the following information in writing:

- The effective date of the transfer, and the date that the mortgagor's first payment to the new servicer will be due;

- The new servicer's name, address and telephone number, and the name of a contact person (or department) that can answer questions;

- Instructions on how to handle payments that become due before the new servicer notifies the mortgagor about where his or her future monthly payments are to be sent;

- Assurance that the legal terms and conditions of the mortgage (other than the name and address of the party to whom payments are made) will not be affected by the transfer;

- Suggestions or instructions about how to handle any optional item that the servicer previously escrowed for--such as mortgage life or accident and health insurance--that the new servicer may not offer; and

- The name and telephone number of a contact person (or department) in the transferor servicer's office that the mortgagor may contact if he or she has any questions about the notification or the pending transfer.

<u>Before the date of the actual transfer</u>, the **transferee** servicer must send each mortgagor a written confirmation of the information contained in the transferor servicer's notice to the mortgagor. In addition, the **transferee** servicer must send the following information to the mortgagor as soon as possible—generally, at least 15 days before it is due to receive the mortgagor's first payment:

- Detailed information about the monthly payment—amount, due date, applicable late charges, etc. (including payment coupons if the servicer normally provides them for its customers);

- The address to which payments are to be sent;
- An explanation of the method the servicer uses for determining escrow deposits for taxes and insurance, any changes that may be made to the monthly payment as the result of the servicer's method of calculating escrow deposits, the reasons for the changes, and the approximate date on which the changed payment will become effective;
- The telephone number of a contact person (or department) that the mortgagor can call if he or she has questions; and
- Information describing the terms and cost of any mortgage life or disability insurance coverage that the servicer offers, if the mortgagor's present optional life insurance coverage is affected by the transfer.

Notifying Third Parties

<u>Before a transfer of servicing actually occurs</u>, the **transferor** servicer must take certain actions to assure that all servicing functions that involve third parties will continue uninterrupted (or will be discontinued) after the transfer of servicing. Specifically, the servicer must take the following actions:

- The servicer must contact each conventional mortgage insurer (MI) that insures any of the mortgages being transferred to request approval of the transfer and the continuation of the mortgage insurance coverage. This is not necessary when an MI's master policy does not require the MI's prior approval when insured mortgages are assigned to another lender that is in good standing. If the current MI will not provide continuing coverage, the servicer must find another MI to take over the insurance—at no increased cost to the mortgagor—and obtain that MI's written commitment to provide the required coverage. (The transferor and transferee servicers may work together to find a new MI.)

- The servicer must notify the hazard and flood insurance carriers to request a policy endorsement to substitute the transferee's name in the mortgage clause and to change the premium billing address to that of the transferee servicer (unless the mortgagor pays the premium directly).
- The servicer must notify any tax service it uses or any accident and health insurers that are providing coverage for any of the mortgages that are being transferred to indicate whether the new servicer will continue using their services.
- The servicer must send appropriate notices of the transfer, providing the transferee servicer's name and address, to FHA or VA (if required), taxing authorities, holders of leaseholds, and other lienholders. The servicer should also notify any public utilities that levy mandatory assessments if the servicer escrows funds for their payment.

Transfer of Individual Mortgage Files

No later than 30 days after the effective date of the transfer, the **transferor** servicer must deliver to the transferee servicer the individual mortgage file for each mortgage included in the transfer. If both servicers agree, this information may be provided on microfiche. Among other things (see Part I, Section 304, of the Servicing Guide), the individual mortgage file should include a history of mortgage payments received and escrow disbursements made for the mortgage during the current year and the two preceding years (making additional historical information available if the transferee servicer requests it), including the most recent escrow analysis and appropriate supporting documentation; a complete history of mortgage payments received and escrow disbursements made since inception if the mortgage is in foreclosure status; copies of any current assumption or payoff statements and any pertinent related information that will avoid delays in processing a subsequent payoff or in refunding the mortgagor's escrow balance; a copy of the notice that was sent to advise the mortgagor of the pending transfer of servicing; and copies of all correspondence or notices related to the servicing transfer that were sent to the mortgagor,

FHA/VA/MI, Fannie Mae, any government authority, or an interested third party. Servicers that use a single letter or magnetic tape to notify third parties about a transfer of servicing may provide this information to the transferee servicer in a master file rather than having to copy it for individual mortgage files.

If the servicer is performing administrative services—such as paying taxes and insurance premiums, making property inspections, performing property maintenance functions, handling evictions, etc.—for properties that Fannie Mae has acquired by foreclosure or acceptance of a deed-in-lieu, the transferor servicer must give the transferee servicer a complete history of its actions from the date the property was acquired, including a list of expenditures, receipts, a summary of management and marketing activities, and any other appropriate supporting documentation.

Transfer of Portfolio Information

<u>By the effective date of the transfer of servicing</u>, the **transferor** servicer must deliver to the transferee servicer information and records related to the entire portfolio of mortgages being transferred (including any acquired properties that have not been sold). Specific information that should be forwarded includes the following:

- Documentation evidencing each MI's approval of the servicing transfer or its commitment to insure the transferred mortgages, or a copy of the MI's master policy evidencing that it is permissible to transfer servicing of insured mortgages without the MI's prior approval;
- Copies of any tax service contracts that will remain in effect, or notification that the contracts will be transferred to the new servicer by a tape process;
- A list of mortgages that have optional mortgage life or accident and health insurance that will remain in effect;
- A list of tax bills, assessments, hazard insurance premiums, mortgage insurance premiums, etc. that are due to be paid

from escrow funds but that are still unpaid as of the effective date of the transfer;

- A list of mortgages that are subject to automatic drafting of the monthly payment;
- A list of the expiration dates of the hazard, flood, and mortgage insurance policies for each mortgage being transferred, whether or not premiums for these policies are escrowed;
- A list of adjustable-rate mortgages, showing the plan identification and parameters, the index used, the next interest rate change date, the next payment change date, the dates on which any conversion to fixed-rate mortgage option may be exercised, and the current status of any changes in process;
- Ledger records, showing activity for the current year and the previous two years;
- Trial balances, as of the close of business on the day immediately preceding the day the records are transferred, showing:
  - the remittance type for each mortgage—either actual/actual, scheduled/actual, or scheduled/scheduled;
  - delinquencies, foreclosures, bankruptcies, and acquired properties;
  - transfers of ownership, payoffs, and other exception transactions that are in process;
  - escrow balances, escrow advances, curtailments; and
  - buydown account balances for mortgages subject to interest rate buydown plans;
- A copy of the custodial bank reconciliation for each custodial bank account maintained, as of the close of the bank's last business day that immediately precedes the day the records are transferred to the new servicer. (If the transferor servicer is unable to complete this reconciliation by the effective date of the transfer, it should complete the reconciliation as promptly as possible and send it to the transferee servicer within five business days after the effective date of the transfer.);

- Copies of all servicing and accounting reports that were filed with Fannie Mae for the three months that immediately precede the date the records are transferred to the new servicer; and
- Definitions of codes used in ledger records, trial balances, or any other documents that are being forwarded to the new servicer.

Both the **transferor** and **transferee** servicers should maintain adequate records—lists, cards, computer tape, microfilm, etc.—of the portfolio transfer in their corporate records to identify the mortgages included in the transfer, the effective date of the transfer, and the parties involved in the transfer.

Transfer of Funds

No later than five days after the effective date of the transfer, the **transferor** servicer must forward all account balances including, but not limited to, unremitted principal and interest collections, escrows funds, curtailments, and buydown funds to the transferee servicer. If the transferor servicer has advanced delinquent interest or scheduled principal and interest to Fannie Mae, the transferee servicer should reimburse the transferor servicer as soon as it receives a final accounting of all monies from the transferor servicer. All net amounts owed must be paid to the appropriate party on the effective date of the transfer.

Transitional Responsibilities

The **transferor** servicer and the **transferee** servicer must ensure that their staff and facilities are adequately prepared to process servicing and accounting transactions and to respond to mortgagor inquiries during the transfer transition period. The **transferee** servicer must assume responsibility for responding to mortgagor inquiries that are received after the effective date of the transfer. It must not refer any mortgagor to the transferor servicer. If any servicing or accounting problem cannot be resolved without the involvement of the transferor servicer, the transferee servicer—not the mortgagor—should initiate the contact.

After the effective date of the transfer, the **transferor** servicer must deliver to the transferee servicer any funds or correspondence related to any of the transferred mortgages or acquired properties that it receives—and must make that delivery within three days after it receives the funds or correspondence.

During the transition period, the **transferee** servicer must give special consideration to a mortgagor's needs and make every effort to resolve disputes to the mortgagor's satisfaction when the dispute arises from a legitimate misunderstanding of the instructions that were contained in the notices of transfer that were sent to the mortgagor. Late charges must be waived and, if necessary, appropriate adjustments must be made to payment and credit records to reflect misapplied or unapplied payments that were owed to the transferee servicer but which were sent to the transferor servicer.

New Procedures Governing Transfers of GNMA Servicing and Requirements for Final Certification of Pools

<u>Transfers of Issuer Responsibility</u>

The following procedures governing the transfer of issuer responsibility (GNMA servicing) are applicable for all pools with an effective transfer date of July 1, 1988 or later.

- Pools may not be transferred within 90 days of issuance nor within 180 days of a prior transfer.
- The buyer of servicing is fully responsible for the final certification and servicing of the pools.
- Requests to transfer 10 or more pools must be submitted on a 5-1/4" diskette along with the customary documentation required for such transfers. The information contained on the floppy diskette will be the same information listed in the ""Exhibit A" which identifies the pools to be transferred. The data format of the floppy diskette will be specified in a subsequent all issuer letter. Requests not conforming to this requirement or diskettes that appear to be damaged or unreadable will be returned and the request will not be processed.
- Requests to transfer 9 or fewer pools may be submitted in either the customary paper manner only or along with the 5-1/4" diskette.
- Pools that are 18 months or older and not finally certified may not be transferred until they are finally certified.

The following rules are applicable to pools that are not finally certified:

- A pool may be transferred only <u>once</u> prior to its final certification.

- The seller remains residually liable for the certification of transferred pools, i.e., if the buyer does not perform.
- Letters of credit held by GNMA under the current tri-party transfer agreement (Addendum to the Assignment Agreement) for transfers concluded prior to July 1, 1988 will be returned, and the agreements dissolved as between GNMA and the other parties, upon application to GNMA by the other parties jointly. GNMA will return the letter of credit upon a determination that the current transfer satisfies all of the rules stated herein.
- Pools currently transferred under an Addendum to the Assignment Agreement may not be transferred again until finally certified.

Although GNMA hereby recognizes the transfer of issuer responsibility as a recurring event in the normal course of business, this recognition should not be misconstrued as GNMA's endorsement of frequent movement of mortgage pools. GNMA expects issuers to maintain the same high standards of servicing after the implementation of this policy as before.

Final Certification of Pools

The following rules regarding final certification apply to all GNMA pools.

- Final certification of a pool must be accomplished on or before the 18th month of the pool issuance. (NOTE: This rule is effective July 1, 1988, but will not be enforced until January 1, 1989. Consequently, final certification deadlines which fall after July 1, 1988 whether subject to existing rules or this new rule will be extended automatically to January 1, 1989, even if this results in more than 18 months being allowed for final certification.)

- Extensions for 45 days will no longer be granted nor required as of July 1, 1988. No extensions beyond the 18 month period will be granted.
- Completed HUD Form 11706 with Final Certifications should be sent directly to GNMA's agent at the following address:

> Chemical New York, Inc.
> 1325 G Street NW
> Suite 640
> Washington, D.C. 20005
> Attention: Final Certification Department
> (202)662-0501

Sanctions

Failure to accomplish final certification within the allotted 18 months is conclusive evidence of a servicing deficiency which will result in automatic default of the servicing portfolio if the deficiency is not cured within 30 days of notice given by GNMA.

Summary of Transfer Policy

Use the following decision tree to determine whether a pool may be transferrable at the time the request is made of GNMA. Requests for transfer must be received no later than the 3rd business day of each month in order for the transfer to be effective as of the 1st of the following month. To be transferrable, a "yes" answer must be given for each question listed below.

A. If the pool is finally certified:

1. Then is the issue date more than two months ago?
2. If yes, then, is the date of the last transfer more than five months ago?
3. If yes, then, the pool is transferrable.

B. If the pool is <u>not</u> finally certified:
    1. Then, is the issue date more than two months ago?
    2. If yes, then, is the issue date <u>less than</u> 18 months ago?
    3. If yes, then, is this the first transfer of the pool? (NOTE: A pool governed by the provisions of any Addendum to the Assignment Agreement has already been transferred once and is not eligible to be transferred again until finally certified.)
    4. If yes, then, the pool is transferrable.

Chart 1   Marginal Cost of Servicing Per Loan Group by Dollar Volume Serviced

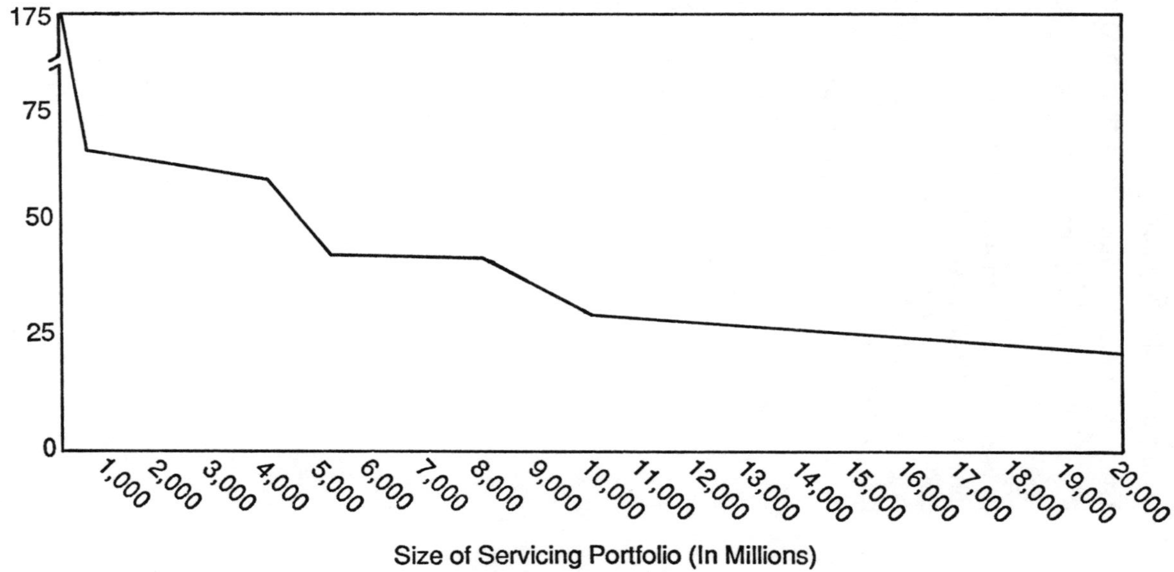

Size of Servicing Portfolio (In Millions)

FREDDIE MAC

Like Fannie Mae, the Federal Home Loan Mortgage Corporation (Freddie Mac) has certain regulations and guidelines to follow when transferring servicing portfolios. Refer to the Freddie Mac's *Sellers' and Servicers' Guide*, Volume 2, Sections 8025 and 6311.
Section 6311 gives the following specifics:

- The servicer may not transfer its servicing portfolio without Freddie Mac's prior written consent. Each request will be reviewed on an individual basis and the servicing portfolio may be transferred only to another approved servicer.

- As a condition of granting approval to a transfer of servicing, Freddie Mac requires that any outstanding obligations of the servicer to Freddie Mac be fulfilled including, but not limited to, any mortgage repurchase obligation and/or any obligation to perform under a contract to Freddie Mac's Securities Sales and Trading Group.

- Form 981, Request for Transfer of Servicing (Exhibit XIV) must be completed and sent to the regional office (Attn: Loan Servicing) as soon as possible in advance of the transfer date as shown on the form.

- When submitting the request, the servicer will warrant the following:
  - Each MI that insures the mortgages has approved the transferee and shall continue to provide coverage for the benefit of the transferee;
  - Or that it has obtained a commitment from another MI company to provide coverage, and written evidence of such approval and/or commitment must be submitted with the required documentation at the time of physical transfer of all applicable files and records;

- Freddie Mac reserves the right to disapprove, in its sole discretion, the transfer of servicing if it determines that the transferee will not be able to adequately service the mortgages.

- For all servicing transfers submitted for approval on or after July 15, 1986, the transferee agrees that it is solely responsible to Freddie Mac for:
  — All warranties and representations concerning the transferred mortgages' eligibility for purchase by Freddie Mac whether or not the transferor was responsible for such warranties and representations
  — Any and all servicing warranty violations, including those that occurred prior to the transfer to the transferee
- For mortgages transferred that were purchased by Freddie Mac pursuant to a negotiated purchase contract, a copy of the contract will be sent by the transferor together with certification by the transferee that the transferee assumes any and all special obligations of the transferor under the contract.
- A transfer fee of $500 will be payable to Freddie Mac on or before the effective date of transfer.

In addition, at the time of transfer Freddie Mac will provide a "Transfer of Servicing Agreement" between Freddie Mac, the transferor and transferee. Exhibit XV is an example of this agreement.

Exhibit XIV FHLMC Form 981—Request for Transfer of Servicing

Request for Transfer of Servicing (Form 981)

Exhibit 109

Page 307

Sellers' & Servicers' Guide, Volume 2

11/1/86

Freddie Mac

Owned by America's Savings Institutions

Request for Transfer of Servicing

Submit to the Servicing Department at the applicable Freddie Mac regional office.

If more space is needed to list accounting groups, please use additional Forms 981.

Requested date for transfer of servicing

	Transferor		Transferee
Seller/Servicer number		Seller/Servicer number	
Seller/Servicer name		Seller/Servicer name	
Address		Address	
City, State, Zip		City, State, Zip	
Contact person		Contact person	
Department		Department	
Phone number ( )		Phone number ( )	

Accounting group(s)

For each accounting group being transferred, complete the following information as of the accounting cycle prior to the requested date for transfer of servicing

	Accounting group number	Active principal balance (Freddie Mac share)	Inactive principal balance (Freddie Mac share)	Real estate owned (REO) principal balance (Freddie Mac share)	For Freddie Mac use only Approval state
1					
2					
3					
4					
5					
6					
7					
8					
9					
10					
11					
12					
13					
14					
15					

Does this request represent all the accounting groups the transferor services for Freddie Mac? ☐ Yes ☐ No

Does the transferor have any pending commitments with Freddie Mac? ☐ Yes ☐ No

Freddie Mac Form 981 (9/86)

EXHIBIT XV—TRANSFER OF SERVICING AGREEMENT

This is an Agreement among the Federal Home Loan Mortgage Corporation ("Freddie Mac"), 1776 G Street, N.W., P.O. Box 37248, Washington, D.C. 20013; (Name of Buyer) Seller/Servicer number (#); ("Transferee") and (Name of Seller) Seller/Servicer Number (#); ("Transferor") with respect to the mortgages specified in Attachment 1 to this Agreement (the "Mortgages").

WHEREAS:

a. Freddie Mac is a corporation duly organized and existing under and by virtue of the laws of the United States and has full corporate power to enter into and perform the obligations of this Agreement; and

b. Transferee is a (type of corporation) duly organized and existing under and by virtue of the laws of (applicable State) and has full corporate power to enter into and perform the obligations of this Agreement; and

c. Transferee is a (type of corporation) duly organized and existing under and by virtue of the laws of (applicable State) and has full corporate power to enter into and perform the obligations of this Agreement; and

d. Freddie Mac owns certain specified interests in the Mortgages; and

e. Transferor wishes to transfer all of its rights and obligations with respect to the Mortgages to Transferee; and

f. Transferee wishes to accept all of the Transferor's right and obligations with respect to the Mortgages; and

g. Freddie Mac has consented to the transfer of all rights and obligations with respect to the Mortgages from Transferor to Transferee.

NOW, THEREFORE, in consideration of the promises and mutual covenants contained in this Agreement, the parties agree as follow:

Article 1. Servicing of Mortgages

A. Transferee shall, from this date forward, be the servicer for each of the Mortgages. Transferee's obligations as servicer shall be those contained in the Purchase Documents, including Volume 2 of the Freddie Mac *Sellers' and Servicers' Guide.*

B. Transferee shall comply in all respects with Volume 2 of the Freddie Mac *Sellers' and Servicers' Guide* as it now exists and as it may, from time to time, be amended.

C. Nothing in this Agreement shall affect in any way Transferee's obligations as servicer of any mortgages owned in whole or in part by Freddie Mac except for the Mortgages described in Attachment 1.

Article 2. Documents.

Transferee hereby acknowledges and warrants to Freddie Mac that it has received and possesses all legal documents, files and records necessary for the discharge of all servicing obligations imposed by Article 1 of this Agreement, including, but not limited to, those items contained on the "Checklist" attached hereto as Attachment 2.

Article 3. Sale and Servicing Warranties.

A. Freddie Mac agrees that Transferor is released and relieved of all liabilities and obligations for all breaches of sale and servicing warranties with respect to the Mortgages.

B. Transferee shall be responsible to Freddie Mac for all breaches of sale and servicing warranties with respect to the Mortgages pursuant to the Purchase Documents.

C. Transferee shall be responsible to Freddie Mac for all breaches of servicing warranties including those that occurred prior to (date), the date of sale and transfer of the servicing of the Mortgages.

Article 4. Compensation.

Freddie Mac shall compensate Transferee for servicing its interest in the Mortgages in the amount and manner prescribed in Volume 2 of the Freddie Mac *Sellers' and Servicers' Guide.*

Article 5. Transfer Fee.

Transfereror shall pay Freddie Mac, on or before the effective date of the transfer, a transfer fee of $500.00.

Article 6. Effect of Headings.

The headings are for convenience only and shall not affect the construction of this Agreement.

Article 7. Governing Law.

This Agreement shall be governed by the laws of the United States. Insofar as there may be no applicable precedent, and insofar as to do so would not frustrate the purposes of the Federal Home Loan Mortgage Corporation Act of 1970, as amended (12 U.S.C. SS1451-1459) or any provision of this Agreement, the local laws of the state of (   ) shall be deemed reflective of the laws of the United States.

SIGNED BY FREDDIE MAC, TRANSFEROR AND TRANSFEREE

As with Fannie Mae and Freddie Mac, Ginnie Mae has a *Servicing Guide* that should be referred to before any attempt to transfer servicing is made. Transferring servicing of Ginnie Mae pools involves what is known as the transfer of issuer responsibility. Basically, this is the same concept as Fannie Mae's, in that when the transfer of servicing is consummated, the new servicer takes on the responsibilities of the originator/seller.

Please refer to the Guide for any and all updates, specifically chapters 2–7 and 11–10. As of this writing, the following guidelines are in effect for the transfer of servicing/issuer responsibility:

- All transfers of servicing/issuer responsibility must be preapproved in writing and carried out using the assignment agreement as prescribed by Ginnie Mae. The buyer must assume all of the duties and obligations under the guaranty agreements.

    NOTE: Only pools that have been finally certified by the document custodian may be transferred. Also, the guide states that transfers should not be part of a continuous, recurring business practice, and it requires transferors to demonstrate that a proposed transfer is required due to special circumstances and that such transfers will not be routine.

- The proposed buyer/substitute issuer must be an approved MBS issuer in good standing with the necessary experience and adequate staff and facilities to handle the pools being transferred.

- The buyer/substitute issuer must have adequate net worth in assets as prescribed by Ginnie Mae.

- Reasons for the transfer must be submitted to Ginnie Mae in writing. These actions must follow sound business practices and promote "stable pool administration arrangements."

- A fee of $250 must be paid by the seller/transferring issuer for each pool being transferred. The fee is considered to be payable and earned when Ginnie Mae approves the transfer.

- When Ginnie Mae gives its approval for the transfer, but prior to the actual transfer itself, the seller/transferring issuer, must submit the following to Ginnie Mae:
  - A corporate resolution from the seller approving the request for transfer
  - Form HUD 11715, Custodial Agreement, signed by the buyer/substitute issuer and the custodian for each pool involved. If a new custodian is to be used, the present custodian must receive a release of documents on form HUD 11708 for each pool which will release them of any responsibility after they transfer the documents to the new custodian.

  NOTE: Form HUD 11726 is used for manufactured home loan pools, HUD 1722 for project loan pools, and HUD 1729 for construction loan pools.

  - Form HUD 11707, Servicing Agreement, which must be executed by the buyer/substitute issuer, for each pool.
  - New forms HUD 11709 and 11720 to establish principal and interest and tax and insurance custodial accounts, which must be executed by the buyer/substitute issuer and the custodian of funds.
  - An assignment agreement in the form prescribed by Ginnie Mae must be signed. (see Appendix 52 in the Guide). This agreement is to be received by Ginnie Mae no later than the first calendar day of the month prior to the month in which the buyer/substitute issuer will pay the securities holders.
  - A check to Ginnie Mae which will cover the fee of $250 for each pool being transferred.
- When Ginnie Mae signs the assignment agreement, the buyer/substitute issuer must, within 90 days, accomplish the following:

— The Note must be endorsed by the seller to the buyer/substitute issuer, without recourse. The buyer will then in turn endorse each one of the instruments in blank without recourse. Form HUD 11706, 11725 or 1721, when properly executed by the custodian, will be an acknowledgement to Ginnie Mae that all notes are endorsed properly.

— Recorded assignments of mortgages from the seller to the buyer for each mortgage in the pool must be forwarded to the custodian. Certified copies of the assignments may be substituted and sent to the custodian.

— The buyer will execute assignments of the mortgages to Ginnie Mae in recordable form, but not recorded, and substitute these assignments for the ones executed by the seller and which are in the possession of the custodian. Execution of Form HUD 11706, 11725 or 1721 by the custodian acknowledges to Ginnie Mae the receipt of the assignments executed by the buyer and the release of the assignments that were executed by the seller.

— The buyer will submit to Ginnie Mae a copy of a written release of documents, Form HUD 11708, issued by the prior custodian to the new custodian. This step is not necessary if there is no change of custodian.

— After the transfer of documents has been completed, an updated copy, certified by the new custodian, of the original Form HUD 11706, Schedule of Pooled Mortgages, showing which mortgages have been deleted or satisfied, shall be sent to Ginnie Mae.

NOTE: For manufactured home loan pools the form is HUD 11725, and for project and construction loan pools the form is HUD 1721.

REMITTANCE SCHEDULE

1   FHLMC

A.   Arc

Cutoff is the 15th, funds being transferred under the accelerated reporting cycle (ARC) on the 3rd business day following
the 15th.

........3 days float

B.   Non-Arc

Cutoff is the 15th, funds transferred on the 1st Tuesday of
the following month.

........10 days float

II   FNMA

A.   MBS

P&I is due on the 1st.
Loan payoffs of previous month and schedule payments of
the current month are due on the 18th. * can reinvest collections prior to remittance.
Pay investors on the 25th.
Paydown is announced by the 5th business day. (paydown
tells how much remittance on the 25th is due).

........collect remittance on the 18th
..........pass to the investor on the 25th
............................7 days float

---

*   This information is from Chuck Clark the secretary of GNMA, in Washington D.C.

III   GNMA

A.   GNMA I

Weighted average is 11 days.

........11 days float

B.   GNMA II

Payment is automatically withdrawn from accounts on the 18th or 19th of every month. This results in no float.

........0 days float

FHLMC MULTI-FAMILY SERVICING

- Remittance is 5 business days after 15th of the month.
- Other remittance characteristics similar to single family serv-icing.
- Securities are issued as PC's under a number of plans.
- Prepayment penalties:

    PLAN A:
    > Prepayment (partial or full) allowed during first five years only with penalty. Penalty declines with ma-turity but is always at least one percent.

    PLAN B:
    > Prepayment (partial or full) is not allowed during first 54 months of the loan's term.

- Servicing fees are, as with single-family servicing, subject to negotiations between Freddie Mac and the seller-servicer.
- All loans in N.E. region are non-recourse.
- Seller-servicer advances the funds for foreclosure and is repaid at the end of the foreclosure process by Freddie Mac with 8% per year interest added.
- In the Northeast region, out of 3083 loans in the portfolio, 8 are in active foreclosure (5 loans are to the same borrower). Out of these, 2 will probably foreclose, and 5 will probably be assumed.
- Out of 3083 loans in the Northeast regional portfolio, 25 are delinquent (11 from the same borrower). Out of these, 8 are 30 days delinquent, 5 are 60 days delinquent, 4 are 90 days delinquent, and 8 are in foreclosure.
- 2.05% National delinquency rate.

Source: Wayne Ferguson, FHLMC Northeast regional office, 4/12/88

Freddie Mac Servicing
(Investor)

Accounting/Reporting System
ACR (Accelerated Remittance Cycle)

Description of System
Seller may change the required net yield to FHLMC. Under the ARC program the RNY is reduced in exchange for the Sellers obligation to remit.

Automated Reporting System

Required Service Fee
.375%

Required Guarantee Fee
NONE

Remittance Type
Scheduled interest/scheduled principal
Program/Product

Cutoff Date
15th

Remittance Date
On the contract specified business day after the 15th of the month cutoff.

Automatic Draft
Yes

Delinquencies Removed from Accounting Group
VIA FHLMC form 116. Must have FHLMC approval to do so.

Prepaids/Delinquents
Remit prepaid principal and delinquent interest

Freddie Mac Servicing
(Investor)

Accounting/Reporting System
  Single Debit Reporting Concept

Description of System
  Effective 1-87, FHA/VA mortgages reported under single debit
  were converted to net yield accounting.

Automated Reporting System

Required Service Fee

Required Guarantee Fee

Remittance Type Actual/Actual

Program/Product

Cutoff Date

Remittance Date

Automatic Draft

Delinquencies Removed from Accounting Group

Prepaids/Delinquents

Fannie Mae Servicing
(Investor)

Accounting/Reporting System
MRS/MBS
(will be known as Laser)

Description of System

Automated Reporting System
Mor Net

Required Service Fee

Required Guarantee Fee
.25% of beginning security balance
Remittance Type
Scheduled interest/scheduled principal
Program/Product

Cutoff Date
30th - month end
Remittance Date
18th of following month
Automatic Draft
Yes
Delinquencies Removed from Accounting Group
No

Prepaids/Delinquents
Remit all curtailments and delinquent payments thru the scheduled section of the report.

Note: These loans are currently being serviced in the MRS/MBS system, which will begin converting to Laser in 1988.

Fannie Mae Servicing
(Investor)

Accounting/Reporting System
   AES (Aggregate Exception System) (not known as Laser).

Description of System
   Assumes that all monthly payments were made when due &
   for the correct amount. Servicer reports exceptions to this assumption.

Automated Reporting System
   Laser

Required Service Fee
   ?

Required Guarantee Fee
   No

Remittance Type
   Actual/Actual

Program/Product

Cutoff Date
   30th - Month End

Remittance Date
   Daily when total amount collected is greater than 2500, or; the
   1st of each month.

Automatic Draft
   Yes

Delinquencies Removed from Accounting Group
   NO

Prepaids/Delinquents
   Remit prepaids, not delinquents.

Note: The actual/actual loans were all converted in 9-86 to the
Laser system. The scheduled/actual loans are being converted
starting with the 10-87 reporting in November.

Fannie Mae Servicing
(Investor)

Accounting/Reporting System
    Participation Accounting System (will be known as Laser)

Description of System

Automated Reporting System

Required Service Fee
    .375%

Required Guarantee Fee
    No

Remittance Type
    Scheduled interest/actual principal

Program/Product

Cutoff Date
    30th - Month End

Remittance Date
    Can not find specific date. Usually by the 4th, 5th day.

Automatic Draft
    Yes

Delinquencies Removed from Accounting Group
    NO

Prepaids/Delinquents
    Remit prepaid principal & delinquent interest.

Note: The scheduled/actual loans are being converted to the Laser system starting with the 10/87 reporting in November.

Fannie Mae Servicing
(Investor)

Accounting/Reporting System
Summary Accounting System (will be known as Laser)

Description of System

Automated Reporting System

Required Service Fee

Required Guarantee Fee

Remittance Type
Scheduled interest/actual principal

Program/Product

Cutoff Date

Remittance Date

Automatic Draft

Delinquencies Removed from Accounting Group

Prepaids/Delinquents

Note: The scheduled/actual loans are being converted to the Laser system starting with the 10/87 reporting in November.

TRANSFER FEES

GNMA

GNMA charges a transfer fee of $250 per pool.

FHLMC

Transfer fee is the larger of $500 or 1 basis point (0.01 percent) of the total dollar amount of FHLMC's participation in the unpaid principal balance of the mortgages being transferred.

FHLMC considers waiving fees for transfers of servicing that meet the following criteria;

1) where one receiving the servicing is the originator of the mortgages;

2) where the transfer of servicing is between affiliates (e.g., a parent to a subsidiary); and

3) where the transfer is a result of a merger and acquisition or a regulatory takeover.

FNMA

FNMA has removed all transfer fees on sales of FNMA servicing between approved sellers. FNMA will not absorb the excess yield or yield differential in servicing transfers.

The FNMA servicing transfer fee had ranged from 5 to 10 basis points assessed on the amount of servicing being sold.

The new program allows final transfer without full certification if there's a letter of credit, posted with GNMA, equalling one half of 1% of the portfolio being transferred. The buyer must agree that final certifications will be complete within a year. It's available only for new production servicing, and GNMA officials tell us such transfers will only be okayed through the rest of this year. Although HUD and VA are generally blamed for certification delays, officials suggest a large part of the problem lies with local recording clerks. They encourage the industry to use local political muscle to get these offices operating more efficiently.

Draft—6/25/90

LASER
June 1990

Making Doing Business with Fannie Mae Easier

Q. What is LASER?

A. LASER is an automated loan accounting system, designed to manage Fannie Mae loans throughout their entire life cycle—from commitment and delivery, through reporting and disposition—and to make doing business with Fannie Mae easier and more efficient. LASER maintains data on a loan-level basis—mirroring the records you keep—and provides you and Fannie Mae with a means to better manage and control the loans you service for us. The purchasing system of LASER was implemented in January 1985, and the reporting system in October 1986.

Q. What do the terms LASER Actual/Actual, LASER Scheduled/Actual, and LASER Scheduled/Scheduled mean?

A. These terms describe the monthly remittance options under which loans may be sold to Fannie Mae, either for cash sales or mortgage-backed securities (MBS) swaps. Using Actual/Actual (A/A), lenders remit to Fannie Mae each month the actual interest and actual principal collected from borrowers to Fannie Mae; on Scheduled/Actual (S/A) loans, lenders remit scheduled interest (whether collected or not) and actual principal; and with Scheduled/Scheduled (S/S) loans, lenders remit scheduled interest and scheduled principal (whether collected or not). While Actual/Actual and Scheduled Actual are generally both available for cash sales, all loans sold under our MBS program must be remitted under Scheduled/Scheduled. Each option has some different LASER reporting and remitting requirements.

Q. How often are remittances made on each type?

A. If reporting under the Actual/Actual option, remittances are due whenever actual collections exceed $2,500 (net of servicing fees), or no later than the first business day of the next month if less than $2,500 is collected. Payoffs and repurchases are due within one business day of receipt.

Remittances for <u>Scheduled/Actual</u> loans are due on the 20th calendar day of the month following activity. Payoffs and repurchases are included in the monthly remittance.

Under <u>Scheduled/Scheduled</u>, a monthly remittance of scheduled principal and interest, plus any unscheduled principal, is due on the 18th calendar day of the month following the reporting period. Or, with MBS Rapid Payment Method (RPM) option, lenders may remit funds on the 10th of the month instead of the 18th in exchange for a 3 basis point reduction in guaranty fee.

Q. **Why does Fannie Mae offer more than one remittance type on loans sold for cash? Can I change remittance types after I have sold the loans?**

A. To better meet our customers' needs, we offer a choice between receiving float on their collections and reduced required yields. While we offer aggressive and flexible pricing on many of our products, our yields are generally lower for loans remitted under A/A.

You may indicate the remittance type at the time you request a commitment. Lenders can switch easily between remittance types after the loans has been purchased to meet their particular needs.

Q. **What are the benefits to lenders of LASER Reporting?**

A. LASER's automated, loan-level reporting system is designed to reduce your monthly processing activities and costs, and provide greater accuracy and control in the reporting of your servicing portfolio. Under the LASER system, you report loan-level "trial balance" type information, similar to that which you routinely maintain on every loan.

Some specific benefits that LASER reporting offers Fannie Mae lenders are:

— Lenders use one standard LASER form and format to report on all of their loans purchased or securitized by Fannie Mae, for all three remittance types;

— Lenders have increased control with loan-level processing;

— LASER provides timely feedback on your reported activity via output reports—no later than the 25th of the month—and makes portfolio reconciliation easier by streamlining the process of identifying and correcting errors; and

— The LASER database contains individual loan data on loans backing ARM MBS, which allows us to provide more detailed MBS investor information in our pool prospectuses and monthly ARM Analysis Tapes.

Q. What type of information do I need to report and how do I report to Fannie Mae every month?

A. It is easy to report under LASER. For most loans, the information reported to Fannie Mae comes directly from your trial balance or payment history. The standard monthly reporting package consists of three forms: Loan Activity Report, LAR (Form 493) is used to report each loan's status and the amount of principal and interest due Fannie Mae; Scheduled/Scheduled P&I Distribution Report (Form 490) is used to summarize the loan level detail; and the Input Control Report (Form 499 or 499A) serves as a cover sheet for all documents in the reporting package.

Three additional forms may be submitted, as needed, to notify us of changes to loans you service. These are: Monthly Payment/Rate Change Form (Form 498); Lender Loan ID Change (Form 495); and Loan Address Change (Form 488).

Q. What are the advantages of reporting loan-level data using LASER versus summary or group level data?

A. There are several advantages to reporting loan-level data with LASER:

— LASER eliminates the need for you to create summary or pool level reports from detailed loan records. You simply can transfer the loan-level trial balance data that you currently maintain for your records to LASER's monthly reporting forms.

— LASER does not require separate reporting for exception cases, such as payoffs. All loans are reported on the Loan Activity Report (Form 493).

Q. Can I use MORNET to report on LASER?

A. Yes. The MORNET PC/LASER Reporting System is available to any Fannie Mae lender. PC/LASER combines the accuracy, timeliness, and cost-effectiveness of the MORNET communications network in an easy to use PC-based software application that prepares and transmits your LASER accounting reports. For more information on MORNET PC/LASER, or to obtain a MORNET sign-up kIT, call the MORNET Hotline at 1-800-752-6440 (in Washington, DC, call 752-6000).

Q. How can I learn more about LASER?

A. To help your loan servicing and investor accounting departments learn more about LASER and how to report on loans easily and efficiently, our Mortgage Operations department can send you our LASER booklets, "Reporting and Remitting to LASER" and "Reconciling under LASER."

Lender Reporting Seminars are also available through your lead regional office.

Q. What if I have questions about LASER?

A. Any questions about LASER can be referred to the LASER Hotline, 1-800-872-0888 (in Washington, DC, call 752-8400). The Hotline is available Monday through Friday, 9 a.m.–6 p.m. eastern time.

To find out more about Fannie Mae's automated LASER Reporting System, contact the LASER Hotline, or the LASER Coordinator in your lead regional office:

Northeastern Region	*Southeastern Region*	*Western Region*
Bob Hearn	JoAnn Billinger	Bob Sanborn
(215)574-1462	(404)365-6049	(818)568-5496

Midwestern Region	*Southwestern Region*	
Patricia Shaw	Maria Pena	
(312)368-6236	(214)770-7443	

Delinquency Calculation

SUBJECT: DELINQUENCY CALCULATION

1. Mortgage Banking Method

Today Is:	Loan Is Due For	Last Paid Installment	Delinquency Rating
4-1-88	3-1-88	2-1-88	30 Days
4-1-88	2-1-88	1-1-88	60 Days
4-1-88	1-1-88	12-1-87	90 Days

2. FHLBB (Thrift) Method

Today Is:	Loan Is Due For	Last Paid Installment	Delinquency Rating
4-1-88	2-1-88	1-1-88	30 Days
4-1-88	1-1-88	12-1-87	60 Days
4-1-88	12-1-87	11-1-87	90 Days

3. Odd Due Date FNMA Method

Today Is:	Loan Is Due For	Last Paid Installment	Delinquency Rating
4-1-88	3-10-88	2-10-88	Current
4-1-88	2-10-88	1-10-88	30 Days
4-1-88	1-10-88	12-10-87	60 Days
4-1-88	12-10-87	11-10-87	90 Days

State Servicing
Information and Laws

State Escrow Handling Assumptions

"MULT" means the factor by which the monthly tax and insurance payment on each loan is multiplied to arrive at an estimate of annual available tax impounds. A state which pays taxes once a year will have a multiplier of 6.5, meaning that, on average, 6.5 times the single monthly tax and insurance impound payment will be on hand. States which pay taxes every six months will have a multiplier of 3.5, etc.

State	Code	Mult	Interest Paid on Impounds
Alabama	AL	6.40	
Alaska	AK	6.50	
Arizona	AZ	3.50	
Arkansas	AR	6.50	
California	CA	3.82	2.00%
Colorado	CO	6.50	
Connecticut	CT	3.50	5.25%
Delaware	DE	6.50	
District of Columbia	DC	3.50	
Florida	FL	6.50	
Georgia	GA	6.50	
Hawaii	HI	3.50	
Idaho	ID	6.50	
Illinois	IL	6.50	
Indiana	IN	3.50	
Iowa	IA	3.50	5.25%
Kansas	KS	6.50	
Kentucky	KY	6.50	
Louisiana	LA	6.50	
Maine	ME	6.50	3.00%
Maryland	MD	6.50	5.25%
Massachusetts	MA	3.50	
Michigan	MI	3.50	
Minnesota	MN	3.58	5.00%
Mississippi	MS	6.50	
Missouri	MO	6.50	
Montana	MT	6.50	
Nebraska	NE	3.50	
Nevada	NV	3.50	
New Hampshire	NH	2.00	5.00%
New Jersey	NJ	2.00	
New Mexico	NM	3.50	
New York	NY	3.50	2.00%
North Carolina	NC	6.50	
North Dakota	ND	6.50	
Ohio	OH	3.50	
Oklahoma	OK	6.50	
Oregon	OR	6.50	4.50%

State	Code	Mult	Interest Paid on Impounds
Pennsylvania	PA	6.50	
Rhode Island	RI	3.50	4.00%
South Carolina	SC	6.50	
South Dakota	SD	3.50	
Tennessee	TN	6.50	
Texas	TX	6.50	
Utah	UT	6.50	5.25%
Vermont	VT	3.50	
Virginia	VA	4.00	
Washington	WA	3.50	
West Virginia	WV	3.50	
Wisconsin	WI	6.50	
Wyoming	WY	3.50	

Tax Payment Frequency By State

State	Code	Annual	Semi-Annual	Quarterly
Alabama	AL	6.5		
Alaska	AK	6.5		
Arizona	AZ		4.0	
Arkansas	AR	6.5		
California	CA		4.5	
Colorado	CO	6.5		
Connecticut	CT		4.0	
Delaware	DE	6.5		
District of Columbia	DC		4.0	
Florida	FL	6.5		
Georgia	GA		4.0	
Hawaii	HI		4.0	
Idaho	ID	6.5		
Illinois	IL		4.0	
Indiana	In	6.5		
Iowa	IA		4.0	
Kansas	KS	6.5		
Kentucky	KY	6.5		
Louisiana	LA	6.5		
Maine	ME		4.0	
Maryland	MD	6.5		
Massachusetts	MA		4.0	
Michigan	MI	6.5		
Minnesota	MN		4.0	
Mississippi	MS	6.5		
Missouri	MO	6.5		
Montana	MT		4.0	
Nebraska	NE		4.0	
Nevada	NV	6.5		
New Hampshire	NH		4.0	
New Jersey	NJ			2.0
New Mexico	NM	6.5		
New York	NY			2.0
North Carolina	NC	6.5		
North Dakota	ND	6.5		
Ohio	OH		4.0	
Oklahoma	OK	6.5		
Oregon	OR	6.5		
Pennsylvania	PA	6.5		
Rhode Island	RI		4.0	
South Carolina	SC	6.5		
South Dakota	SD	6.5		
Tennessee	TN	6.5		
Texas	TX	6.5		
Utah	UT	6.5		
Vermont	VT	6.5		
Virginia	VA		4.0	
Washington	WA		4.0	
West Virginia	WV	6.5		
Wisconsin	WI	6.5		
Wyoming	WY	6.5		

State Servicing Laws

ARKANSAS, Stat. Ann. Sec. 67-2205

All companies that originate or service loans secured by property located in Arkansas must file proof of exemption from the state's mortgage banking licensing act. Mortgage lending is regulated in Arkansas by the Securities Department, and the law exempts from the registration requirements the following entities: banks, savings banks, trust companies, savings and loan associations, consumer finance companies, industrial loan companies, insurance companies, small business investment companies, REITs, attorneys, real estate brokers rendering services in the performance of normal duties, and mortgage loan companies that are subject to licensing, supervision or auditing by FNMA, VA, GNMA, or HUD as approved seller/servicers. A 1985 amendment to the licensing act required all such persons doing business under one of the above exemptions of file proof of the exemption with the Securities Commissioner along with a $100 filing fee. Mortgage loan companies have always been required to submit an annual audited financial statement to the Securities Department regardless of their exempt status.

CALIFORNIA, Bus. and Prof. Code Secs. 10130 et seq.

The statutory definition of "real estate broker" includes, in relevant part . . . a person who for compensation or in expectation of compensation, regardless of the form or time of payment, does or negotiates to do one or more of the following acts for another or others:

1. Solicits borrowers of lenders or, negotiates loans or collects payments or performs services, for borrowers or lenders or note owners in connection with loans secured directly or collaterally by liens on real property or on a business opportunity.

2. Sells or offers to sell, buys or offers to buy, or exchanges or offers to exchange a real property sales contract or a promissory note secured directly or collaterally by a lien on real property or on a business opportunity and performs services for the holders thereof.

Exemptions from the definition include:

1. Any person or employee thereof doing business under any law of this state, any other state, or of the United States relating to banks, trust companies, savings an loans associations, industrial loan companies, pension trusts, credit unions, or insurance companies.

2.   Any lender making a loan guaranteed or insured by an agency of the federal government or for which a commitment of so guarantee or insure has ben made by the agency.

3.   Any person licensed as a personal property broker, a consumer finance lender, or a commercial finance lender when acting under the authority of that license.

4.   Any person who makes collection of payments for lenders or on notes of owners in connection with loans secured directly or collaterally by liens on real property, if: (a) The person makes collection on ten or less loans, or in amount of forty thousand dollars ($40,000) or less any calendar year; or (b) the person in a corporation licensed as an escrow agent and the payments are deposited and maintained in the escrow agent's trust account.

COLORADO, Rev. Stat. Sec. 38-38-113 *et seq*

Any person who regularly engages in the collection of payments on a mortgage or deed of trust must comply with the following:

1.   Promptly credit all payments received and promptly perform all duties imposed by law and by the note, mortgage, or deed of trust creating the indebtedness.

2.   Within 20 days of a servicing transfer, the transferor must mail a notice to each borrower that contains the name, address, and telephone number of the new servicer. The debtor may continue to make payments to the transferor until a notice of the servicing transfer is received from the transferee. Such notice may be combined with that sent by the servicing transferor. It will be the responsibility of the transferor to forward any payment received and due after the date of transfer to the new servicer.

3   Servicers must respond in writing within 20 days of receipt of a written request from a debtor or his agent for information concerning a loan that: (a) is readily available to the servicer from its books and records, and (b) would not constitute the rendering of legal advice. All responses must include the telephone number of the servicer. Servicers will not be liable for any damage or harm that might arise from the release of any information pursuant to this section.

The statute also imposes liability on the servicer for a violation of these requirements (contained in section 38-38-113) if the violation is not remedied in a reasonable, timely, and good faith manner. If not resolved, and the debtor has made a good faith effort to resolve the dispute, the debtor may bring an action for such violations and the court may award, in addition to actual damages, $500 together will costs and reasonable attorney fees.

No transferee of servicing or collection rights will be liable for any action or omission of a transferor who might otherwise be liable under this section.

HAWAII, Rev. Stat. Secs. 454D-1 <u>et seq</u>

Regulates the activities of mortgage and collection servicing agents. A person shall be deemed to engage in the business of a "mortgage servicing agent" or "collection servicing agent" if he, by himself or through others offers to undertake to collect for another person the amounts due under any agreement that provides for installment payments and is secured by an interest in real property . . . whether or not the agent receives any compensation or other consideration for the services.

Exemptions: These provisions do not apply to the following:

1.   Licensed real estate brokers and salesman residing in the state who provide collection services limited to a particular transaction or where the broker is covered by an errors and omissions insurance policy that covers such activities.

2.   Banks, collection agencies, credit unions, escrow depositories, industrial loan companies, savings and loan associations, and trust companies authorized to do business in Hawaii.

3.   A financial institution that services only FHA and VA loans and is a HUD approved lender, provided that it files proof of that status annually with the Department of Commerce and Consumer Affairs and continues to service any FHA and VA loans.

4.   Persons performing these services under court order.

5.   Persons performing these services, but with respect to fewer than five agreements ant any one time.

Servicing agents are required to obtain a $50,000 surety bond or an irrevocable letter of credit in the same amount. There must be a designated agent in the state authorized to act on the he servicer's behalf. Every servicing agent must maintain a separate trust account in a federally insured depository institution for funds collected and must keep a permanent record of all receipts and disbursements with the designated agent. The records must be kept for at least six years following the last installment payment collected.

The Director of Commerce and Consumer Affairs is empowered to register mortgage and collection servicing agents, establish registration and biennial renewal fees and fines, and to suspend or revoke a registration for cause.

Any persons who willfully or knowingly violate any provisions of the act for which there is no other penalty specifically provided will be fined not less than $100 nor more than $1,000 for each violation.

Any false certificate, entry, or memorandum upon any of the servicing agents' books or records, or knowingly altering, destroying, mutilating, or concealing such books or records, will result in a fine of up to $1,000, six months' imprisonment, or both.

Any person who willfully or knowingly causes the commingling of funds of a servicing agent with customer trust funds will be fined $1,000, imprisoned up to sex months, or both. Embezzlement or misappropriation of customer trust funds will result in a fine of up to $5,000, five years imprisonment, or both.

ILLINOIS, Public Act 85-735, Laws of 1987 (Effective January 1, 1988)

Whenever the servicing of a residential mortgage is transferred or sold by a licensee under the mortgage banker/mortgage broker licensing act, notice of the transaction must be given to the mortgagor simultaneous with the sale or transfer. The notice must contain: (1) an address and person to whom the mortgagor may address questions relating to the mortgage; (2) the exact name, address and telephone number to whom at least the next three months' payments are to be submitted; and (3) the total amount required by the servicer for each of those monthly payments.

Ann. Stat. Ch. 17 Sec. 48.2

Provides that any bank affiliates or subsidiaries that engage in making residential mortgage financing transactions must provide the following information with respect to each such transaction: If the servicing of a residential mortgage is transferred from he original mortgagee, a written notice by certified mail within 45 days of the transfer must be sent to the mortgagor setting forth the same information as required above. In addition, if the servicing is transferred again, or if the information contained din the original notice changes, a notice with corrected information must be provided within 45 days of each subsequent transfer or information change by the current servicing transferee.

The Illinois licensing law regulation all entities engaged in the business of brokering, funding, originating, servicing or purchasing of residential mortgage loans.

KENTUCKY, Rev. Stat. Secs. 292.010 *et seq*

The Kentucky licensing law defines a "mortgage loan company" as any person who directly or indirectly holds himself out as being able to:

1.   Make or purchase loans secured by mortgages on residential real property;

2.   Service loans secured by mortgages on residential real property; and

3.   Buy or sell notes secured by mortgages on residential real property.

Exempted from the licensing requirements are, among others, mortgage loan companies regulated by HUD. Persons relying upon an exemption must file a claim of exemption with the Commissioner of Financial Institutions.

MAINE, Rev. Stat. Ann. tit. 9.A Sec. 9-304

Consumer credit transactions secured by a mortgage on real estate may not be assigned unless: (1) the creditor retains the servicing and either maintains a place of business in Maine or has a toll-free telephone number, or other free means of oral communication, that is disclosed to mortgagors and staffed during normal business hours; or (2) the assignee or servicing agent retained to collect the accounts maintains a toll-free telephone, or other free means of oral communication that is disclosed to mortgagors in each coupon book or on each periodic billing notice or statement of account. The telephone line must be staffed during normal business hours for mortgagors to use to communicate with the servicer concerning the loan transaction.

Consumers are not obligated to make payments to any creditor, other than the original creditor, until notification is received of the assignment of rights to payments, and that payment is to be made to the assignee. The notification must clearly and conspicuously identify the new servicer or it will be considered ineffective. If requested by the consumer, the assignee must furnish reasonable proof that the transfer has been made or the consumer may continue to pay the original creditor.

(The above provisions apply to creditors making loans secured by first lien real estate mortgages who are not supervised lenders.)

MARYLAND, Com, Law Sec 13-316

Defines a mortgage servicer as a person responsible for the collection and payment of principal, interest, escrow, and other monies under an original mortgage. "Mortgage" includes a mortgage, deed of trust, security agreement, or other lien on one to four-family residential real property located in Maryland.

Effective July 1, 1987, mortgage loan servicers who service such loans are required to comply with the following provisions:

Within seven days of acquiring mortgage servicing, the servicer must send a written notice to each mortgagor that contains information regarding the mortgage on the date of transfer. The notice must state: (1) the name, address and telephone number of the new servicer and the address where mortgage payments are to be forwarded; (2) the principal balance and escrow balance of the loan; (3) the telephone number of a designated contact person to whom mortgagors may direct complaints and inquires; (4) the responsibilities of the contact person (detailed below); and (5) a statement that the servicer's violation of this act will result in the servicer being held liable for any economic damages caused by such violation.

The designated contact person is required to respond in writing to each written complaint or inquiry within 15 days when a reply is requested.

Servicers are required to make timely payments of taxes and insurance premiums as loan as the mortgagor has paid an amount sufficient to pay such assessments and, with regard to taxes, as loan as the servicer is in possession of either the tax bill or notice from the taxing authority.

MICHIGAN, Public Act 173, Laws of 1987 (Effective November 18, 1987.)

Michigan's licensing law requires mortgage loan servicers to either register or obtain a license in order to service Michigan loans. Servicers that are approved as a seller/servicer by FNMA or FHLMC, or as an issuer or servicer by GNMA, must submit a registration form and pay an annual fee of $300 to the Bureau of Financial Institutions.

Lenders that are exempted from this provision include financial institutions, subsidiaries and affiliates of financial institutions, financial institution holding companies, and mortgage servicers servicing 10 or fewer loans within a 12-month period. Servicers must deliver an annual statement of the borrower's account showing the unpaid principal balance of the mortgage loan, the interest paid during the preceding 12 months, and the amounts deposited and disbursed from escrow during the period. In addition, within 25 days written request from a borrower, a servicer must deliver a ledger history of the borrower's account for a period not to exceed the immediately preceding 12 months. Such a request may not be made more than once during any 12-month period and a fee may not be charged to the borrower.

MINNESOTA, Stat. Ann. Sec. 47.205

When the servicing of mortgage loan financing one- to four-family, owner-occupied residences located in the state is sold or assigned to another person, the selling lender must notify the mortgagor of the sale no more than ten days after the actual date of transfer. The notification must include the name, address, and telephone number of the person who will assume responsibility for servicing and accepting payments for the mortgage loan. The notification must also include a detailed written financial breakdown including but not limited to interest rate, monthly payment amount, and current escrow balance. The purchasing lender must issue corrected coupon or payment books, if used, and must notify the mortgager within 20 days after the first payment to the purchasing lender is due of the name, address, and telephone number of person from whom the mortgagor can receive information regarding the servicing of the loan. In addition, the purchasing lender must inform the mortgagor of any changes made regarding the mortgage escrow account or servicing requirements including but not limited to interest rate, monthly payment amount, and current escrow balance. The purchasing lender must respond within 15 business days to a written inquiry from a mortgagor. A written response must include the telephone number of the company representative who can assist the mortgagor. If a lender fails to comply with the above requirements, her will be liable to the mortgagor for actual damages caused by the violation. In addition, the lender is liable to the mortgagor for $500 per occurrence if the violation was due to the lender's failure to exercise reasonable care.

NEW MEXICO, Chapter 343, Laws of 1987

Requires mortgage loan servicers to maintain an office or agent in the state. The act states that any business, organization, or similar entity that services single-unit residential mortgages secured by real property located in the state must either maintain its principal office, a branch office, or an agent in New Mexico for the purpose of providing loan information and data to mortgagors or their agents. In addition, the law requires that. response to a mortgagor's inquiry must be made within ten working days from the date of inquiry. (Effective June 19, 1987).

The maintenance of a post office box in New Mexico is not sufficient for the purpose of maintaining "an agent" in New Mexico pursuant to Chapter 343. (87 Op. Att'y Gen. 40).

Mortgage Escrow Accounts

(States which require the payment of interest on escrow accounts are marked with an asterisk).

ARIZONA, Rev. Stat. Ann. Sec. 6-911.05 (D)

If periodic payments ar to be collected from the mortgagor to provide for the payment of taxes, assignments, insurance premiums, ground rents, or other current charges against the real estate security, the estimated payment amount stated to the mortgagor by the mortgagor by the mortgage banker must be such that the total will approximate the actual tax or payment(s) when due. All such periodic payments must be accounted for annually to the borrower and, to the extent monies have been collected, be paid promptly by the mortgage banker. (Applies to licensees under the mortgage banking licensing act.)

ARKANSAS, Code Ann. Sec. 23-39-309

All monies paid to a mortgage loan company (required to be licensed under state law) for the payment of taxes or insurance premiums on property secured by a loan made by the company shall be deposited in an insured account and kept separate, distinct and apart from funds belonging to the mortgage loan company. The company shall, upon reasonable notice, account to the mortgagor and to the Commissioner for all funds in the account. Such funds are not subject to execution or attachment on any claim against the company.

Act 737, Laws of 1987 -

Requires all banks, savings and loan association, other financial institutions, and all persons, firms and corporations that are holders of escrow funds for payments of real property taxes to notify the county collector within 30 days after sufficient funds for the payment of property taxes have accumulated in each such account. If sufficient funds for the payment of one year's taxes on such real estate have accumulated prior to the commencement of the period during which the taxes may be collected, the above notification must be made within 30 days after the collector is authorized by law to commence collecting property taxes for given year.

In addition, escrow fund holders must, during 1988, remit payment for property taxes within 90 days of receipt of the tax bills from the collector. After 1988, such payments must be remitted within 60 days of receipt of the tax bills.

Failure to comply with these provisions will be subject to a penalty of 10 percent of the amount of the total taxes due. In no event will such penalties be charged against the escrow account. (Effective April 7, 1987).

* CALIFORNIA, Civil Code, Secs. 2954-2955 (Effective March 3, 1976)

Impound accounts maintained in connection with mortgages secured by single-family, owner-occupied dwellings are optional unless: (1) required by state or federal regulatory authority; (2) the state or federal government makes, guarantees or insures the loan; (3) the borrower or purchaser is delinquent in paying two consecutive tax installments; (4) the original principal amount of the loan is 90 percent or more of the appraised value of the property; or (5) whenever the combined principal balance of all loans secured by the real property exceeds 80 percent of the appraised value of the property securing the loans. Every mortgagor must receive one itemized accounting of the impound account per year without charge and may request additional similar accountings for one or more months upon written request and advance payment of a set fee. Any increase in monthly payments must be preceded by a n itemized accounting, a statement f the new monthly rate and an explanation of the cause of the increase. Violation of these provisions is punishable by a fine of not less than $25 nor more than $100. Lenders are responsible for making timely payments of property taxes and insurance premiums.

Every bank, savings and loan association, credit union or any other person or organization making loans secured by real property containing on- to four-family residence shall pay a minimum 2 percent simple interest charge on impound account funds collected in connection with such loans. Interest is payable annually or upon termination of the account, whichever is earlier. Lenders may not impose any fee in connection with the maintenance or disbursement of an account that will reduce the effective interest rate below 2 percent per annum. Exempted from the interest requirement are monies required by a state or federal regulatory authority to be placed by a financial institution other than a bank in a non-interest-bearing demand trust fund account at a bank. All monies held in impound accounts for the payment of taxes or insurance premiums shall be retained in the state and, if invested, may only be invested within the state. (62 Op. Att'y Gen. 351 ruled that this provision is constitutional.)

Special Note:

For several years Section 2954.8 of the Civil Code has required the payment of 2 percent interest on impounds unless the impounds were kept in non-interest bearing accounts. Most mortgage bankers were required by the Real Estate Commissioner's Regulations to keep the money in "demand" accounts which do not pay interest. Therefore they were not required to pay interest on impound accounts.

A. B. 575, effective January 1, 1980, changed Section 2954.8 to provide that interest mut be paid unless the funds are required to be kept in non-interest bearing accounts. Effective February 16, 1980. the California Real Estate Commissioner's regulations were changed to permit impounds to be placed in interest-bearing accounts. The Commissioner has adopted a new Section 2830.1 to read:

Section 2830.1, Interest on Impounds. A real estate broker who receives funds in trust from or on behalf of an obligor for the payment of property taxes, assessments, insurance or other purposes relating to real property containing only a one- to four-family residence shall not be precluded by provisions of Section 2830 from depositing and maintaining said fund in an interest-bearing account in bank, savings and loan association or other financial institution provided that the account is insured by an agency of the federal government. This, in effect, removed the exemption that had applied to mortgage bankers.

COLORADO, Rev. Stat. 39-1-119

Escrow account balances may not exceed three months' total escrow charges. Each year, lenders must refund on or before May 30 any amounts in excess of three-twelfths of the taxes paid in such year. Payments into such escrow accounts for the payment of taxes due in subsequent years shall be adjusted annually, based upon the amount of taxes paid in the previous year. If the lender reasonably believes that substantial improvements have been made to a property, a reasonable estimate of newly assessed taxes may be used as a basis for establishing payments for the escrow account. Any person willfully failing to make a refund for any whole month or more shall be liable for interest at a rate of 6 percent per annum and an equal amount as penalty.

Sec. 38-38-113 -- Mortgage loan servicers are liable for any interest or late fees charged by any taxing entity if funds for the full payment of real property taxes have been held in escrow by the servicer and are not remitted to the taxing entity when due.

Sec. 39-1-119 -- The amount of payments in an escrow account for the payment of taxes due in subsequent years may be increased only upon official notification of an increase in the amount of taxes levied on the property. The amount may not be increased solely upon notification of an increase in the valuation for assessment of such property.

* CONNECTICUT, Gen. Stat. Sec. 49-2a et seq.

Requires each bank, trust company, savings and loan association, savings bank, insurance company and other mortgagee or mortgage servicing company holding funds of a mortgagor in an escrow account to pay interest on such funds at a rate not less than 5 1/4 percent per annum (effective October 1, 1985). Lenders had been required to pay interest at a rate of 4 percent per annum since January 1, 1978. These provisions apply to mortgages secured by one- to four-unit, owner-occupied residences and housing cooperatives occupied solely by the shareholders. Interest payment shall be annually credited towards the payment of taxes and insurance premiums in the ensuing year. If the debt is paid prior to the end of the year, the interest to the date of payment shall be paid to the mortgagor. Violation of these provisions by a mortgagee or mortgage servicing company shall result in a fine not to exceed $100 for each offense.

Interest may <u>not</u> be required to be paid on escrow account where (1) there is a contract between the parties, entered into before October 1, 1975, which contains an express disclaimer on the part of the mortgagee to pay such interest; (2) the payment of such interest would violate a federal law or regulation, or (3) the account is maintained with a mortgage servicing company, neither affiliated with nor owned in whole or in part by the mortgagee, under a written contract or any mortgage agreement, entered into before October 1, 1975, that does not permit the company to earn or receive a return from the he investment of such account; or (4) that account is maintained in connection with a loan entered into on and after October 1, 1977, which is serviced and held for sale for not more than one year by a mortgage servicing company, neither affiliated with not owned in whole or in part by the purchaser of the mortgage loan.

A rate of 2 percent per annum applies where a contract that contained an express provision to pay 2 percent was entered into prior to October 1, 1977. In addition, lenders must pay 2 percent on escrow accounts established after October 1, 1973 and prior to January 1, 1978.

DISTIRCT OF COLUMBIA, Code Ann. Sec. 28-3301 (f)(2)

Any loan which is secured by a mortgage or deed of trust on residential real property shall be subject to the following provision . . . any borrower who has made a downpayment equaling 20 percent or more of the total purchase price of the property or who has an equity interest in the property equal to or greater than 20 percent is not required by the terms of the loan to make advance payments of real estate taxes or casualty insurance premiums to enable the lender to have fund on hand for disbursement for payment of such taxes or insurance premiums. Lenders are required to inform borrowers, in writing, of this right to pay such taxes and insurance premiums directly.

FLORIDA, Stat. Ann. Sec. 501.137

All lenders of money whose loans are secured by mortgages on real estate located in the State and who maintain escrow accounts for the payment of property taxes or hazard insurance premiums shall promptly pay such taxes or insurance premiums when they become due and adequate escrow funds are deposited sot hat the maximum tax discount available may be obtained and so that insurance coverage on the property does not lapse. If the escrow account is deficient, the lender must notify the depositor within fifteen days after receipt of the tax or insurance notification. Each mortgagee must issue an annual statement of the escrow account to the mortgagor at the expiration of the annual accounting period.

Lenders will be liable for any loss suffered by property owners as a result of the lender's negligent failure to pay any taxes or insurance premiums when due if there were sufficient funds in the account at that time. The extent of such liability shall not exceed the amount of taxes or other charges assessed by the tax collector or the coverage limits of any lapsed insurance policy.

The above provisions relating timely payments of insurance premiums becomes effective October 1, 1984.

* GUAM, Laws 1980, Bill No. 419

Requires interest to be paid on home mortgage escrow accounts at a rate not less than that on regular passbook savings accounts by a Guam bank or savings and loan association. The law applies to mortgage escrow accounts established pursuant to mortgages executed both before and after the effective date of the law, September 1, 1980.

HAWAII, Rev. Stat. Sec. 449-16.5

In all escrow agreements involving the sale of real property . . . in which an escrow depository acts as a fiduciary party holding the funds in escrow, any interest earned on such funds shall accrue to the credit of the purchaser unless otherwise instructed in writing by the purchaser and seller in the escrow agreement. (This section does not apply to band, trust companies, building and loans, savings and loans or insurance companies, when acting as escrow depositories.)

IDAHO, Code Sec. 26-1931(8)

Savings and loan associations may require borrowers to pay monthly, the equivalent of one-twelfth (1/12) of the estimated annual taxes, assessments, insurance premiums and other charges upon real estate securing a loan. The amount of such monthly charges may be increased or decreased so as to provide reasonably for the payment of these charges. The association at its option may hold such funds in transit and commingle them with other such funds or place the funds in savings accounts or hold in open account and advance like amounts for such purposes or credit such funds as received to the mortgage account and advance a like amount for the purposes stated. Associations have no obligation to pay interest earnings or other increment to the borrower nor to invest these monies for the benefit of the borrower, unless such funds have been in a savings account.

ILLINOIS, Ann. Stat. Ch. 17 Secs. 4901-5001

In lieu of establishing an escrow account, a borrower may pledge an interest bearing time deposit with the mortgage lender in an amount sufficient to secure the payment of anticipated taxes. "Mortgage Lenders" are defined as banks, savings and loan associations, building and loan associations, or other institution, association, partnership, corporation or person who extends that loan of monies for the purpose of enabling another to purchase a residence.

When a mortgage loan is reduced to 65 percent of its original amount by timely payments of the borrower, a mortgage lender must notify the borrower that he may terminate the escrow account or elect to continue the account until he requests a termination, or until the loan is pad in full, whichever occurs first. Borrowers shall not have the right of termination in conjunction with mortgages insured, guaranteed, supplemented or assisted by the state or the federal government that require an escrow arrangement for their continuation.

If, after terminating an escrow account, the borrower does not furnish to the lender sufficient evidence of timely payment of taxes, the lender, after verifying the nonpayment, may reestablish an escrow arrangement with the borrower within 30 days after the payment due date.

All lenders must furnish to borrowers written notice of the requirements of this act at the date of closing. Failure of any lender operating within the state to comply with the provisions of this act shall entitle the borrower to actual damages in court action. Mortgage lenders using the capitalization method of accounting (crediting tax payment directly tot he loan principal upon receipt and increasing the loan balance when the taxes are paid) are exempted from the provisions of this act.

No mortgage agreement securing a singe-family residence shall contain any requirement that the mortgagor must maintain more than 150 percent of the previous year's assessed real property tax in an escrow account, except in the first year of the mortgage's life.

* *IOWA, Code Ann. Sec. 524.905(2)*

Effective July 1, 1982, banks, savings and loan associations, credit unions, and industrial loan companies that maintain escrow accounts in connection with loans secured by one- to two-family, owner-occupied dwellings, must pay interest to the borrower on those funds at the rate the institution pays to depositors of funds in ordinary savings accounts. Interest must be calculated on a daily basis and a written annual of all account transactions must be delivered to each mortgagor.

A state bank may act as an escrow agent with respect to real property and shall act as a fiduciary for all such funds. A bank maintaining such an account, whether or not the mortgage has been assigned to a third person, shall deliver to the mortgagor a written summary of all transactions made during each calendar year. Credit unions and savings and loan associations are also authorized to act as escrow agents, but only in connection with real property loans made by he institution. The loan document may include a provision requiring the borrower to pay monthly an amount equal to one-twelfth of the estimated annual real estate taxes, special assessments, insurance premiums or any other payment agreed to by the borrower and the bank in order to secure the loan.

KANSAS, Stat. Ann. Sec. 17-5510

Limits the collection of escrow funds by savings and loan associations to one-twelfth of the estimated annual taxes and insurance premiums.

KENTUCKY, Rev. Stat. Sec. 294.130

All monies paid to a mortgage loan company (required to be licensed under Chapter 294) for the payment of taxes or insurance premiums on property secured by a loan made or serviced by the company shall be deposited in an insured account and kept separate, distinct and apart from funds belonging to the mortgage loan property. Any interest earned on the funds shall belong to the borrower and will be applied to the expenses that will be paid from such account. The mortgage company must, upon reasonable notice, account for all funds deposited by a borrower and, upon reasonable notice, account to the Commissioner of Banking and Securities for all funds deposited. Escrow account funds are not subject to execution or attachment on any claim against the mortgage company.

LOUISIANA, Rev. Stat. Sec. 6.828

Savings and loan associations are permitted to require borrowers to pay monthly, in advance, the equivalent of one-twelfth of the estimated annual taxes, insurance premiums and other expenses upon real estate securing a loan so as to enable the association to pay such charges as they become due from the funds so received. The funds are to be held, without interest, for the credit of the borrower.

* MAINE, Rev. Stat. Ann. Art. 9-B Sec. 429, Art. 9-A Sec. 3-312

Any mortgage holding mortgagor funds in an escrow account on behalf of itself or another mortgagee for the payment of taxes or insurance premiums for property location in Maine must pay a minimum of 3 percent per year interest on such accounts. "Mortgagee" includes commercial banks, savings banks, industrial banks, savings and loan associations, credit unions, and supervised lenders (includes mortgage companies operating in the sate). The payment of interest applies only to escrow accounts established in connection with mortgages on owner-occupied residential property consisting of one- to four-family dwelling units.

These requirements apply to any funds in an escrow account on October 1, 1985, and to any funds deposited in an escrow after that date. The 1984 law that placed mortgage companies within the scope of the statute required interest to be paid only on funds held in escrow in connection with mortgages executed on or after September 1, 1984. The 1985 amendment (Chapter 327, Laws of 1985) makes the interest requirement apply to all funds held in escrow on October 1, 1985 regardless of the date of the mortgage loan origination. Interest payments must be computed on the daily balances in each account from the date of receipt to the date of disbursement and credited to the mortgagor's account on the last business day of each quarter of a calendar or fiscal year. Payments may not be reduced by any charge for the service or maintenance of an account. A statement showing all interest credited to the account must be sent to each mortgagor at least once a year. The payment of interest does not apply to mortgage transactions under which such payment of interest on escrow accounts is prohibited by federal law. Prior to September 1, 1984, mortgage companies were exempted from paying interest on escrow accounts. "Financial Institutions" were required to pay mortgagors quarterly dividends or interest at a rate 1/2 of the highest annual interest rate paid by the institution or regular savings accounts (effective September 14, 1979).

MARYLAND, Com. Law Secs. 12-109, 12-109.1

Requires any bank, savings bank, or savings an loan association doing business in Maryland that lends money secured by a first mortgage or first deed of trust on only interest in residential real property and creates or is the assignee of an escrow account in connection with such a loan, top ay interest on the funds at a rate which is the greater of: (a) 3 percent per annum simple interest; or (b) the rate regularly paid by the lending institution on regular passbook savings accounts. All interest shall be computed on the average monthly balance and credited annually to the borrower's account. The lending institution must provide an annual statement of the account balance. This section applies only to loans made after May 31, 1974.

These provision do not apply to institutions which provide for the payment of taxes, insurance or other expenses under the direct reduction method by which there expenses when paid by the lender, are added to the outstanding principal balance of the loan. Loans purchased by an out-of-state lender through FNMA, GNMA or the FHLMC are exempted if the purchasing lender elects to service the loan. However, interest payment requirements shall apply if the out-of-state lender sells the loan to or places the loan with a Maryland lender for servicing.

Funds held in escrow accounts may not be used to reduce the loan principal or to pay interest or other loan charges except upon foreclosure or release unless there is periodically an overage in the account. In these cases, the borrower shall be given, at least annually, the option of receiving a refund, applying the overage to the payment of principal and Interest or leaving the excess amount in the account. If the borrower does not reply to the lender's notice of these options within 60 days, the lender must return the overage to the borrower.

Sec. 13-316 (D)

Servicers are required to make timely payments of taxes and insurance premiums so long as the mortgagor has paid an amount sufficient to pay such assessments and, with regard to taxes, so lang as the servicer is in possession of either the tax bill or notice from the taxing authority. (This section becomes effective July 1, 1987.)

* MASSACHUSETTS, Ann. Laws Ch. 183, Sec. 61

Requires a mortgagee holding a first mortgage lien on a dwelling house located in the commonwealth of a one- to four-unit, owner-occupied dwelling who requires advance payments for ht payment of real estate taxes to pay interest on such funds. Interest shall be paid at least annually at a rate and in a manner to be determined by the mortgagee. Mortgages must file an annual statement with the commissioner of banks showing the rate of interest paid on such amounts and the methods by which such interest was paid. The report must include a statement showing the amount of net profit or loss from the investment of such amounts, including calculations of relevant gross income and expense.

Banks, national banking associations, federal savings banks, and federal credit unions do not have to include the above-mentioned statement if they have paid interest in an amount equal to the rate paid on their regular saving or share accounts.

If the lender shows a net loss from these investments, the commissioner may grant an exemption from the interest requirement. These provisions apply only to advance deposits for the payment for the payment of taxes on mortgaged property made after July 1, 1975.

MICHIGAN, Comp. Laws Sec. 565.161

Any mortgagee or agent receiving escrow funds from a mortgagor for the payment of taxes, insurance premiums or improvements to the property, must furnish the mortgagor with an annual statement of the escrow account within 60 days of the close of the calendar year.

The annual statement is not required where the mortgagor is provided with a monthly billing form or mortgage passbook that lists the account balance and records tax expenditures. Mortgagees will be liable for any fees or penalties incurred by the mortgagor as a result of failure to make timely payments of taxes when due.

Sec. 438.31 (c) (13-14)
An interest-bearing deposit account held in a depository institution may be established as a condition of the making of a mortgage or land contract where the primary security is an owner-occupied dwelling. The account shall be pledged to the lender as additional security for the mortgage or land contract. The lender may make withdrawals as agreed upon in the mortgage and such withdrawals will be applied against the periodic payments otherwise due from the borrower pursuant to the terms of the mortgage. All interest earned on the pledged deposit amount shall be credited to the account. Lenders who make five r more mortgage in any one calendar year may not require the establishment of such an account on more than 20 percent of mortgages made during the year.

* MINNESOTA, Stat. Ann. Sec. 47.20 (9)

Requires all banks, trust companies, savings and loan associations, mortgage banks, mutual savings banks, insurance companies, credit unions or assignees of the above that require a mortgagors' funds to be paid into an escrow or similar account for payment of taxes or insurance in connection with a mortgage on a one- to four-family, owner-occupied residence in the state to pay interest on the funds at a rate not less than 5 percent per annum. Interest shall be computed on the average monthly balance on the first of each month and be annually credited to the remaining balance on the mortgage or, at the election of the mortgagee, be paid to the mortgagor, or credited to the escrow account. If the interest exceeds the remaining balance, the excess shall be paid to the mortgagor. The payment of interest is not required fit he escrow is mandatory under federal law, is maintained in connection with a conventional loan in an original principal amount in excess of 80 percent of the lender's appraised value a at the time the loan is made, or if the loans is insured or guaranteed by HUD, the VA or the FNMA. The requirement to pay interest is retroactive (effective date June 1, 1986).

Lenders not requiring the maintenance of an escrow account may permit a mortgagor to elect to maintain a non-interest bearing escrow account to be serviced by the mortgagee at no extra charge if the mortgagor is also offered the option of managing the payment of insurance and taxes himself or opening a passbook savings account for that purpose. A mortgagee that is not a depository institution offering passbook savings accounts shall notify its mortgagors, (1) that they may open accounts at a depository institution and (2) of the current maximum legal interest rate on such accounts. These options do not apply to escrow accounts which are specifically exempted from the Interest paying requirements.

Lenders are specifically prohibited from charging a direct fee for the administration of escrow accounts are required to make timely payments of tax and insurance bills provided that there are sufficient funds in the account. Failure to make such payments shall subject the mortgagee to lability for all damages caused. Mortgagors must be promptly notified of any account shortages.

Sec. 47.205(3) - Each lender requiring escrow accounts with respect to a mortgaged one-to four-family owner-occupied residence located in the state shall make payments for the taxes or insurance from the escrow account in a timely manner as these obligations become due provided that funds paid into the account are sufficient for the payment. If there is a shortage of funds, the lender shall promptly notify the mortgagor of the shortage. If the lender fails to make the timely payments, her will be liable to the mortgagor for actual damages caused by he late payment and is liable to the mortgagor for $500 per occurrence if the violation was due to the lender's failure to exercise reasonable care. Lenders are permitted to make a payment on behalf of the mortgagor even though there are not sufficient funds in a particular account to cover the payment.

MONTANA, Code Ann. Secs. 71-1-113 through 71-1-115

Limits escrow accounts to no more than 110 percent of the projected amount needed unless parties agree in writing to a larger amount.

Lending institutions that maintain reserve accounts for the payment of taxes and insurance premiums in connection with a mortgage on real property must keep itemized records of such accounts and annually mail a statement of total receipts and disbursements to each borrower.

NEBRASKA, Rev. Stat. Sec. 8-330

Building and loan associations may pay interest on funds held in an escrow account for the payment of taxes, insurance and similar payments, if agreed to in writing by the borrower and association.

Sec. 45-101.05 - Lenders are prohibited from requiring a borrower to deposit, in any one month, an amount larger than one-twelfth of the total yearly amount of estimated taxes and insurance premiums. However, if the lender determines there will be a deficiency on the due date, he will not be prohibited from requiring additional monthly deposits in such escrow accounts of pro rata portions of the deficiency corresponding to the number of months from the date of the lender's determination of such deficiency to the date upon which such taxes and insurance premiums become due and payable.

NEVADA, Rev. Stat. Secs. 645B.165, 645B.170, 645B.180

All money paid to a mortgage company (licensed under Chapter 645B) for the payment f taxes and insurance shall be deposited in a bank and kept separate, distinct and apart from funds belonging tot he company and shall be designated as an "impound trust account". The company shall, upon reasonable notice account for any funds paid by a mortgagor and, upon reasonable notice, account to the commissioner of savings associations for all funds held in the impound trust account. Such funds are not subject to execution or attachment on any claim against the mortgage company.

* NEW HAMPSHIRE, Rev. Stat. Secs. 384.16c - 384.16e

Any bank which requires or accepts monies for deposit in escrow accounts maintained for the payment of taxes, insurance premiums or other expenses related to loans on property secured by a real estate mortgage shall credit each account with interest at a rate of not less than 2 percent below the rate paid on regular savings deposits in said bank. (Effective January 1, 1974.) Effective July 1, 1985, the minimum rate of interest is raised to 5 percent.

Any company that is in the business of making loans for the purpose of financing the acquisition of single-family homes and which requires or accepts money for deposit in escrow accounts maintained for the payment of taxes, insurance premiums or other related expenses must credit each such escrow account with interest at a rate of not less than 4 percent per annum. (Effective January 1, 1984.) Effective July 1, 1985, the minimum rate of interest is raised to 5 percent.

NEW JERSEY, Stat. Ann. Sec. 17.9A-65.2

No banking institution, saving and loan association, or mortgage company shall require a mortgagor to increase payments to an escrow tax account until such institution has received official notification of an increase in taxes from the taxing district in which the property is located. The amount of any such increase shall not exceed the amount required to meet the actual increase in taxes.

NEW MEXICO, Stat. Ann. Sec. 48-7-8

Mortgagees may impose a monthly charge to be held in escrow fr the payment of taxes, insurance premiums and the charges under the terms of a mortgage. Any balance exceeding two months' total escrow charges shall, upon the he demand of the mortgagor but not more than once each year, be credited to the principal amount of the mortgage within 60 days of the demand. Failure of mortgagee to credit such excess shall cause a penalty at the rate of 6 percent per year, payable to the mortgagor.

* NEW YORK, McKinney's Banking Law, Section 14-b, General Obligation Law, Scetion 5-601

Requires any mortgage investing institution (bank, trust company, savings bank, savings an loan association, private bank, investment company, insurance company or other entity which makes, extends or hold mortgage loans) that maintains an escrow account in connection with a loan secured by a 1-6-family, owner-occupied residence or loan any property owned by a cooperative apartment corporation to pay interest at a rate not less than 2 percent per annum or a rate prescribed by the banking board, whichever is higher. The banking board shall prescribe the method or basis of computing interest and the minimum rate paid shall be a net rate over and above any service charges imposed. Interest shall be computed on daily balances and credited to the account as of the last business day of each quarter of the calendar year or the bank's fiscal year. Service charges in connection with the maintenance of an escrow account are prohibited unless expressly authorized in a loan contract executed prior to this act's effective date (July 1, 1974).

Interest is not required where: (1) there is a contract between the mortgagor and the mortgage investing institution entered into before the effective date of the act (1974) which contains an express disclaimer of an obligation on the part of the mortgage investing institution to pay interest on such accounts; (2) the payment of such interest would violate any federal law or regulation; or (3) such accounts are maintained with a mortgage servicing company, neither affiliated with nor owned in whole or impart by the mortgage investing institution, under a written contract, entered into before the effective date of this act, which contract does not permit the mortgage investing institution to earn or receive a return from the investment of such accounts.

Banking Law, Sec. 9-e - Any mortgagee of real property located in the state that is secured by one- to four-family residential property who receives money from a mortgagor for the payment of real property taxes, must, at least annually, provide to the mortgagor any paid bill received for the payment of taxes. This requirement does not apply to billings for taxes transmitted by computer tape by a city with a population greater than $1 million.

Lien Law, Section 71-a(3) - Requires that any initial advance pursuant to a residential real estate sale or construction contract on a residential condominium on not more than a two-family residence be placed in an interest-bearing escrow account in a bank, trust company or savings and loan association. Alternatively, the recipient of the advance may post a bond guaranteeing the return of the money otherwise required to be held in escrow. A boldface statement of the purchaser's right to demand an escrow or bond must be contained in the contract of sale.

Gen. Oblig. Law Sec. 5-602 - Mortgage investing institutions are required to pay interest on insurance draft deposits held in escrow that represent compensation for damages to a 1-6 family, owner-occupied residence or cooperative apartment on which it holds a mortgage or loan and maintains an escrow account. (Effective November 14, 1986.) Interest shall be credited on a quarterly basis at a rate of 2 percent per year or at any higher rate prescribed by the banking board. The banking board is directed to promulgate regulations concerning the method or basis of computing any minimum rate of interest. Any such minimum rate will be a net rate over and above any service charge that may be imposed by an mortgage lending institution for maintaining an escrow.

Real Prop. Law Sec. 447-h - Every banking organization and mortgage service organization holding escrow deposits shall, without charge, on or before January 31 of each year, furnish to each owner of mortgaged real property a statement showing the amount of tax bills paid from the he escrow account, the payment date, the remaining balance, and the total amount of interest paid of the mortgage during the preceding year. The statement must also contain the principal balance remaining on the obligation as of the previous December 31.

Banking Law, Sec. 9-1 - Requires every mortgage escrow agent located within the state that receives money from a mortgagor for the payment of real property taxes to, within 45 days of the commencement of the escrow account and within 45 days of the termination of the account, notify each applicable jurisdiction of such commencement or termination.

"Mortgage escrow agent" is defined as including every banking organization, insurance company, foreign banking corporation licensed to do business in the state, national banking association, savings bank or savings and loan association, credit union, bank, trust company, licensed mortgage banker, or any other person, entity, or organization that, in the regular course of its business requires, maintains, or services escrow accounts n connection with mortgages on real property located in New York. (Effective August 9, 1987.)

* OREGON, Rev. Stat. Secs. 86.205 - 86.275 (effective September 1, 1975)

Lenders (any person who makes, extends or holds a real estate loan agreement including, but not limited to, mortgagees, beneficiaries under trust deeds and vendors under conditional land sale contracts) may require a lender's security provision in connection with a real estate loan agreement either as a direct reduction provision, an escrow account or a pledge of an interest-bearing savings account in an amount not to exceed the maximum amount which a lender may require a borrower to deposit in an escrow account and bearing interest at a rate not less than the rate required on the lender's security protection.

"Real estate loan agreement" is defined as a loan for $100,000 or less that is secured by owner-occupied residential property, including multi-family, that is located in the state.

Interest on escrow accounts shall be paid quarterly at a rate not less than 4 1/2 percent. Interest shall be computed on the average monthly balance of the account. Lenders are prohibited from imposing a service charge in connection with an interest-bearing escrow account.

Lenders are prohibited from requiring a borrower to deposit, in any month, a sum in excess of 1/12th of the total amount of estimated property taxes, insurance premiums, or similar charges that will be due and payable during the 12-month period unless the lender determines there will be a deficiency on the due date. If this occurs, the lender may required additional monthly deposits of pro rata portions of the deficiency.

If a lender fails to ay the borrower's taxes in time to take advantage of any authorized discounts, the lender shall credit to the account an amount equal to the discount plus any accrued interest on the unpaid property taxes t the date the taxes are paid. If the lender's failure to make the timely payments is willful or if the lender fails to credit the borrower's account with the correct amount, the borrower shall have a cause of action against the lender to recover an amount equal to 15 times the amount of discount that the borrower should have received, plus any interest that would have accrued. Borrowers recovering damages shall be entitled to attorney fees as determined by the count in addition to costs and necessary disbursements. Violation by the lender of any of these provisions shall render the lender's security provision voidable at the option of the borrower, and make the lender liable to the borrower in an amount equal to actual damages or $100, whichever is greater, and court costs and attorney fees in the case of a successful action by the borrower.

These provisions do not apply to a loan agreement which is serviced or held for sale within one year by a mortgage servicing company neither affiliated with not owned in whole or in part by the purchaser and which is made or held by a purchaser whose principal place of business is outside of the state.

PENNSYLVANIA, Stat. Ann. Tit. 21 Sec. 705

Requires bank, savings and loan associations, or other lending institution holding a residential mortgage to send written notification by first class mail to a mortgagor when their mortgage has been fully paid. Any moneys remaining in an escrow account established for the payment of taxes or insurance premiums must be returned within 30 days to the mortgagor.

* RHODE ISLAND, Gen. Laws Ann. Sec. 19-5-22

Requires all banks, trust companies, savings and loan associations, mutual savings banks, insurance companies and other mortgagees holding funds of a mortgagor in escrow for the payment of taxes and insurance premiums to pay or credit interest on such funds at a rate not less than 4 percent per annum. This requirement is effective June 26, 1985, and applies to escrows maintained in connection with mortgage loans secured by one- to four-unit, owner-occupied residential properties located in the state. Prior to June 26, 1985, lenders were required to pay interest at a rate of 2 percent per annum (effective July 1, 1979). Interest shall be credited annually toward the payment f taxes and insurance premiums in the ensuing year. If the mortgage debt is paid prior to June 30th in any year, the interest to the date of payment shall be paid to the mortgagor. These provisions may be waived and violation of this act by a mortgagee will result in fine not to exceed $100.

FMHA, HUD, VA or privately insured mortgages are exempt. The bank commissioner is empowered to make rules and regulations necessary to carry out these provisions and shall furnish forms to mortgagees for the purpose of reporting to mortgagors the interest due.

Sec. 34-26-2 - Escrow funds must be disbursed to a mortgagor within 30 days after the final payment of a mortgage loan.

* UTAH, Code Ann. Secs. 7-17-1 et seq.

Applies to any person who regularly makes, extends or holds real estate loans and includes, but is not limited to, mortgagees, beneficiaries under trust deeds and vendors under conditional land sales contracts who regularly require or maintain reserve accounts. (Effective June 30, 1979.)

Each lender is required to pay at lest 5.25 percent interest per annum on mandatory reserve accounts maintained in connection with a mortgage secured by a one- to four-unit, owner-occupied residence. Interest shall be computed on the average of the month end balances at the end of the calendar year. Within 60 days after the end of each calendar year, the interest shall be credited to the remaining principal balance on the loan, paid to the borrower or credited to the account, at the election of the lender. In the event of payoff of the loan, the interest must be paid or credited to the borrower within 30 days after the payoff date. Lenders may not require or impose a service charge for the administration of the account. Payment of interest is not required: (1) if the account is required by a governmental insurer or guarantor; (2) the original principal amount of the loan exceeded 80 percent of the appraised value of the property at the time the loan was made (when the principal balance of the loan is paid down to 80 percent, this exception shall not apply); (3) if such payment of interest is prohibited by federal law. Lenders not requiring the establishment of reserve accounts shall offer the following options to the borrower: (1) borrower may maintain a non-interest-bearing account to be serviced by the lender at no charge to the borrower, or 92) borrower may manage the payment of insurance premiums and taxes from his own account. If the borrower selects option (2) and is delinquent more than once in the payment of the taxes or insurance premiums, the lender may require a reserve account without interest or other compensation for the use of the funds.

Lenders must furnish an itemized statement to the borrower, within 60 days after the end of each calendar year, showing monies received for interest and principal repayment and received and held in or disbursed from a reserve account. Negligent failure by the lender to make timely payments for taxes and insurance premiums shall subject the lender to liability for all damages directly resulting from the failure. Failure of the borrower to promptly deliver all notices of tax assessments or assigns shall relieve the lender from such lability. A lender who violates this act is liable to the borrower form actual damages suffered or $100, whichever is greater. If an action is commenced, the regailign party may be awarded reasonable attorney's fees. No action may be brought more than one year after the date of the violation.

Sec. 7-7-33(6) - A savings and loan association may require (subject to the above provisions) a borrower to pay monthly, in advance, equivalent of one-twelfth of the estimated annual taxes, assessments, insurance premiums, and other charges upon the real estate securing the loan. If the association advances its own funds, that amount shall be secured by the mortgage or trust deed with the same priority as the original amount advanced under the mortgage or trust deed.

VERMONT, Stat. Ann. Tit. 9 Sec 44

Agreements to maintain with the lender non-interest bearing reserves or deposits with which to pay when due taxes and insurance premiums shall not be construed to be interest or a prohibited charge.

VIRGINIA, Code Sec. 6.1-2.8

Any bank or lender maintaining escrow accounts for the payment of taxes and insurance which, upon receipt of a notice thereof, fails to make timely payment and incurs a penalty or late charge or a cancellation for nonpayment if there are sufficient funds in the account at least five days before the payment due date, shall be liable for the penalty or late charge assessed and for any loss as a result of the property being uninsured for nonpayment. Lenders must give written notice to any obligor of the payment of such penalty or late charge within five days after payment is made.

* WISCONSIN, Stat. Ann. Sec. 183.051(5)

Requires a bank, credit union, or mutual savings bank which originates a loan and which requires an escrow to assure the payment of taxes or insurance premiums to pay interest on the outstanding principal balance of the escrow of not less than 5.25 percent per annum (effective 1981).

Sec. 138.052(5), effective January 1, 1983, requires a bank, credit union, mutual savings bank, savings and loan association, or mortgage banker which originates a loan and requires an escrow to assume the payment f taxes or insurance premiums to pay interest on the outstanding principal balance of the escrow of not less than 5.25 percent unless the escrow funds are held by a third party in a non-interest-bearing account (effectively exempting mortgage bankers from this requirement).

Parties may agree to waive payment of all or part of the interest if more than 75 percent of the lender's interest in the loan is sold to a third party who is not a person related to the lender and the escrow funds are held by a third party.

INTEREST ON ESCROWS - STATE REQUIREMENTS

State	IOE Rate	Method to be Used in Calculating IOE	When IOE is to be Credited
California	2 Percent	Simple Interest	Annually or upon termination of loan, which ever is earliest.
Connecticut	5 1/4 Percent (effective October 1, 1985)	Not stated	Annually or upon termination which ever is earliest.
Guam	Not less than rate on passbook savings accounts		
Iowa	Not less than ordinary savings account rate	Daily balances	Not stated
Maine	3 Percent	Daily balances	Last business day of each quarter of calendar or fiscal year.
Maryland	Regular passbook savings rate of 3 percent simple interest	Average monthly balance	Annually
Massachusetts	Not stated (rate determined by mortgage)	Not stated	Annually
Minnesota	5 Percent	Average monthly balance	Annually or upon termination of loan, is earliest.

State	IOE Rate	Method to be Used in Calculating IOE	When IOE is to be Credited
New Hampshire	5 Percent (effective 7/1/85)	Not stated	Not stated
New York	2 Percent	Daily simple interest	Quarterly
Oregon	4 1/2 Percent	Average monthly balance	Quarterly
Rhode Island	4 Percent (effective 6/26/85)	Not stated	Annuall or prior to June 30 if loan is terminated
Utah	5 1/4 Percent	Average monthly balance	Annually
Wisconsin	5 1/4 Percent	Outstanding principal balance	Not stated

Index

A

Acceleration zone, 167
Acquisitions, 45
Action plans, 11
Adjustable rate mortgages, 23
  loan characteristics, 32, 52
  and servicing fees, 59
  and weighted average note range, 58
"Adjustment date," 111
Advancing funds on delinquent loans,
  71-72
"Agency Authorization," 135
Age stratification of portfolios, 53
"Agreement," 111
American call option, 164
Amortization, and mortgage defaults,
  166
Analysis preparation, 49, 51-54
Analysis questions, and due diligence,
  147-48
Ancillary income, 35, 60
"Applicable Law," 137
"Assignment Agreement," 111
"Assignment of Mortgages," 115-16
Assignment of trade, 211, 212-13
"Association," 111
Assumptions, and due diligence, 150
Auction, 103-4, 196
"Authority and Capacity," 117-18, 124
Auto-regressive prepayment model, 175

Average loan size, 21
  and portfolio evaluation, 58

B

Balloon loans, 55
  and due diligence, 149
Base zone, 167
Basis risk, 188
Bear hedge, 181, 184, 185
Bidding and closing, 101-38
  auction, 103-4, 196
  bidding process, 40, 42, 45-46, 98, 104-
    6, 196
  closing the sale, 107
  negotiating, 106-7
  offer sample, 108-10
  purchase and sale agreement, sample,
    111-38
  transaction types, 102-3
Bidding process, 40, 42, 45-46, 98, 104-
    6, 196. *See also* Bidding and clos-
    ing
Bid expiration date, 105-6
Bid page, of portfolio, 18
Bid price, 105
"Binding Effect; Severability," 137
Brokers, of mortgage servicing sales, 39-
    42
  and bidding process, 104-5
  marketing and, 43-46

433

in negotiating phase, 106-7
premarketing and, 42-43
Broker sale, 102-3
"Broker's Fees," 135-36
Bulk transactions vs. flow transactions, 214-15
Bull-hedge, 180-81, 182, 183
Burnout zone, 167
Business action plans, 11
"Business day," 111
Business objectives and strategies, 9-10
Business planning. *See* Strategic planning
Buyer's market, 99
Buyer's responsibilities, in transfer of servicing, 154-58

C
Cash flow, 1, 2-3
augmenting, 3
and present value analysis, 48-49
"Certificates of Seller," 129
"Certification of Pools," 131
Closing the sale, 107. *See also* Bidding and closing
Cohane Rafferty, and plain vanilla deal example, 192-200
Co-issuance, 211, 213
Collateralized mortgage obligations, 53
Collateral level yield hedge, 178-0, 181-83, 184, 185, 186
Collections file, 160
Combined cash flow model, 177
Company appraisal, 7-8
Company goals, statement of, 6-7
Competition, 47
"Compliance with Conditions," 129-30, 132
"Compliance with Insurance and Guaranty," 119-20
"Compliance with Law," 122

"Compliance with Requirements," 118, 119
Computer conversion, and transfer of servicing, 155
Computer reports, servicing portfolio, 18, 19
Computer system, 34
Conditions precedent to obligations of purchaser, 129-31
Conditions precedent to obligations of seller, 132
"Confidentiality of Information," 135
Consideration, 116-17
Contents page, of portfolio, 19, 20-21
Contingency plans, 11-12
Conventional servicing, 179-81
"Cooperation," 115
"Correctness of Representations and Warranties," 129, 132
Correlation risk, 188
Cost analysis, 7
"Cost and Expenses," 132
"Counterparts," 137
Coupon rate, 21
Covenants, 125-28
Cover page, of portfolio, 17-18
Cross selling, 35
"Custodian," 111-12
Customer base, broadening, 3

D
Database, of brokers, 40, 41
Date of information, 19
Days float
on payoffs, 61
on principal and interest payments, 60-61
Defaults prepayment subclass, 164, 166
Delinquencies, 24, 26, 106, 198
calculation methods, 27
and due diligence, 148

in loan mix, 37-38
national survey of residential mortgage loans, 36
and portfolio evaluation, 68-69, 97
and transfer of servicing, 156
"Delinquent Mortgage," 112
"Delivery of Loan Documents," 126
"Delivery of Servicing Records," 126
Discount price, of PO's, 172
Discount rate of capital, 49
Discount rate/required return, 74
Due diligence and portfolio transfer, 139-52, 154
  planning session, 140
  sample detailed report, 142-52
  task force, 140-41
"Due Incorporation and Good Standing," 117
"Due Organization," 124

E
Early servicing offerings, 14, 15
Early payoffs, reserve requirements for, 61
Earnings rate on P&I and early payoff float, 62
Economic analysis, 47-100
  analysis preparation, 49, 51-54
  determining values, 54-74
  evaluating mortgage servicing, 47-48
  market value vs. economic value, 98-100
  present value analysis, 48-49, 50
  sample evaluation, 75-81
  sensitivity analysis, 81-97
Economic indicators, and loan origination, 8
Economic refinancing, 164-65
Economic trends, 8-9, 68
"Effective Agreement," 124-25
Efficiency, in managing portfolio, 26

"Entire Agreement; Amendment," 136-37
Escrow
  balance, 26, 62-64
  gaining float from, 3
  HUD regulations and, 63-64
  interest on, by state, 35
  packaging information, 35, 37
  payments, 4
  and portfolio evaluation, 62-65
  revenues, effects on, 48
  and transfer of servicing, 159
"Escrow Analysis," 123
Essential details page, of portfolio, 19, 22, 201, 205, 207
  sample due diligence report, 142
  sample portfolio evaluation, 77
Evaluating portfolios. *See* Economic analysis
"Excess Funds," 131
Exclusive servicing offering, 199
Exclusive with one broker transaction, 103

F
Federal Accounting Standards Board (FASB), 73
Federal deposit insurance, on P&I accounts, 62
"FHA," 112
FHA-insured loans, 3
  foreclosure costs on, 70
Files, in transfer of servicing, 155, 156, 160-61
"Filing of Reports," 118
Financial projections, 11
Fixed rate loan characteristics, 32
Float, 4, 60-61
  and escrow earnings, 64
Floating rate hedges, 185
Flow deals, 211-15

advantages to buyer and seller, 214-15
assignment of trade, 211, 212-13
co-issuance, 211, 213
definition and formats, 211-13
flow transactions vs. bulk transactions,
    214-15
Flow servicing, 211
FNMA/FHLMC loans, 23, 34
    days float on principal and interest pay-
        ments, 60
    delinquencies and, 72
    foreclosure costs on, 70
    and hedging, 185, 187
    payoffs on, 61, 67
    prepayment profiles, 167
Foreclosure/bankruptcy file, 155, 156,
    161
Foreclosure by advertisement, 72
Foreclosures, 24, 26, 52
    and due diligence, 148
    foreclosure completion time, 72-73
    and portfolio evaluation, 69-71

G
Generic deal. *See* Plain vanilla deal
Geographical distribution, 204
Geographic concentration, 24
Geographic stratification of portfolios,
    53
Geography breakdown page, 26-27, 28-
    29
GNMA I and II loans, 23, 29, 34
    delinquencies and, 72
    as hedging tool, 181, 183, 186
    payoffs on, 67
"Good Standing," 125
Graduated payment mortgages, 52-53
"Guide," 112

H
"Hazard Insurance," 122

"Headings; Interpretive Principles," 137
Hedge sensitivity analysis, 179-80
Hedging, 163-90
    combined cash flow model, 177
    dynamics of servicing, 164-71
    floating rate hedges, 185
    interest rate model, 172-74
    premium servicing bidding strategy,
        188
    prepayment models, 174
    principal-only stripped mortgage-
        backed securities, 171-72, 173,
        176, 185-87
    relative risks, 188
    strategies, 177-83
    zero-return hedge, 183
Historical prepayment model, 174-75
HUD, and escrow, 63-64

I
Implied prepayment model, 175
Income tax rate, and portfolio evalua-
    tion, 58
"Incorporation of Exhibits," 137
Indemnification, 105
"Indemnification by Seller', 132-33
Inflation
    factors determining, 174
    and servicing cost per loan, 67
"Inspection of Records," 127-28
Insurance files, 161
"Interest on Escrows," 123
Interest rate model, 172-74
Interest rate risk, 188
Interest rates, 21
    effect on residential mobility, 166
"Interim Servicing Agreement," 112
Investment type, 19
Investor information, 36
Investor reporting, and due diligence,
    142-46

Investor stratification, of portfolio, 51

L

Late fees, and portfolio evaluation, 59, 69
"Legal Opinion," 130-31
Legislation, and portfolio market, 99
"Letter Agreement," 112
Life insurance, 37
"Litigation," 119
Loan breakdown section, of portfolio, 29, 32-34
Loan file, 155, 160
Loans
    annual servicing costs, and portfolio value, 65-67
    characteristics, 203
    delinquencies, 68-69, 71-72
    loan type stratification, and portfolio value, 52-53
    number of and average size, 19, 21
    payoff costs per, 67
    sources, 33
Loan to value, 33
Lock box set up, 156
Long range goals, achieving, 7

M

Macauly duration, calculation of, 190
Mailing follow ups, 44
Management philosophy, 5
Market expectations implied prepayment model, 175
Marketing, 39-46
    premarketing, 42-43
Market value
    determining, 47
    vs. economic value, 98-100
Matched coupon level yield hedge, 178, 181, 183
Mathematical prepayment models, 175

"MBSs," 112
Mergers, 45
"Misapplied Payments," 127
Monitoring phase, 12
Monthly principal and interest constant, 24
Monthly tax and insurance constant, 24, 25
Mortgage-backed securities, 112, 171
Mortgage Bankers Association of America, 38, 68
Mortgage banking boom of 1980's, 2
"Mortgage Documents," 120-21
"Mortgage Payments Received After Transfer Date," 127
"Mortgage Payments Received Prior to Transfer Date," 127
"Mortgage Pools," 124
Mortgage rate, 21
"Mortgages," 112
Mortgage servicing portfolios
    bidding and closing, 101-38
    brokering of, 39-42
    buying, 3-4, 12
    due diligence and portfolio transfer, 139-52
    economic analysis of. *See* Economic analysis
    evolution of, 14-17
    flow deals, 21-15
    hedging, 163-90
    marketing, 39-46
    packaging, 13-38
    plain vanilla deal, 191-209
    sample computer reports, 16
    sample portfolio, 169-70
    selling, 2-3, 12
    streamlining, 2, 3
    transfer of servicing, 153-61
Mortgage Servicing Purchase and Sale Agreement, 111-38

Mortgage servicing transactions, 102-3
"Mortgagor," 113
Mortgagor, and notification of transfer
    of servicing, 157-59

N
Negotiating, 106-7
Net servicing fee, 25. *See also*
    Weighted net servicing fee
Network, evaluating, 43-44
Note rate distribution, 27, 29, 30-31,
    202, 206, 208
Note rate range, 21
  and portfolio evaluation, 58
  and prepayment risk, 54
Note type stratification, and effect on
    portfolio value, 51-52
"Notices," 128, 136
"Notice to Insurers and Guarantors,"
    125-26
"Notice to Mortgagors," 125
"No Violations," 118
Number of loans, 19
  and portfolio evaluation, 55

O
"Obligations of Purchaser," 115
"Obligations of Seller," 115
Offer, sample, 108-10
Opportunity cost of capital, 49
Options-based prepayment model, 176
Original term stratification of portfolios,
    53, 55
"Other Costs," 117

P
Packaging, of portfolio, 19-38
  evolution of servicing portfolio, 14-17
  broker's assistance in, 41
  special considerations, 37-38
Pass-thru rate, 21

"Payment," 116
Payment of delinquent loans, 106
Payment terms, 105
Payoff files, 155, 156
Payoffs, 61-62, 67
  and due diligence, 149
"Payoff Statements," 123
Plain vanilla deal, 191-209
PMI Information, 33
Points, 165
"Pool," 113
Portfolio evaluation
  assumption, 54-55, 56-57, 75-81
  sample evaluation, 75-81
Portfolios. *See* Mortgage servicing port-
    folios
Power-of-sale, 72
Premarketing, 42-43
Premium servicing bidding strategy, 188
Prepayment
  models, 175-76
  rates, 74
  risk, 48, 52-53, 54, 163-64, 170-71, 188
  sensitivity, 172
  subclasses, 164-66
  typical profiles, 167, 169-70, 173
"Prepayments and Assumptions," 126
Present value analysis, 48-49, 50
Price, calculation of, 189
Price sensitivity, 81-97
Pricing, determining, 45
Principal balance, 19
Principal and interest constant, 26
Principal and interest payments, and
    portfolio evaluation, 59, 60, 61, 62
Principal-only stripped mortgage-
    backed securities, 171-74, 186
  model, 176-77
"Prior Services," 113
Private sale, 102
Productivity, 1, 4

Pro forma projections, 11
Property types, 33, 53-54
Property values, and mortgage defaults, 166
Prospects, targeting, 44
Public Securities Association, 53
Purchase and sale agreement, 111-38
Purchase price, on offer, 108-10, 113, 116
Purchase price amortization, 73-74
"Purchase Price Percentage," 113
"Purchaser," 113
Purpose, statement of, 5

Q-R
Questions, of prospective buyers, 44
Rate of return or yield, calculation of, 189
Real Estate Settlement Procedures Act, 63, 99
Refinancing, 165
Regression model, 175
"Regulatory Approvals," 125, 130, 132
"Related Escrow Account Balances," 126
"Related Escrow Accounts," 113, 119
Representations and warranties as to mortgages, 120-24
Representations and warranties of purchaser, 124-25
"Repurchase of Delinquent Mortgages," 131
"Repurchase of Servicing," 134-35
"Requirements," 113
Residential mobility, 164, 165-66

S
"Sale Date," 113
"Sale Documents," 113
Salespeople. *See* Brokers, of mortgage servicing sales

"Schedule of Insurance," 123
"Schedule of Items," 131
Secondary market, emergence of, 14, 15, 39
"Security Interest," 121
Security rate, 21
"Seller," 113
Seller's representations and warranties, 117-20
Seller's responsibilities, in transfer of servicing, 158-60
Sensitivity analysis, sample, 81-97
"Servicing," 114
"Servicing Agreements," 114
Servicing agreements for private investors, and due diligence, 151
Servicing dynamics, 164-71
Servicing evaluation model, 176
Servicing fees, 23, 59
    annual servicing cost per loan, 65-67
    effects on, 48, 54
Servicing portfolios. *See* Mortgage servicing portfolios
Short lists, 44-45, 196
"Solicitation of Accounts," 128
Specific investor information, 34
Spread, 168
Statement of company goals, 5-6
Statement of purpose, 5
"Statistical and Other Information," 128
Stochastic prepayment model, 175
Strategic assumptions, 8-9
Strategic business planning, 4-5
Stratetic mortgage servicing, 12
Strategic planning, 1-12
    business action plans, 11
    business objectives and strategies, 9-10
    company appraisal, 7-8
    contingency plans, 11-12
    portfolios, purposes for buying and selling, 2-4

pro forma projections, 11
statement of company goals, 5-6
statement of purpose, 5
strategic assumputions, 8-9
strategic business planning, 4-5
strategic mortgage servicing, 12
"Substitution of Purchaser," 115
Supplemental information pages, of portfolio, 36-40
"Supplementary Information," 135
"Survival of Representations and Warranties," 136
System requirements, and due diligence, 151-52

T-U
Table of contents page, of portfolio, 21, 22-23
Taxes and insurance, and due diligence report, 146-47
"Tax Identification," 122-23
Tax & insurance constant, 24, 25
Tax liability, 58
Tax payment frequency by state, with multiplier, 25-26
Tax service, 34, 105
Tax-shield benefit, 73-74
Telecommunications, 45
"Termination," 133-35
Thrift legislation, and portfolio market, 99
Ticor, 34
Timelines, 11
"Title Insurance," 120
Title page, of portfolio, 18
"Title to the Servicing," 118-19
Transamerica, 34
Transfer and Assumption, 114-16
Transfer/conversion costs, and portfolio evaluation, 65
Transfer date, 105, 114

"Transfer of Responsibilities as Servicer," 114-15
Transfer of servicing, 153-61
buyer's responsibilities, 154-58
files, 160-61
seller's responsibilities, 158-60
Transfer project manager, 154
"Transfers," 123-24
Treasury options, and hedging, 187
Trial balances, and transfer of servicing, 156
Trends, effect of, 8-9, 68
Twelve-month average escrow balance, 23-24
"Unpaid Balance," 121

V
VA-insured loans, 3, 38
foreclosure costs, 70-71
"Validity of Note; Legal Proceedings," 121-22
Valuation of current portfolio, 8. *See also* Economic analysis
Veterans Administration, 114. *See also* VA-insured loans

W-Z
"Waivers," 136
Weighted average life in years, calculation of, 190
Weighted average net servicing fee, 23, 27
and portfolio evaluation, 59
Weighted average note range, 22
and portfolio evaluation, 58
Weighted average original term, 23
Weighted average remaining terms, 23
and portfolio evaluation, 55
Zero return hedge, 183